The Texa

Texas Litigators' Guide to Departing Employee Cases

2022

Mark A. Shank
Author and Editor

Greg McAllister and Dave Wishnew
Assistant Editors

www.stoneycreekpublishing.com

Published by Stoney Creek Publishing
www.stoneycreekpublishing.com

in association with

The Texas Lawbook

The Texas Lawbook
texaslawbook.net

Distributed by Texas A&M University Press

ISBN (paperback): 978-1-7368390-2-7
ISBN (ebook): 978-1-7368390-3-4
Library of Congress: 2021922628

Cover and interior design by A.J. Reid Creative

Printed in the United States

The Texas Lawbook

Texas Litigators' Guide to Departing Employee Cases 2022

Mark A. Shank
Author and Editor

Greg McAllister and Dave Wishnew
Assistant Editors

www.stoneycreekpublishing.com

About the Contributors

John DeGroote serves as a mediator and arbitrator in complex business, technology, and intellectual property matters involving parties and interests around the country and beyond—often before litigation is filed.

Prior to establishing his current practice John spent more than 10 years at KPMG Consulting, later known as BearingPoint, Inc., a $3 billion technology consulting firm with more than 15,000 employees worldwide, where he served as Chief Litigation Counsel and, later, as BearingPoint's Executive Vice President and General Counsel.

Mr. DeGroote received his mediation training from Pepperdine University's Straus Institute for Dispute Resolution in 2005, his J.D. from the Duke University School of Law in 1990, and his B.A. from Mississippi State University in 1986. John is a past chair of the State Bar of Texas's ADR Section and the Dallas Bar Association's ADR Section.

He lives in Dallas with his wife and three boys.

Bennett Hampilos is an associate at Lynn Pinker Hurst & Schwegmann, LLP. He received a bachelor's degree from New York University and a J.D. from Cornell Law School. Bennett previously clerked for the Honorable Royce C. Lamberth on the U.S. District Court for the District of Columbia.

Patrick Maher graduated from the University of Texas School of Law in 1981 with high honors. At Texas, he was an Editor on the Texas Law Review and a member of the Chancellors and Order of Coif.

Following graduation, he clerked for Judge Joseph Sneed, on the United States Court of Appeals for the Ninth Circuit. Mr. Maher is a past Chair of the State Bar of Texas Labor & Employment Law Section, a Fellow of the College of Labor and Employment Lawyers and has been listed in *Best Lawyers in America* (Woodard Press 2005 – 2020) and *Texas Super Lawyers* (Texas Monthly Magazine 2004 – 2020). Mr. Maher is Senior Counsel at Ogletree, Deakins, Nash, Smoak & Stewart in Dallas, Texas.

Greg McAllister is a partner at the Rogge Dunn Group. Greg's business and employment litigation practice focuses on representing executives and employees in contract disputes, noncompetition and nonsolicitation, change of control, discrimination, and other matters.

His practice at Gruber Hurst Johansen Hail Shank, Littler Mendelson, and RDG helped him learn from many great lawyers —especially Mark Shank and Rogge Dunn because they exemplify leadership, know the law, exude passion for what we do, and roll up their sleeves to work side-by-side on our cases.

Rob Radcliff is a Dallas-based employment lawyer that focuses on non-compete disputes and other employment transition issues. He handles matters throughout the United States in both the courtroom and in arbitration.

Josh Sandler is consistently recognized as one of the best trial lawyers in Texas. He was one of only one hundred attorneys in the State of Texas identified by Texas Super Lawyers as a Top 100 Up-and-Coming Texas Rising Star.

Josh is a partner at Lynn Pinker Hurst & Schwegmann, LLP in Dallas. For numerous years, D Magazine has named him one of the Best Lawyers in Dallas. And Benchmark Litigation placed Josh on their Hot List, an exclusive designation of the most promising talent in litigation communities in the U.S. and Canada that is given to attorneys who have earned praise from clients and peers regarding the quality of their work.

Josh is an experienced trial lawyer who represents businesses and high net worth individuals in a wide range of disputes involving probate, trust, estate, and fiduciary litigation; commercial litigation, including commercial real estate litigation; and business and employment disputes in the state and federal courts of Texas and the Southwest.

Holly Stubbs is an associate at Lynn Pinker Hurst & Schwegmann, LLP. She earned her law degree from Columbia Law School. Holly clerked for the Honorable Michael J. Seng of the United States District Court for the Eastern District of California and for the Honorable Micaela Alvarez on the United States District Court for the Southern District of Texas prior to joining Lynn Pinker.

Shelby K. Taylor is an attorney at Littler Mendelson, P.C in Dallas, Texas. She concentrates her practice on advising and representing employers in a broad range of labor and employment matters arising under both state and federal laws. She attended law school at Southern Methodist University Dedman School of Law and is active in the Dallas Association of Young Lawyers community.

Jason Weber is a Dallas-based shareholder at Polsinelli and a member of the firm's Restrictive Covenants, Enforcement and Trade Secrets (RCETS) practice. Jason is Board Certified in Labor and Employment Law by the Texas Board of Legal Specialization and focuses his practice on business disputes and employment-related consulting and litigation. He has extensive experience drafting, enforcing and defending against restrictive covenants, both in Texas and nationally. Jason received his B.A. from Baylor University and his J.D. from Baylor Law School, where he served on Law Review. Jason has received multiple distinctions including "Top 100 Lawyers Under 40" by *Texas Super Lawyers Magazine* and *Texas Monthly*, "Best Lawyers Under 40 in Dallas" by *D Magazine*, "Ones to Watch" by *Best Lawyers*, and "Litigator of the Week" by *Texas Lawyer*.

Dave Wishnew had his first taste of a departing employee case in 2010 when he joined Mark Shank at Gruber Hail Johansen Shank LLP. Over the next several years, Dave and his mentor Mark successfully handled dozens of departing employee cases. In 2018, Dave and his partners Trey and Michael formed Crawford, Wishnew & Lang PLLC. A zealous advocate for his clients, Dave's diverse litigation practice focuses on complex commercial and employment disputes. Dave has substantial experience litigating departing employee cases, obtaining injunctions for employers, defeating injunctions for employees, and winning substantial financial recoveries. Dave had his 15 minutes of lawyer fame when news agencies across the world published stories of a substantial jury verdict Dave obtained on behalf of his client, a Dallas wedding photographer, in a defamation case against two former clients who pursued an extensive news and social media campaign against her. Dave has consistently been recognized by his peers as a premier litigator.

Dave is also involved in a number of civic and charitable organizations, and pays it forward by mentoring young lawyers.

Robert Wood is a labor and employment attorney with Wood Edwards LLP in Dallas.

Acknowledgement of
Greg McAllister and Dave Wishnew, Assistant Editors

Greg and Dave have assisted with this project from day one, writing, editing and providing ideas. They agreed to accept increased roles for this edition. I am very thankful for their excellent support and assistance.

TABLE OF CONTENTS

PART I

THE LAW

Chapter 1
Overview

Edited by Jason Weber

1-1 DEPARTING EMPLOYEE CLAIMS

Employers' confidential business information, proprietary technology, goodwill, or "know-how" often constitutes valuable property that provides a competitive advantage in the marketplace. These employers spend great amounts of time, effort, and money developing and protecting this information. Most cases involving departing employees center around such confidential, proprietary, and trade secret information—which is often intangible. If such intangible property becomes known in the industry, particularly to competitors, then the employer can lose its competitive advantage, its property's trade secret status, and protections available under the law. Of course, the employer, usually by necessity, exposes its employees to such intangible property in their day-to-day work. Usually, when employees are "in the tent" and drawing a paycheck, they are perfectly content to honor the information's confidentiality and use it only for the employer's benefit. When an employee departs—or prepares to depart—an employer, that employee's willingness to protect this information often dissipates, particularly if the parting is not amicable. This book discusses various aspects of the give-and-take between employee and employer on these issues, as well as other monetary and nonmonetary issues that affect the relationship between employers and departing employees. Also, this book deals with causes of action, remedies, defenses, and strategies and tactics before and during suit.

1-2 TYPES OF RESTRICTIVE COVENANTS

There are at least three common types of restrictive covenants found in most employment agreements: confidentiality, nonsolicitation, and noncompetition. Although these covenants often appear in the same employment agreements, each distinct covenant raises different but related issues.

1-2:1 CONFIDENTIALITY COVENANTS

Seldom does an employment agreement omit a confidentiality covenant. A confidentiality covenant (sometimes called a nondisclosure agreement/covenant or "NDA") defines, labels, and protects trade secrets (if applicable) and other confidential information. Although common law typically protects the confidentiality and misuse of sensitive information without such a covenant,[1] a confidentiality covenant usually broadens the scope of the information protected and serves as evidence of the employer's attempts to protect this information. This common law protection should be treated as a backstop and—preferably—never exclusively relied upon by the employer because the absence of a confidentiality covenant exposes an employer to the counterargument that the material at issue is not genuinely "confidential."[2] Moreover, because a confidentiality covenant

1. *See e.g.*, *Keel Recovery, Inc. v. Tri Cnty. Adjusters, Inc.*, No. 05-19-00686-CV, 2020 WL 5269603, at *4 (Tex. App.—Dallas Sept. 4, 2020, no pet. h.) (recognizing an employee has a common law duty to not "carry away confidential information" (quoting *Whooters v. Unitech Int'l, Inc.*, 513 S.W.3d 754, 763 (Tex. App.—Houston [1st Dist.] 2017, pet. denied)); *Rugen v. Interactive Bus. Sys., Inc.*, 864 S.W.2d 548, 551 (Tex. App.—Dallas 1993, no writ) (noting the "well established" rule preventing employees from using confidential information or trade secrets gained while employed, even if not subject to restrictive covenants).

2. As discussed below, confidentiality covenants are also important because the confidential information contemplated or promised in such covenants often serves as

is contractual in nature, a former employee's breach may give rise to a claim for attorney's fees under Texas statute.[3] Unlike nonsolicitation and noncompetition covenants, confidentiality covenants are not subject to the heightened requirements of Texas's Covenants Not to Compete Act (Act).[4]

A typical confidentiality covenant generally includes the following language:

> In consideration of the training and support provided by the Employer to Employee, and the compensation and other consideration to be paid to Employee under this Agreement, Employee agrees that Employee will not, without the written consent of the Employer, disclose or make any use of such Confidential Information except as may be required in the course of rendering services under this Agreement. Further, Employee agrees to immediately deliver to the Employer all Confidential Information and all copies thereof upon termination of employment.

The confidentiality covenant should also (1) define "confidential information," (2) establish the employee's understanding of the confidential information's significance, (3) express the employer's promise to provide confidential information, and (4) possibly establish a time limitation for nondisclosure. In addition, the confidentiality covenant should be presented to and executed by the employee *before* any confidential information is disclosed

---

the foundational "protectable interest" that an employer may rely upon in justifying the necessity of nonsolicitation and noncompetition covenants. *See supra* Chap. 3-2:2.

3. Tex. Civ. Prac. & Rem. Code Ann. §§ 38.001, *et seq.*

4. *E.g.*, *Marsh USA, Inc. v. Cook*, 354 S.W.3d 764, 768 (Tex. 2011) ("Agreements not to disclose trade secrets and confidential information are not expressly governed by the Act"); *see also Guy Carpenter & Co., Inc. v. Provenzale*, 334 F.3d 459, 465 (5th Cir. 2003) ("As a preliminary matter, non-disclosure covenants do not restrain trade and competition in the same way that non-solicitation covenants restrain trade and competition. As a result, § 15.50 does not govern or impair the enforceability of non-disclosure covenants.").

to him (ideally at the inception of employment rather than "midstream").

Employers should also take care to draft (or revise) their confidentiality covenant so they do not violate the National Labor Relations Act (NLRA). For example, in 2014, the Fifth Circuit held that a confidentiality covenant in an employee agreement violated the NLRA because it defined "Confidential Information" to include "personnel information," *i.e.*, wage and benefit information.[5] While the Fifth Circuit has since clarified that confidentiality covenants will generally not run afoul of the NLRA so long as they do not expressly encompass wage and benefit information,[6] employers should still be cautious about implementing catch-all definitions of "confidential information." Incorporating a savings cause—*e.g.*, "nothing herein will affect an employee's right to discuss the terms or conditions of employment with other employees or third parties"—may also help minimize the risk of a confidentiality covenant infringing on employees' statutory rights.[7]

While Texas common law—likely—continues to govern the protection of confidential information (absent a confidentiality covenant), trade secrets are now governed by the Texas Uniform Trade Secrets Act (TUTSA).[8] To qualify as a trade secret under TUTSA, the information must meet two requirements: (1) the owner of the trade secret must take reasonable measures under the circumstances to keep the information secret; and (2) the information must derive independent economic value, actual

5. *Flex Frac Logistics, L.L.C. v. N.L.R.B.*, 746 F.3d 205, 210 (5th Cir. 2014).

6. *T-Mobile USA, Inc. v. N.L.R.B.*, 865 F.3d 265, 276 (5th Cir. 2017).

7. *See, e.g., First Transit Inc.*, 360 NLRB 619, 621 (2014) (a savings cause "may, in certain circumstances, clarify the scope of an otherwise ambiguous or unlawful rule").

8. Tex. Civ. Prac. & Rem. Code Ann. §§ 134A.001–.008 (first enacted in 2013 and later amended in 2017). Before the enactment of TUTSA, trade secret protection in Texas was a conglomeration of common law, the Restatement (Third) of Unfair Competition, the Texas Theft Liability Act, and the Texas Penal Code. *See In re Bass*, 113 S.W.3d 735, 739 (Tex. 2003); *see also* Tex. Civ. Prac. & Rem. Code Ann. § 134.002(2); Tex. Pen. Code Ann. § 31.05(a)(4); Restatement of Torts, § 757, cmt. b (1939).

or potential, from not being generally known to, and not being readily ascertainable through proper means by, another person who can obtain economic value from the disclosure or use of the information.[9] Subject to the two requirements above, a "trade secret" expressly includes:

> [A]ll forms and types of information, including business, scientific, technical, economic, or engineering information, and any formula, design, prototype, pattern, plan, compilation, program device, program, code, device, method, technique, process, procedure, financial data, or list of actual or potential customers or suppliers, whether tangible or intangible and whether or how stored, compiled, or memorialized physically, electronically, graphically, photographically, or in writing[.][10]

TUTSA displaces both common law trade secret and Texas Theft Liability Act (TTLA) claims.[11] Conversely, Texas courts have come to differing conclusions on whether TUTSA's preemption provision encompasses the misappropriation of information that is not a trade secret.[12]

As stated above, because confidentiality covenants are directed at protecting information—rather than prohibiting conduct, and are therefore far less restrictive to the departing employee than other

9. Tex. Civ. Prac. & Rem. Code Ann. § 134A.002(6).

10. *Id.*

11. *StoneCoat of Tex., LLC v. ProCal Stone Design, LLC*, 426 F. Supp. 3d 311, 332 (E.D. Tex. 2019) (TUTSA "displaces both common-law misappropriation-of-trade-secret and TTLA theft-of-trade-secret claims).

12. *Compare DHI Group, Inc. v. Kent*, 397 F. Supp. 3d 904, 923 (S.D. Tex. 2019) ("fail[ing] to see how the plain language of the TUTSA's preemption provision can be read to preempt civil remedies for the misappropriation of information that is not a trade secret") *with Embarcadero Technologies, Inc. v. Redgate Software, Inc.*, No. 1:17-CV-444-RP, 2018 WL 315753, at *3 (W.D. Tex. Jan. 5, 2018) ("TUTSA's preemption provision encompasses all claims based on the alleged improper taking of confidential business information.").

restrictive covenants—they are broadly enforced under Texas law.[13] As discussed in later chapters of this textbook, on some occasions (typically when an employee's action is particularly egregious) courts will fashion remedies to limit the post-employment activities of former employees even absent restrictive covenants. This remedy usually occurs when an employee departs to work for a competitor and will inevitably use or disclose his former employer's trade secrets or confidential information in carrying out duties for the competitor. This concept is adopted in other states but not expressly adopted by Texas courts.[14] Although Texas has not expressly adopted the inevitable disclosure doctrine, Texas courts have—in order to protect trade secrets—fashioned remedies similar to those fashioned by courts that adopted the inevitable disclosure doctrine.[15] In general, however, absent a

---

13. *See e.g., Alliantgroup, L.P. v. Feingold*, 803 F. Supp. 2d 610, 622 (S.D. Tex. 2011) ("Under Texas Law, nondisclosure provisions are more readily enforced than noncompete clauses because the non-disclosure provisions are restraints on trade, they do not prevent the employee from making use of general experience he acquired during employment, and they do not offend public policy." (internal citations omitted))*; Mobile Storage Group, Inc. v. Fleet Trailer Leasing, LLC*, No. EP-08-CA-185-FM, 2008 WL 11334007, at *4 (W.D. Tex. Oct. 31, 2008) ("Non-disclosure agreements will still be enforced by the Court even if a non-compete covenant is otherwise found to be invalid or unenforceable. Non-disclosure agreements remain enforceable because they are not considered to be restraints on trade."); *but see Oxford Glob. Res., Inc. v. Weekley-Cessnum*, No. 3:04-CV-00330, 2005 WL 350580, at *2 (N.D. Tex. Feb. 8, 2005) ("If a nondisclosure covenant has the practical effect of prohibit[ing] the former employee from using, in competition with the former employer, the general knowledge, skill, and experience acquired inf former employment, then it is more properly characterized as a noncompetition agreement." (internal citations omitted)).

14. *Compare PepsiCo, Inc. v. Redmond*, 54 F.3d 1262, 1269–70 (7th Cir. 1995) (endorsing inevitable disclosure) *with Cardoni v. Prosperity Bank*, 805 F.3d 573, 589–90 (5th Cir. 2015) (collecting cases and recognizing the "inevitable disclosure" doctrine "is not yet the law in Texas"); *Cardinal Health Staffing Network v. Bowen*, 106 S.W.3d 230, 242 (Tex. App.—Houston [1st] 2003, no pet.) (finding "no Texas case expressly adopting the inevitable disclosure doctrine, and it is unclear to what extent Texas courts might adopt it or might view it as relieving an injunction applicant of showing irreparable injury"); *see also DGM Services, Inc. v. Figueroa*, No. 01-16-00186-CV, 2016 WL 7473947, at *5 (Tex. App.—Houston [1st Dist.] Dec. 29, 2016, no pet.) ("Like the *Cardoni* court, we conclude that the inevitable disclosure doctrine has not been adopted by Texas courts and is not a blanket rule applicable to all nondisclosure provisions in Texas.")

15. *See Conley v. DSC Commc'ns Corp., No. 05-98-01051-CV, 1999 WL 89955, at *8 (Tex. App.—Dallas Feb. 24, 1999, no pet.) (not recognizing inevitable disclosure doctrine but finding injunction appropriate when it was probable that former employee would use confidential information for his benefit or to the detriment of former employer); Rugen v. Interactive Bus. Sys., Inc.*, 864 S.W.2d 548, 552 (Tex. App.—Dallas 1993, no writ)

valid (or reformable) restrictive covenant promising otherwise, a departing employee may compete with a former employer after the employment relationship ends.[16]

1-2:2 NONSOLICITATION COVENANTS

1-2:2.1 NONSOLICITATION OF EMPLOYEES

A covenant not to solicit employees restricts the departing employee's ability to recruit former co-employees from joining him at a new employer. These nonsolicitation covenants are sometimes called "non-raiding" or "non-poaching" provisions. It is usually far more devastating for an employer when a departing employee entices several former co-employees to change jobs (*i.e.*, "raiding" or "poaching" the former employer), than for merely one employee to leave. Courts usually enforce covenants not to solicit employees (or non-raiding provisions). Post-*Marsh*, Texas courts have consistently held that nonsolicitation of employee covenants must meet the requirements of the Act.[17] Nonetheless,

---

(former employee "is in possession of [former employer's] confidential information and is in a position to use it. Under these circumstances, it is probable that [former employee] will use the information for her benefit and to the detriment of [former employer]."); *see also T-N-T Motorsports, Inc. v. Hennessey Motorsports, Inc.*, 965 S.W.2d 18, 24 (Tex. App.—Houston [1st Dist.] 1998, pet. dism'd); *see also Conley v. DSC Commc'ns. Corp.*, No. 05-98-01051-CV, 1999 WL 89955, at *3–5 (Tex. App.—Dallas Feb. 24, 1999, no pet.).

16. *See Johnson & Brewer & Pritchard, P.C., 73 S.W.3d 193, 201 (Tex. 2002); John R. Ray & Sons v. Stroman*, 923 S.W.2d 80, 88 (Tex. App.—Houston [14th Dist.] 1996, writ denied); *see also Miller Paper Co. v. Roberts Paper Co.*, 901 S.W.2d 593, 603 (Tex. App.—Amarillo 1995, no writ).

17. *See Marsh USA Inc. v. Cook*, 354 S.W.3d 764, 768 (Tex. 2011) ("Covenants that place limits on former employees' professional mobility or restrict their solicitation of the former employers' customers and employees are restraints on trade and are governed by the" Act.); *Smith v. Nerium Int'l, LLC*, No. 05-18-00617-CV, 2019 WL 3543583, at *4 (Tex. App.—Dallas Aug. 5, 2019, no pet.) ("the supreme court holds that a covenant restricting former employees from soliciting their "former employers' customers *and employees*" is a restraint of trade subject to § 15.50"); *Cooper Valves, LLC v. ValvTechnologies, Inc.*, 531 S.W.3d 254, 265 (Tex. App.—Houston [14th Dist.] 2017, no pet.) (recognizing employee non-solicitation covenants must comply with the Act); *Weber Aircraft, L.L.C. v. Krishnamurthy*, No. 4:12-CV-666, 2014 WL 12521297, at *11 (E.D. Tex. Jan. 27, 2014), *report and recommendation adopted sub nom. Weber Aircraft, LLC v. Krishnamurthy*, No. 4:12-CV-666, 2014 WL 12918853 (E.D. Tex. July 29, 2014) (same).

as a practical observation, such covenants are generally more liberally enforced—likely because such covenants typically impose a negligible restraint on a departing employee's freedom to work. Here is an example of a nonsolicitation of employees covenant:

> During the term of Employee's employment with Employer and for twenty-four (24) months thereafter, Employee shall not, alone or together with others, directly or indirectly, induce, influence, solicit, encourage, or advise any of Employer's employees, officers, contractors, or agents with whom Employee had contact as an employee of Employer within the twenty-four (24) months immediately preceding the termination of Employee's employment, to terminate their relationship with Employer.

1-2:2.2 NONSOLICITATION OF CLIENTS

Some states treat covenants not to solicit clients differently than noncompetition covenants. Texas does not.[18] However, similar to above, Texas courts tend to more readily enforce covenants not to solicit clients than broader form noncompetition covenants.[19]

18. *Marsh*, 354 S.W.3d at 768; *Shoreline Gas, Inc. v. McGaughey*, No. 13-07-364-CV, 2008 WL 1747624, at *10 (Tex. App.—Corpus Christi Apr. 17, 2008, no pet.) ("nonsolicitation agreements are subject to the same analysis as covenants not to compete"); *Miller Paper Co. v. Roberts Paper Co.*, 901 S.W.2d 593, 600 (Tex. App.—Amarillo 1995, no writ) (stating that "other than the moniker assigned it, nothing truly differentiates the [non-solicitation] promise at bar from a covenant not to compete"); *see also Guy Carpenter & Co. v. Provenzale*, 334 F.3d 459, 464–65 (5th Cir. 2003) (applying Texas law and stating that nonsolicitation covenants restrain trade and competition and are governed by the [Act]); *Mach 1 Air Services, Inc. v. Bustillos*, No. EP-13-CV-00088-DCG, 2013 WL 12108595, at *4 (W.D. Tex. May 10, 2013) ("Although *DeSantis* involves a non-compete clause, as opposed to a non-solicitation clause, the Court finds that the difference is irrelevant because Texas courts hold that 'non-solicitation agreements are subject to the same analysis as covenants not to compete.'"); *Rimkus Consulting Grp., Inc. v. Cammarata*, 255 F.R.D. 417, 438–39 (S.D. Tex. 2008) (holding that a "nonsolicitation covenant is also a restraint on trade and competition and must meet the criteria of section 15.50 of the Texas Business and Commerce Code to be enforceable").

19. *See, e.g., York v. Hair Club for Men, L.L.C.*, No. 01-09-00024-CV, 2009 WL 1840813, at *4–6 (Tex. App.—Houston [1st Dist.] June 25, 2009, no pet.) (trial court struck through noncompetition covenant and enforced nonsolicitation covenant related to

This enforcement is in part because covenants not to solicit clients tend to be far less restrictive than noncompetition covenants. Moreover, there seems to be an inherent logic and sensibility to protecting a former employer from the direct solicitation of its current clients. Typically, the departing employee was exposed to and gained valuable information about the former employer's clients—information that he would not have otherwise obtained. Consequently, enforcing a covenant not to solicit clients is a way of protecting confidential and proprietary information about these clients. Nevertheless, such covenants should still generally be tied to clients with whom or which the departing employee interacted with or was exposed to confidential information about during the employment period.[20] Additionally, the length of time necessary to protect this information is almost always a subject of contention. Here is an example of a nonsolicitation of clients covenant:

> During the term of Employee's employment with Employer and for twenty-four (24) months thereafter, Employee shall not, without the Employer's written consent, directly or indirectly, in any individual or representative capacity whatsoever or through any form of ownership, solicit, induce, or attempt to induce any client or prospective client of Employer in Dallas County (i) with whom Employee had any Material Business Contact during the twenty-four (24) months preceding termination of employment with the Employer or (ii) about whom Employee learned Confidential Information as a result of employment with

(1) defendants' former clients serviced at plaintiff's business and (2) plaintiff's employees).

20. *D'Onofrio v. Vacation Pubs., Inc.*, 888 F.3d 197, 211–12 (5th Cir. 2018) ("Under Texas law, covenants not to compete that extend to clients with whom the employee had no dealings during her employment or amount to industry-wide exclusions are overbroad and unreasonable."); *Gallagher Healthcare Ins. Servs. v. Vogelsang*, 312 S.W.3d 640, 654 (Tex. App.—Houston [1st Dist.] 2009, pet. denied) ("[a] restrictive covenant is overbroad and unreasonable when it extends to clients with whom the employee had no dealings during his employment" (internal citations omitted)).

> Employer, to withdraw, curtail, divert, or cancel any client's or prospective client's business with Employer or in any manner modify or fail to enter into any actual or potential business relationship with Employer. Material Business Contact means contact between Employee and each client or potential client (i) with whom or which Employee dealt on behalf of Employer, (ii) whose dealings with Employer were coordinated or supervised by Employee, or (iii) whose development and/or production of Employer's products and services, including but not limited to sales of Employer's services, led to commissions or other direct earnings for Employee within the twenty-four (24) months immediately preceding the termination of Employee's employment.

1-2:3 NONCOMPETITION COVENANTS

Noncompetition covenants are the form of restrictive covenants most commonly associated with the Act (codified in the Texas Business and Commerce Code).[21] Similar to nonsolicitation covenants, in order for a noncompetition covenant to be enforceable, it must strictly comply with the requirements set forth in Tex. Bus. & Com. Code Ann. § 15.50. Typically, noncompetition covenants differ from nonsolicitation of clients covenants by breadth and subject matter. Noncompetition covenants go beyond reference to clients and directly limit the (1) activities which the departing employee can engage in and/or (2) employers for whom the departing employee can work. For example, noncompetition covenants may limit the departing employee's ability to engage in his former employer's business (*e.g.*, he may not sell plumbing parts, work in a certain industry, or manage a restaurant in a certain area). Noncompetition covenants often preclude the departing employee from working in any competitive capacity

21. Tex. Bus. & Comm. Code Ann. §§ 15.001, *et seq.*

for an employer within a certain geographic area. Enforcing these covenants is generally a higher bar for the employer than enforcing other covenants—partly because of the human element of restricting one's freedom to work. The reasonableness and necessity of a noncompetition covenant is often the focal point of litigation. Employers bear the burden of establishing that the covenants contain:

> . . . limitations as to time, geographical area, and scope of activity to be restrained that are reasonable and do not impose a greater restraint than is necessary to protect the goodwill or other business interest of the [Employer].[22]

Even if the covenant is not enforceable (as is or via reformation), its mere existence creates difficulties for departing employees. A prospective employer may be unwilling to hire that employee in the face of noncompetition covenants that could subject the (1) employee to litigation and (2) prospective employer to liability on a tortious interference claim and/or enjoined conduct. In any event, the departing employee, win or lose, may have to spend significant attorney's fees litigating the issue. Finally, a noncompetition covenant's mere existence limits the mobility of the employee, who will not know precisely what activities he may engage in until the court tells him—and the combination of the case law and the predilections of judges make such a result difficult to predict. Here is an example of a noncompetition covenant:

> During the term of Employee's employment with Employer and for twenty-four (24) months thereafter, Employee will not directly or indirectly (i) compete with Employer in Competing Business in Dallas County or (ii) participate in the ownership, management, operation, financing, or control of, or be employed by or consult for or otherwise render services to, any person, corporation, firm,

22. *Id.* at § 15.50(a).

> or other entity that competes with Employer in Competing Business in Dallas County in a role that relates to the Competing Business. Notwithstanding the foregoing, Employee is permitted to own up to 2% of any class of securities of any corporation in competition with Employer that is traded on a national securities exchange or through NASDAQ. For purposes of this paragraph, "Competing Business" shall mean those portions of Employer's business in which Employee actively participated within the immediate twelve (12) months preceding Employee's termination of employment with Employer.

1-2:4 OTHER, RELATED PROVISIONS

1-2:4.1 PROPHYLACTIC CLAUSES

Prophylactic provisions take various forms, but they are largely designed to protect employers when hiring employees. These provisions (sometimes referred to as "comfort letters") typically make clear to the employee that he (1) should not violate any enforceable restrictive covenants with former employers (and warrants that he will not do so), (2) promises not to bring or use trade secrets or confidential information of another employer to the workplace, and (3) will generally live up to any promises that he made to former employers. This clause typically has value for hiring employers defending against potential tortious interference claims and suits involving injunctive relief. Here is an example of such a prophylactic clause:

> Employee represents to Employer that (i) except as disclosed to Employer in writing on or before the date hereof, Employee is not a party to any agreement or understanding, written or oral, which may restrict Employee in any manner from

> engaging in any activities which Employee may be required or expected to perform in connection with Employee's duties with Employer, (ii) Employee will not disclose or use any confidential information that belongs to a former employer or other third party for Employer's benefit without the prior consent of such party, and (iii) Employee returned or destroyed any papers in Employee's possession, which contained a former employer's or other third party's confidential information which Employee has a duty not to disclose.

Requiring a prospective employee to certify that he is not bringing confidential information to the workplace will limit tortious interference claims and often diffuse tension between competing employers.

1-2:4.2 GARDEN LEAVE

Garden leave is a lesser-used concept that originated in Europe but has started to become statutorily adopted—to various degrees—by states.[23] The term "garden leave" comes from the notion that an "employee will stay home and work in his garden" for a certain amount of time between resignation and going to work for a competitor.[24] Under garden leave clauses, employers traditionally require departing employees to give notice for a period of days, weeks, or months. During that period, the employee has no duties but is paid his regular salary and benefits. This provision effectively extends the employment—and therefore, the departing employee's duty of loyalty and any restrictive covenants—allowing the employer to get its "ducks in a row" so it

23. *See, e.g.*, Mass. Gen. Laws Ann. ch. 149, § 24L ("To be valid and enforceable, a noncompetition agreement . . . shall be supported by a garden leave clause or other mutually-agreed upon consideration between the employer and the employee, provided that such consideration is specified in the noncompetition agreement.").

24. Greg T. Lembrick, *Garden Leave: A Possible Solution to the Uncertain Enforceability of Restrictive Employment Covenants*, 102 Colum. L. Rev. 2291, 2296 (2002).

can fend off any efforts of the departing employee to immediately start competing.[25] Here is an example of a garden leave provision:

> At any time after Employee or Employer gives notice to the other to terminate the employment in accordance with the terms of this Agreement or after Employee purported to terminate the employment without giving full notice and Employer does not accept such resignation on such terms, Employer may require that during any such notice period or any part or parts of such notice period Employee does not enter or attend Employer's premises ("Garden Leave"), and during any period of Garden Leave, Employee must not:
>
> (i) undertake any work for any third party as an employee or otherwise;
>
> (ii) have any contact or communication with Employer's clients, customers, vendors, or suppliers; or
>
> (iii) have any contact or communication with Employer's employees, managers, members, officers, directors, agents, or consultants.
>
> During any period of Garden Leave, Employee will remain an employee of Employer and the employment shall continue (notwithstanding that Employee resigned as a board director or from any offices of the Employer) and Employee is not entitled to become employed or engaged by any other company, partnership, person, or entity in any capacity. Employee will continue to be paid salary and be provided with contractual benefits during any period of Garden Leave in the usual

25. *See id.*

> manner under the Agreement, except Employee will not be entitled to receive any bonus or commission accumulated during or in respect of Garden Leave.

1-2:4.3 DUTY OF LOYALTY

Common law imposes a duty of loyalty on employees to act primarily for the benefit of their employer in matters connected with their employment.[26] Many employers reinforce this duty through contract. Here is an example of a duty of loyalty provision:

> During Employee's employment with Employer, Employee shall (i) devote Employee's full business time and effort to the furtherance of the business of Employer, (ii) carry out and implement all proper direction and instruction from Employer that conform with reasonable and sound business practices, (iii) abide by Employer's written policies and procedures, and by such other policies and procedures of which Employee has received notice, (iv) use best efforts to avoid any action that might maliciously damages, harm, or discredit the reputation of Employer's products and services, and (v) not engage in any activity that competes with Employer's business or interferes with the performance of Employee's duties hereunder.

1-2:4.4 DISCOVERIES AND INVENTIONS

Many employers choose to rely solely on nondisclosure covenants to protect inventions or discoveries that are developed by their employees. Others include a separate provision to protect discoveries, inventions, ideas, contributions, and improvements related

26. *Daniel v. Falcon Interest Realty Corp.*, 190 S.W.3d 177, 185 (Tex. App.—Houston [1st Dist.] 2005, no pet.).

to the employer's business (often known as "work for hire" covenants). Here is an example of a "work for hire" covenant:

> Employee has no license or any other ownership or right in any intellectual property used by Employer ("Employer's IP"). Any addition to or improvement upon Employer's IP arising in connection with Employee's employment with Employer shall be deemed the property of Employer. To the extent that such additional work or improvement is not automatically deemed the property of Employer, Employee hereby assigns such additional work or improvements over to Employer free and clear of all liens or claims of third parties and the same is deemed "work for hire" under the copyright laws of the United States.

1-2:4.5 SAVINGS CLAUSES

As briefly discussed above, when implementing confidentiality covenants, employers should be mindful of employees' rights under the NLRA (which applies to most private-sector employees—and not merely unionized employees). The same is true for nondisparagement covenants. The bedrock of the NLRA is Section 7, which guarantees employees the right to "engage in concerted activities" including the right to discuss their terms and conditions of employment (*e.g.*, compensation, working conditions) with each other. An employer engages in an unfair labor practice (ULP) when it denies or limits the Section 7 rights of employees. The National Labor Relations Board (NLRB) has taken the position that confidentiality and nondisparagement covenants may violate an employee's Section 7 rights—and thereby become a ULP—if the covenants could reasonably be construed to restrict Section 7-protected communications, such as the discussion of wages among co-workers or criticism of labor practices. While a savings clause does not provide immunity, it is still useful for minimizing the likelihood of a covenant being construed as infringing on Section 7 rights.[27] Here is an example of a savings clause:

> Employee has the right to engage in protected concerted activity, and nothing in this agreement (or any policy of Employer) is designed to interfere with, restrain, or prevent Employee from communicating with other co-workers or third parties regarding the terms and conditions of their employment.

1-3 STEPS TO TAKE WHEN EMPLOYEES DEPART

1-3:1 GATHER INFORMATION DIRECTLY FROM THE DEPARTING EMPLOYEE

It is almost always best to engage in active discussions with the departing employee once he indicates he is leaving. Do not be afraid to ask very pointed questions, such as: where is the employee going, what does he plan to do, does he plan to compete, is he aware of his common law and contractual obligations regarding confidentiality and other applicable restrictive covenants? There are a host of questions that you can and should ask, in a businesslike manner, while making clear that you, as the employer, intend to enforce your rights.

> **Taking steps at the time the employee leaves will be worth the effort in preventing costly disputes later.**

27. *Quicken Loans, Inc. & Lydia E. Garza*, 361 NLRB No. 94 (N.L.R.B. Nov. 3, 2014) *review denied, enforcement granted sub nom, Quicken Loans, Inc. v. Nat'l Labor Relations Bd.*, 830 F.3d 542 (D.C. Cir. 2016).

1-3:2 PROTECT YOURSELF

Regardless of the amicability of the relationship, the employer should actively protect itself against potential nefarious activity by a departing employee. Indeed, the law requires taking such protections as a prerequisite to the employer enforcing its rights. Simple steps that the employer should take include requiring that the employee return all pieces of paper (in any location) that constitute property of or involve the employer's business. Computer access needs to be changed; the employer's laptops, phones, or other devices need to be retrieved; and access to the employer's electronic information needs to be limited or denied (and preserved). Moreover, steps should be taken against inadvertent or intentional deletion of information. These issues are discussed in greater detail in subsequent chapters.

1-3:3 DO YOU SEND A WARNING LETTER?

When an employer knows or suspects that a departing employee is violating some contractual, statutory, or common law duty, a question frequently arises about whether it is advisable to send a warning letter before filing a lawsuit. A letter may be appropriate in some cases, such as when a competitor (*i.e.*, the new employer) is unaware that its new hire is subject to restrictive covenants. The letter may also serve the purpose of a "shot across the bow," heightening a competitor's sensitivity to the need to protect confidential information and avoid being sued. Often, warning letters signal to a court that the owner of trade secret or confidential information made immediate efforts to find a business solution before resorting to judicial intervention. Also, the letter may diminish or eliminate any negative inference that might otherwise be drawn from delay in responding to such behavior. Of course, such a communication places the new employer on notice and might allow it to prepare more quickly for the possibility of litigation and allow unscrupulous new employers and departing employees to destroy important evidence. Warning letters should also be carefully drafted to avoid a possible claim that the former employer is improperly interfering with the departing employee's livelihood and/or a competitor's business.

Lastly, an employer should be careful that sending a warning letter is not the first step of waiver. In *Ally Fin., Inc. v. Gutierrez*, Ally (the former employer) warned Gutierrez (the departed employee), via demand letter, that an enforcement action would be taken because she had breached the nonsolicitation covenant.[28] One month later, however, the company gave Gutierrez her third payment under the Compensation Incentive Plan, a provision of which stated that previous award payments would be repaid under a claw-back provision if the nonsolicitation covenant was violated.[29] The court found that Ally's intentional conduct was inconsistent with the intent in the demand letter to enforce the nonsolicitation covenant and, therefore, waived its right to enforce the covenant.[30] It is important for employers to effectively communicate internally in the aftermath of a departing employee to ensure that one department does not act inconsistently (*e.g.*, finance sending a third payment) with another department (*e.g.*, legal sending a warning letter) and consequently waive its right to seek enforcement of a restrictive covenant.

1-4 FACT GATHERING

It is this author's opinion that thorough initial fact finding is crucial to preparing for and succeeding in litigation. Cases involving restrictive covenants typically involve injunctive relief, so it is critical that factual and documentary information be gathered quickly and efficiently. Therefore, employers must promptly investigate suspected misappropriation of trade secrets or the taking of confidential information. Thorough investigations will include searching the departing employee's office, reviewing all inbound and outbound e-mails, preserving and searching

28. *Ally Fin., Inc. v. Gutierrez*, No. 02-13-00108-CV, 2014 WL 261038, at *3 (Tex. App.—Fort Worth Jan. 23, 2014, no pet.).

29. *Id.* at *4.

30. *Id.* at *7–8.

computer hard drives, and checking any other computerized files. Certain software programs enable recovery of information where there was attempted "deletion" from the computer. Competent computer forensics vendors can sort unusual activity, such as the copying or printing of large volumes of information, access to abnormal files, or otherwise duplicating information. Interviews of a former employee's staff and co-workers often uncover information. Other fertile places to look are telephone records, calendars, phone slips, expense reports, travel logs, and sales activity reports (a drop in production may be indicative of a departing employee deliberately saving leads or sales for his new employer). "Swipe in" and "swipe out" records also may show abnormal access by the departing employee to the employer's office during off hours. This type of investigatory diligence is often the difference between winning and losing one of these types of cases.

Former employers should also be alert to opportunities for researching departing employees' activities with a new entity, including verifying dates of incorporation (particularly with a startup of business), office locations, other filings, marketing material, websites, LinkedIn, Facebook, and other social media.

1-5 WHETHER TO SUE

Costs are always an issue and should be balanced with what is at stake. How valuable is the information, technology, know-how, client goodwill, or other assets that the employer is trying to protect? Does the information have only temporary value, is it outdated, or is the information of critical importance to the employer's business plan? Is there a principled reason to pursue litigation? Does the employer want to take a stand regarding this departing employee—or his new employer—in hopes that it will "send a message" to competitors or future departing employees? Did the departing employee have management responsibilities or specific fiduciary duties? Is proprietary data at stake, or is there a belief that the departing employee has taken information? Is the new employer a significant competitor such that the activities of the departing employee might have significant competitive ramifications?

There are other important considerations. Will a siege with a departing employee take away from the day-to-day competitive activities of the employer in the marketplace? Stated differently, will winning the litigation battle cause the employer to lose the war on the business side? Conversely, is it important to the employer to take a consistent policy of enforcing its rights as a strong deterrent to others who may be considering unlawful activities or competition? And will the lawsuit cause other competitors to think twice before approaching the employer's employees?

One should always consider "fallout" from the litigation. Where the issues involve noncompetition or nonsolicitation covenants, it is often clients or potential clients who are key witnesses to what really happened in a dispute. Typically, employers are very reticent to send subpoenas or deposition notices to clients or potential clients. Another concern is publicity from newspapers, bloggers, or other interested media providing coverage, which might be unwelcome and might allow competitors to become aware of information that they would otherwise not seek.

In a later section of this book, we will talk at length about injunctive relief. Typically, these types of cases involve requests for temporary restraining orders (TROs) or temporary injunctions. To pursue rights in courts of equity, employers must move quickly, lest they be seen as "sitting on their rights" prior to seeking equitable relief. Typically, a disgruntled former employee, who takes confidential and proprietary information, leaves suddenly, and violates restrictive covenants, is not particularly sympathetic. However, once the new employee settles in, and the new employer spends time and money training or integrating the employee, the balancing of the equities becomes less favorable to the former employer. Another often overlooked consideration is that of "unclean hands." Has the former employer engaged in violating restrictive covenants? Has it engaged in other wrongdoing regarding the employee, such as wage and hour violations, sexual harassment, or discharge without good cause? Moreover, an employer who discharges an employee for poor performance may have difficulty establishing that the employer is harmed by that departing employee being permitted to compete despite a restrictive covenant. Finally, one should always consider the significant pressure and time demands that seeking a TRO puts on the involved management employees in a short period of time, disrupting normal schedules and diverting normal business activity.

1-6 WHO TO SUE

Potential defendants in these types of cases usually include departing employees and a company that either employs or is started by the departing employee. Moreover, any person or entity who received trade secrets or confidential information might also be a potential co-defendant. "Necessary parties," and the procedural considerations of who should be joined at the TRO/temporary injunction stage, are discussed in greater detail in subsequent chapters.

1-7 WHERE TO SUE

Venue is often a very important tactical decision. A contract's forum selection clause may dictate where suit may be filed. There also may be an arbitration clause, which removes all or part of the case from the courthouse. Usually, employers want to sue close to "home" for convenience, to maximize chances of success, and to reduce litigation expenses. Often, this puts the departing employee at a disadvantage—particularly if the employer's "home" is not where the employee lives or works. Other important considerations are (1) choosing between state or federal court and (2) whether the case is removable—considerations that may impact which claims are pled and/or which parties are joined.

Less likely considerations are (1) whether the departing employee moved to a different state and may file a declaratory action in that state[31] and (2) the location of an employer's computer server.[32] The conclusion may vary in different parts of Texas, but it is generally very advantageous to stay in a state court where the rules require hearings under specific timetables and typically allow greater access to the court. Finally, judicial temperament and precedent are also important venue considerations. Some venues are regarded as more "business friendly" than others. Judicial precedent is also not the same in every venue. By way of example, Texas appellate courts are divided on whether restrictive covenants may be reformed at the TRO/temporary injunction stage[33]—the availability (or lack thereof) of which can have monumental implications on injunctive relief and damages in a departing employee lawsuit. These practical and procedural venue considerations are discussed in greater detail in subsequent chapters.

31. *Application Group, Inc. v. Hunter Group, Inc.*, 61 Cal. App. 4th 881 (Cal. App. 1st Div. 1998).

32. *MacDermid, Inc. v. Deiter*, 702 F.3d 725 (2d Cir. 2012) (Connecticut employer was able to assert long-arm jurisdiction over an employee residing in Canada. The employee was domiciled and worked in Canada for her employer's subsidiary. The employee, knowing she was facing termination, e-mailed confidential information from her work e-mail to her personal e-mail. The employer's servers were located in Connecticut and—under Connecticut's long-arm statute—the employee was subject to jurisdiction in Connecticut.).

33. *Compare Cardinal Health Staffing Network v. Bowen*, 106 S.W.3d 230, 237–39 (Tex. App.—Houston [1st Dist.] 2003, no pet.) (holding that a restrictive covenant may only be reformed as a final remedy, not as a means to support a temporary injunction); *Gray Wireline Serv., Inc. v. Cavanna*, 374 S.W.3d 464, 470–71 (Tex. App.—Waco 2011, no pet.) (agreeing that "reformation pursuant to section 15.51(c) . . . is a remedy to be granted at a final hearing, whether on the merits or by summary judgment, not as interim relief") *with Tranter, Inc. v. Liss*, No. 02-13-00157-CV, 2014 WL 1257278, at *10 (Tex. App.—Fort Worth Mar. 27, 2014, no pet.) (finding that although a noncompete agreement was overbroad, the employer had "established a probable right to recovery" because of the likelihood that the agreement could be "reformed to contain reasonable limitations"); *see also McKissock, LLC v. Martin*, 267 F. Supp. 3d 841, 857–58 (W.D. Tex. 2016) (reforming a noncompete covenant while granting a preliminary injunction).

1-8 SUMMARY

This first chapter is merely intended to provide an overview of the substantive and tactical issues you will likely encounter in a case involving a departing employee. Subsequent chapters will address various causes of action, defenses, remedies, and strategies you will need to address depending on the types of issues you confront.

Chapter 2
Injunctions

Edited by Robert Radcliff

2-1 OVERVIEW

Cases involving departing employees (particularly those leaving on poor terms) often include injunctive relief. Such relief is sought because a departing employee's offending conduct often involves activities that (1) damage her former employer's business and (2) are not remedied with damages. This lack of damages frequently exists because damages are hard to prove or because the departing employee is not responsible in damages. Under Texas law, there are three procedural injunctions.

2-1:1 TEMPORARY RESTRAINING ORDER

A Temporary Restraining Order (TRO) is intended, on an emergency basis, to preserve the status quo until a temporary injunction hearing is held. Judges typically make their decisions based upon a movant's sworn papers.

2-1:2 TEMPORARY INJUNCTION

A temporary injunction hearing occurs within 14 or 28 days after a TRO is entered.[1] Entry of a TRO is not a prerequisite to

1. Tex. R. Civ. P. 680.

a temporary injunction hearing. Temporary injunction hearings are evidentiary with live witnesses. The purpose of temporary injunctions is to preserve the status quo. As a practical matter, a temporary injunction typically resolves most of a case's issues.

2-1:3 PERMANENT INJUNCTION

A permanent injunction is entered after a final trial on the merits.[2] Injunctions are classified as either prohibitory (*i.e.*, prohibiting a party from performing an action) or mandatory (*i.e.*, requiring a party to perform an action). Because there are inherent difficulties with mandatory injunctions, injunctive relief is typically prohibitory.

2-2 RULES GOVERNING INJUNCTIONS IN GENERAL

Injunction practice is governed by Chapter 65 of Texas's Civil Practices & Remedies Code (CPRC) and Rules 680 to 693(a) of the Texas Rules of Civil Procedure (TRCP). CPRC Section 65.001, entitled "Application of Equity Principles," states: "The principles governing courts of equity govern injunction proceedings if not in conflict with this chapter or other law."

Chapter 65 makes it clear that the principal of equity applies to injunctions. CPRC section 65.011, entitled "Grounds Generally," states that injunctions may be granted if:

> 1) The applicant is entitled to the relief demanded and all or part of the relief requires the restraint of some act prejudicial to the applicant; or . . .
>
> 2) The applicant is entitled to a writ of

2. *Citizens State Bank v Caney Invs.*, 746 S.W.2d 477, 478 (Tex. 1988) (per curiam). *See In re Choice! Energy, L.P.*, 325 S.W.3d 805, 808 (Tex. App.—Houston [14th Dist.] 2010, no pet.) (interpreted the meaning of a "current" employee in 2009 in the context of a 1998 permanent injunction and final judgment.).

> injunction under the principals of equity and the statutes of this state relating to injunctions.

2-3 RELATIVE CONDUCT IN INJUNCTION CASES

Because injunctive relief is equitable, the relative "cleanliness" of the conduct of the parties will always be at issue. Therefore, some good, old-fashion Texas mudslinging should be expected. Successfully labeling your client as "good" and opposing counsel's as "bad" is fundamental in the court's determination of whether or not an injunction should be issued. Certainly, prudent counsel should expect the other side to take a similar approach. "Cleanliness" can determine both whether an injunction is obtained and its scope. If you convince the court to believe that a noncompete has been violated, trade secrets have been stolen, or confidential information has been taken, it will be substantially more inclined to grant (or broaden) injunctive relief. Consequently, conquering the high road for your client, while effectively characterizing the other side as "bad" and culpable, is imperative in cases seeking injunctive relief.

Courts are unanimous in their intolerance of thievery, and they will often go to great lengths to remedy a theft. Therefore, if an employee stole confidential information or trade secrets, abused a confidential relationship, or gained an unfair advantage (either by taking confidential information or diverting customers), an injunction would be issued. The *Miller Paper* case clearly illustrates this concept.[3] In that case, several employees of Roberts Paper left to start a competing business. They took customer lists and stole an item called "the Book."[4] The Book was compiled

3. *Miller Paper Co. v. Roberts Paper Co.*, 901 S.W.2d 593, 596-97 (Tex. App.—Amarillo 1995, no writ). *See also Gonzales v. Zamora*, 791 S.W.2d 258 (Tex. App. Corpus Christi 1990), which has slightly modified the *Miller* outcome in certain circumstances. Meaning, while a former employee can be enjoined from using or disclosing confidential information related to trade secrets that was acquired while an employee, the former employee cannot be enjoined from using general knowledge.

4. *Miller Paper Co. v. Roberts Paper Co.*, 901 S.W.2d 593, 601 (Tex. App.—Amarillo 1995, no writ).

over the course of fifty-two years and was not generally accessible on Roberts' computer system, although copies were periodically distributed to the sales force as the Book was updated. In addition to the customer lists and the Book, the employees sent nearly two thousand letters to former clients and made untrue statements about Roberts, including that it was no longer in business, had lost staff, or was acquired by Miller Paper.[5] Not surprisingly, the trial court granted an injunction preventing Roberts from using the "documents, records, files and hard copy taken from" the plaintiff.[6] The Amarillo Court of Appeals reasoned that the trial court had not prohibited the employees from competing but had, instead, merely prevented them from utilizing "the materials developed by or on behalf of Roberts."[7]

Departing employees should quickly gather defenses to thwart the "bad guy" allegations that will almost certainly be slung their way. There are several ways that a departing employee can prevent such allegations. The best defense would be to prove that she did not take anything prohibited when she left her former employer. Alternatively, she could prove that anything taken was taken inadvertently—a common, understandable occurrence in the age of computers and electronic information. A third argument could be that the information taken was not a trade secret and was, in fact, commonly known, readily ascertainable, available through independent investigation, or provides no competitive advantage. Finally, failing those arguments, defendant or counsel should consider quarantining or sequestering the property (whether digital or hard copy) as soon as possible. However, counsel should remain mindful of the duties of preservation and spoliation. This action allows the defendant to maintain that she simply cannot use what she does not have access to.

5. *Miller Paper Co. v. Roberts Paper Co.*, 901 S.W.2d 593, 601 (Tex. App.—Amarillo 1995, no writ).

6. *Miller Paper Co. v. Roberts Paper Co.*, 901 S.W.2d 593, 600 (Tex. App.—Amarillo 1995, no writ).

7. *Miller Paper Co. v. Roberts Paper Co.*, 901 S.W.2d 593, 602 (Tex. App.—Amarillo 1995, no writ).

First impressions are important, and they only happen once. The counsel who is successful in impressing upon the court the negative characterization of the opposition and the positive characterization of his client will likely secure the desired injunction holding.

2-4 TEMPORARY RESTRAINING ORDERS

Texas Rule of Civil Procedure 680 governs TROs. Injunction practice is very technical. Accordingly, requirements governing injunctions must be met exactly, or an injunction may be void. TRO applicants must plead the prerequisites for injunctive relief.[8] Applicants for TROs and temporary injunctions must plead and prove three specific elements:

1. Cause of action;
2. Probable right to the relief sought; and
3. Probable injury to the movant.[9]

2-4:1 CAUSE OF ACTION

In most instances, pleadings need to tie the injunction application to a specific cause of action.[10] There are rare instances when a suit for permanent injunction is authorized by statute.

---

8. *In re MetroPCS Commc'ns., Inc.*, 391 S.W.3d 329, 337 (Tex. App.—Dallas 2013, no pet.) (orig. proceeding) ("[a] temporary restraining order is basically a writ of injunction within the meaning of Tex. R. Civ. P. 682. Additionally, rule 687, which sets forth the requisites for a 'writ of injunction,' provides specific requirements in the event such 'writ of injunction' is a 'temporary restraining order.' Tex. R. Civ. P. 687(e). Accordingly, we cannot agree . . . that a temporary restraining order is not a 'writ of injunction' subject to the requirements of rule 682.") (citations omitted).

9. *Butnaru v. Ford Motor Co.*, 84 S.W.3d 198, 204 (Tex. 2002) ("To obtain a temporary injunction, the applicant must plead and prove three specific elements: (1) a cause of action against the defendant; (2) a probable right to the relief sought; and (3) a probable, imminent, and irreparable injury in the interim."). *See generally* Hilda Galvan and Kevin T. Kennedy, *Covenants Not to Compete and Injunctive Relief*, State Bar of Tex. (Mar. 2015).

10. *See* Tex. Civ. Prac. & Rem. Code § 65.001; *see also* Tex. Bus. & Comm. Code § 1551.

2-4:2 PROBABLE RIGHT TO RELIEF

Pleadings must demonstrate that a movant has a probable right to relief on a particular cause of action. This requirement does not mean that the movant must prove the cause of action with certainty, but only that the movant "probably" will prevail.[11]

2-4:3 PROBABLE INJURY

To prove probable injury, movants must plead and prove (1) imminent harm, (2) irreparable injury, and (3) inadequate remedy at law.[12]

As stated earlier, TRCP 680 governs the entry of TROs and must be complied with in every respect. TROs are issued to preserve the status quo, *i.e.*, the last peaceable act before the incident in question.[13]

---

11. *Jenkins v. TransDel Corp.*, No. 03-04-00033-CV, 2004 WL 1404364, at *4 (Tex. App.—Austin June 24, 2004, no pet.) (mem. op.) ("Rule 683 does not mandate that an order set out each and every element that must be shown by a party seeking a temporary injunction. Instead, it requires a trial court to set out with reasonable specificity and detail the reasons for the injunction and the acts to be enjoined." *Transport Co. of Tex. v. Robertson Transps., Inc.*, 261 S.W.2d 549, 552-53 (Tex. 1953) ("[Tex. R. Civ. P.] 683 does not require order to state specifically why applicant will probably prevail on final trial, only why probable right to recover will be endangered without injunction; enjoined party may seek findings of fact and conclusions of law). This order does precisely that. The trial court explained what [defendant] had done and explained what he was forbidden to do in the future. Those statements sufficiently describe the situation and how [company] stands to suffer injury in the absence of an injunction.").

12. *Zuniga v. Wooster Ladder Co.*, 119 S.W.3d 856, 860-61 (Tex. App.—San Antonio 2003, no pet.) ("A showing of probable injury requires proof of imminent harm, irreparable injury, and an inadequate remedy at law.") (citing *Fasken v. Darby*, 901 S.W.2d 591, 592 (Tex. App.—El Paso 1995, no writ)); *Guillermo Benavides Garza Inv. v. Benavides,* 04-13-00453-CV, 2014 WL 3339555, at *1 (Tex. App. —San Antonio July 9, 2014, no pet.) (mem. op.) (To satisfy "irreparable harm, it is not sufficient that the application show the actions he seeks to enjoin will harm him personally; rather the alleged irreparable harm must threaten the appellant's right to recover on his cause of action. *See State v. Cook United, Inc.,* 464 S.W.2d 105, 106 (Tex. 1971)").

13. *Allied Home Mortg. Capital Corp. v. Fowler*, 14-10-00992-CV, 2011 WL 2367086, at *4 (Tex. App.—Houston [14th Dist.] June 9, 2011, no pet.) (mem. op.) ("The status quo is the last actual, peaceable, noncontested status which preceded the pending controversy.") (citing *RP & R, Inc. v. Territo*, 32 S.W.3d 396, 402 (Tex. App.—Houston [14th Dist.] 2000, no pet.)).

2-5 REQUIREMENTS FOR AN INJUNCTION APPLICATION

Applications for a TRO must:

1. If the TRO is *ex parte*, state that an *ex parte* TRO is necessary;[14]
2. Identify the person or entity to be restrained;[15]
3. Define the injury and describe why the injury is irreparable;[16] and
4. Be verified. The verification requirement can be satisfied by supporting affidavits or actual verification of the application. Verification must be based upon personal knowledge.[17] Verification can be waived: "A verified petition for injunctive relief is not required to grant a temporary injunction, however, when a full evidentiary hearing on evidence independent of the petition has been held."[18]

Injunction practice is highly technical. Prudent lawyers should take care to comply with all requirements of the rules.

---

14. Tex. R. Civ. P. 680.

15. Tex. R. Civ. P. 683.

16. Tex. R. Civ. P. 680, 683.

17. *In re MetroPCS Commc'ns., Inc.*, 391 S.W.3d 329, 336-37 (Tex. App.—Dallas 2013, no pet.) (orig. proceeding) ("'Verified by his affidavit' means 'proved to be true or correct.'") (citing *City of Arlington v. Dallas-Fort Worth Safety Coach Co.*, 270 S.W. 1094, 1095 (Tex. Civ. App.—Fort Worth 1925, no writ) ("Verification on information and belief is held to be insufficient nor is an affidavit that the allegations sought to be verified are true and correct 'to the best of my knowledge and belief' sufficient.")); *see Williams v. Bagley*, 875 S.W.2d 808, 810 (Tex. App.—Beaumont 1994, no writ).

18. *Mattox v. Jackson*, 336 S.W.3d 759, 763 (Tex. App.—Houston [1st Dist.] 2011, no pet.) (citing *Georgiades v. Di Ferrante*, 871 S.W.2d 878, 882 (Tex. App.— Houston [14th Dist.] 1994, writ denied)).

2-6 CONFERENCING REQUIREMENTS

Many jurisdictions' local rules include a conferencing requirement as part of the application. For example, Dallas County's courts require movants to show whether (1) the defendant is represented, (2) the defendant wants to be heard or can be reached, (3) there is irreparable, imminent harm and insufficient time to notify the defendant or its counsel, and/or (4) notification would impair or annul the court's right to grant requested injunctive relief.[19]

2-7 VENUE

Venue normally depends on whether the request for injunctive relief is (1) the primary reason for the suit or (2) ancillary to the suit. Usually, injunctive relief is ancillary to the lawsuit. In that case, venue is determined by the lawsuit, not by the request for injunction.[20] When the injunctive relief is the primary relief requested in the application, then the mandatory venue statute controls.[21] Local rules may require the movant to notify the court if the movant's case is subject to transfer.[22]

---

19. *See* Dallas Cnty. Local R. 2.02(a)-(b); *see also* Harris Cnty. Local R. 3.3.6; *see also* Bexar Cnty. Local R. 6(C).

20. *In re City of Corpus Christi*, 13-12-00510-CV, 2012 WL 3755604, at *4 (Tex. App.—Corpus Christi Aug. 29, 2012, no pet.) (mem. op.) (writ of mandamus) (" . . . the possibility that the trial court will resort to its injunctive powers to enforce a judgment rendered in this case does not by itself transform the suit into one for a 'writ of injunction' within the meaning of [Tex. Civ. Prac. & Rem. Code §] 65.023(a). In short, based on the pleadings and relief sought, we cannot conclude that the relief sought by [petitioner] in this matter is purely or primarily injunctive. Accordingly, [Tex. Civ. Prac. & Rem. Code §] 65.023 does not apply to compel mandatory venue in Nueces County.") (citations omitted).

21. Tex. Civ. Prac. & Rem. Code § 65.023; *In re Daniel*, 12-06-00232-CV, 2006 WL 2361350, at *2 (Tex. App.—Tyler Aug. 16, 2006, no pet.) (mem. op.) (orig. proceeding) ("The question of proper venue is raised by a party by simply objecting to a plaintiff's venue choice through a motion to transfer venue. If the plaintiff's chosen venue rests on a permissive venue statute and the defendant files a meritorious motion to transfer venue based upon a mandatory venue provision, the trial court must grant the motion.") (citations omitted).

22. *See e.g.*, Dallas Cnty. Local R. 2.02(c).

2-8 BOND

TRO applications must state the movant's willingness to post a bond.[23] Bond is required and may not be waived.[24] The bond's amount is discretionary with the court and usually set in an amount related to the potential damages caused by entry of the TRO. A writ of injunction is not effective until the bond is posted.[25] Thus, an injunction is not effective until the bond is posted.

2-9 SERVICE

TROs must be served. They may be served through a sheriff, constable, or private process server.[26] Therefore, before going to the courthouse to seek a TRO, prudent practitioners should determine the (1) process to obtain a citation, (2) amount of time to obtain a citation, (3) location of the defendant(s), and (4) the best way to serve the defendant(s). This knowledge is important

---

23. Tex. R. Civ. P. 684.

24. *City of McAllen v. McAllen Police Officers' Union*, No. 13-10-00609-CV, 2011 WL 2175606, at *3, n.7 (Tex. App.—Corpus Christi June 2, 2011, no pet.) (mem. op.) ("whether the [defendant] agreed to the waiver [of Rule 684's bond requirement] is immaterial because the failure of the temporary injunction order to comply with rule 684 renders the order void, and 'a party who agrees to a void order has agreed to nothing.'"); *Chambers v. Rosenberg*, 916 S.W.2d 633, 635 (Tex. App.—Austin 1996, writ denied) ("The [Supreme Court of Texas] has held that temporary orders filed without the bond are void, not merely voidable. Though none of the cited cases explicitly concerns an agreed order, we find the strong theme of literal construction of the rule convinces us that we should construe the rule literally in this ease; we are particularly persuaded to do so because the parties here did not explicitly waive the protection of a bond. The temporary injunction was void for lack of a bond.").

25. *See Nationwide Life Ins. Co. v. Nations*, 654 S.W.2d 860, 861 (Tex. App.—Houston [14th] Dist. 1983, no writ) ("Under Tex. R. Civ. P. 684 a bond is specifically required as a condition precedent to the issuance of a temporary injunction. Failure of the applicant to file such a bond renders the injunction void ab initio.") (citing *Goodwin v. Goodwin*, 456 S.W.2d 885 (Tex. 1970)). See also Texas A & M Univ. v. Carapia, 10-14-00280-CV, 2015 WL 3451609, at *5 (Tex. App.—Waco May 28, 2015, no pet. h.) ("The intent of the Texas Supreme Court in promulgating Rule 684 was to require a bond payable to a party against whom a [TRO] or injunction is issued before the order may lawfully issue . . . [w]ithout such a bond the order is void . . . [t]hus, for this additional reason, [this] temporary injunction is void.").

26. Tex. R. Civ. P. 686; *see* Tex. R. Civ. P. 689.

because *service* of the TRO puts movants in a position to seek contempt after noncompliance.[27]

Many practitioners also use any reasonable method to give defendants actual notice of the prohibited conduct (choosing to use e-mail, fax, or even taping the notice to a defendant's front door) to make certain that defendants have actual knowledge of the prohibited conduct. Most TROs prohibit conduct by anyone who "has actual knowledge" of the TRO.[28]

2-10 WATCH OUT!

TRO applications are almost always drafted and executed in haste. Consequently, even the most thoughtful and careful practitioner may overlook crucial issues. Thus, someone on the client representation team needs to be wary of certain issues.

For example, one or more applicable documents, (*e.g.*, employment agreements, stock option agreements, nondisclosure agreements, covenants not to compete) may have a venue selection provision. Texas courts generally give deference to such provisions.[29]

---

27. *See* Tex. R. Civ. P. 692 ("Disobedience of an injunction may be punished by the court or judge, in term time or in vacation, as a contempt."); *see also Tex. Dep't of Pub. Safety v. Morris*, 411 S.W.2d 620, 623 (Tex. Civ. App.—Houston [1st Dist.] 1967, no writ) ("A citation is required to be issued and a writ of injunction must command the person or persons enjoined to desist and refrain from the commission or continuance of the acts enjoined and such person or persons may be held in contempt for disobedience thereof.").

28. *See Credit Bureau of Laredo, Inc. v. State*, 515 S.W.2d 706, 708-09 (Tex. Civ. App.—San Antonio 1974, writ granted, aff'd on other grounds) ("the attorney who signed the agreed judgment, testified that he had represented [Appellant] . . .; that he was representing [Appellant] when the permanent injunction here involved was entered and that he was acting as their legal representative; that he was paid by appellant for such representation; that he signed the judgment and represented to the court that he was acting as their legal representative. The president of [Appellant] testified that he had actual knowledge that an injunction had been issued by the District Court of Webb County enjoining such corporation from deceptive practices. There is testimony that the court costs were paid by check of appellant. . . . [court summarizes *Ex parte Foster*, 188 S.W. 2d 382 (1945)] . . . we hold that the trial court correctly held that the [Appellant] participated in the injunction proceeding as a real party and was bound by the injunction.") (emphasis added) (citing *Ex parte Foster*, 188 S.W. 2d 382 (1945)).

29. *In re AutoNation, Inc.*, 228 S.W.3d 663, 669 (Tex. 2007) ("even if [*DeSantis v. Wackenhut Corp.*, 793 S.W.2d 670 (Tex. 1990)] requires Texas courts to apply Texas

Also, be vigilant in searching for arbitration clauses. An omnibus arbitration clause may purport to require arbitration of "all disputes between employer and employee." Courts have held that such arbitration clauses include disputes between former employers and departing employees.[30] Many arbitration clauses have a "carve out" for injunctive relief. These clauses allow employers to seek injunctive relief in court and later try the damages phase of the case in arbitration.

If there is no carve out, then the employer will probably need to seek injunctive relief in arbitration. The arbitration process—depending on the case administrator and arbitrator—can be clumsier and more time consuming than litigation. Moreover, it is likely that confirmation of an arbitrator's award of injunctive relief is required before a defendant can be subject to contempt for violating the arbitrator's ruling.[31] Employer-plaintiffs should be careful to comply with arbitration provisions because a court-issued TRO may be void or voidable. Such action may breach a contract and thus subject the employer to an attorneys' fees claim under the TCPRC.[32]

Because of arbitration clauses' broad reach in Texas, even if there are multiple agreements (one of which carries with it an arbitration clause and another which explicitly resorts injunctive relief

---

law to certain employment disputes, it does not require suit to be brought in Texas when a forum-selection clause mandates venue elsewhere. No Texas precedent compels us to enjoin a party from asking a Florida court to honor the parties' express agreement to litigate a non-compete agreement in Florida, the employer's headquarters and principal place of business."); *see also In re MetroPCS Commc'ns., Inc.*, 391 S.W.3d 329, 336-37 (Tex. App.—Dallas 2013, no pet.) (orig. proceeding) (Texas's "Supreme Court has consistently granted petitions for writ of mandamus to enforce forum selection clauses because a trial court that improperly refuses to enforce such a clause has clearly abused its discretion.").

30. *Nitro-Lift Techs., L.L.C. v. Howard*, 568 U.S. 17, 18 (2012) (per curiam) ("By declaring the noncompetition agreements in two employment contracts null and void, rather than leaving that determination to the arbitrator in the first instance, the state court ignored a basic tenet of the [Federal Arbitration] Act's substantive arbitration law. The decision must be vacated.").

31. See *Int'l Longshoremen's Ass'n v. Phila. Marine Trade Ass'n*, 389 U.S. 64 (1967).

32. *See* Tex. Civ. Prac. & Rem. Code § 38.001.

to the courthouse in violation of restrictive covenants), failure to arbitrate may still be dangerous due to concerns of a potential claim to dissolve the TRO or for breach of contract in the face of an arbitration provision.

> Always ensure that anything a client swears to or verifies is accurate. Anticipate a line of questioning in a hearing or deposition where the opposing party scrutinizes what the client swore was true and correct in the initial pleading.

2-11 REQUIREMENTS OF A TEMPORARY RESTRAINING ORDER

As stated earlier, Rule 680 must be complied with precisely to effect a valid TRO. The TRO must:

1. State why the TRO was granted without notice if it was granted *ex parte*;[33]
2. Identify the person or entity to be restrained;[34]
3. Be in writing (any extension must also be written);
4. Describe the reason why a TRO was issued, define the injury, and describe why the injury is irreparable;[35]
5. Define in reasonable and understandable detail the act(s) to be restrained;[36]

33. Tex. R. Civ. P. 680.

34. Tex. R. Civ. P. 683.

35. Tex. R. Civ. P. 680.

36. Tex. R. Civ. P. 683.

6. Be self-contained (TROs cannot refer to other pleadings or documents);[37]
7. State the date and hour of issuance;[38]
8. State the expiration date[39] (TROs expire at midnight, 14 days after signed);[40]
9. Fix the amount of the TRO bond;[41] and
10. State the date of the temporary injunction hearing.[42]

2-12 OTHER DOCUMENTS TO PREPARE WHILE DRAFTING TRO APPLICATION

2-12:1 EXPEDITED DISCOVERY MOTION AND PROPOSED ORDER

Before asking a judge to grant a TRO application, efficient movants typically draft a Motion for Expedited Discovery with attached discovery requests and a proposed order. Movants often request disclosures, documents, interrogatory responses, admissions, and/or depositions under an expedited schedule.

---

37. Tex. R. Civ. P. 683.

38. Tex. R. Civ. P. 680.

39. Tex. R. Civ. P. 680.

40. *In re Walkup*, 122 S.W.3d 215, 217-18 (Tex. App.—Houston [1st Dist.] 2003, no pet.), (orig. proceeding) (The TRO expired at midnight, not at 2:30 PM when it was signed.)

41. Tex. R. Civ. P. 684; *Yong Dong Chen v. Xiu Rong Chen*, 09-10-00440-CV, 2011 WL 497157, at *2 (Tex. App.—Beaumont Feb. 10, 2011, no pet.) (mem. op.) ("A bond for a temporary restraining order does not continue on and act as security for a temporary injunction unless expressly authorized by the trial court." *Bay Fin. Sav. Bank, FSB v. Brown*, 142 S.W.3d 586, 591 (Tex. App.—Texarkana 2004, no pet.) (holding temporary injunction order void for noncompliance with Rule 683 and 684 when the order neither fixed bond nor "state[d] that the bond previously filed for the temporary restraining order continued as the bond for the temporary injunction" and did not set the cause for trial on the merits); *see Ex parte Coffee*, 160 Tex. 224, 328 S.W.2d 283, 291 (Tex. 1959).").

42. Tex. R. Civ. P. 680.

2-12:2 PRODUCTION REQUESTS

Movants may request documents before the temporary injunction hearing.[43] Time is limited, so movants often request documents (1) in very specific categories and (2) be produced within five days after the court signed the TRO. Movants often need an opportunity to receive and review documents before pre-hearing depositions.

2-12:3 DEPOSITION — REQUEST, NOTICE, AND SUBPOENAS

When a movant seeks to depose people before a temporary injunction hearing, the movant should prepare notices and subpoena duces tecum to be served on future deponents. Practitioners are aware that (depending on the deposition's timing) the parties might not be able to obtain a deposition transcript before the temporary injunction hearing.

2-12:4 BOND

Get client approval for a bond amount before the hearing. Then, draft a form to file a bond payable to the adverse party (or parties). The bond should have two or more good and sufficient sureties and track the language of TRCP 684.

2-12:5 PRESERVATION

Parties may notify adverse parties regarding their duty to preserve information by (1) sending a letter to the adverse party or (2) requesting a court order. The letter should specifically inform the recipient that it (and its agents, employees, etc.) has a duty to preserve data. These letters are normally sent to various recipients, such as adverse parties, related parties, and server hosts. In most cases, each party sends preservation letters.

---

43. *See* Tex. R. Civ. P. 196.3(a).

2-13 EXTENDING A TEMPORARY RESTRAINING ORDER

Courts may extend TROs for an additional 14 days (for a total of 28 days).[44] Before TROs expire, applicants often—by filing a motion that shows good cause—ask courts to extend TROs.[45] TROs may be extended for longer than 14 days if the parties agree.[46]

2-14 CHALLENGING A TEMPORARY RESTRAINING ORDER

Typically, the TRO is challenged by a motion to dissolve, modify, and/or increase bond.

2-14:1 MOTION TO DISSOLVE

Respondents may request dissolution of an *ex parte* TRO. Respondents must give two days' notice, unless shortened by court order.[47] Respondents may move to dissolve a TRO on grounds that the TRO is void, does not comply with Texas Rules (*e.g.*, noncompliance with bond requirements of TRCP 680), or that some other defect exists.

---

44. Tex. R. Civ. P. 680 (" . . . and shall expire by its terms within such time after signing, not to exceed fourteen days, as the court fixes, unless within the time so fixed the order, for good cause shown, is extended for a like period or unless the party against whom the order is directed consents that it may be extended for a longer period.").

45. Tex. R. Civ. P. 680.

46. Tex. R. Civ. P. 680 ("No more than one extension may be granted unless subsequent extensions are unopposed."). *See also In re Hauck*, 03-14-00640-CV, 2014 WL 5315370, at *1 (Tex. App.—Austin Oct. 13, 2014, no pet.) (mem. op., not designated for publication) ("The Texas Supreme Court has held that 'Rule 680 governs an extension of a temporary restraining order, whether with or without notice, and permits but one extension for no longer than fourteen days unless the restrained party agrees to a longer extension.' *In re Texas Natural Res. Conservation Comm'n*, 85 S.W.3d 201, 204-05 (Tex. 2002)."

47. Tex. R. Civ. P. 680 ("On two days' notice to the party who obtained the temporary restraining order without notice or on such shorter notice to that party as the court may prescribe, the adverse party may appear and move its dissolution or modification and in that event the court shall proceed to hear and determine such motion as expeditiously as the ends of justice require.").

2-14:2 MOTION TO MODIFY

Respondents may request modification of an *ex parte* TRO. Like dissolution, respondents must give two days' notice, unless shortened by court order.[48] Respondents can move to modify a TRO or temporary injunction on various grounds. For example, respondents may argue that (1) an injunction granted more relief than was requested, (2) an injunction was overbroad, (3) pleading prerequisites were not met, or (4) there is some other defect in the TRO or relief granted (*e.g.*, unconstitutional prior restraint).[49]

2-14:3 MOTION TO INCREASE BOND

Determining a bond amount's adequacy is made on a case-by-case basis and is based upon the record before the reviewing court.[50] "As a general rule, the amount of the bond required on the issuance of a temporary injunction rests within the sound discretion of the trial court and will not be disturbed on appeal in the absence of an abuse of discretion."[51]

48. Tex. R. Civ. P. 680.

49. Currie v. Int'l Telecharge, Inc., 722 S.W.2d 471, 475 (Tex. App.—Dallas 1986, no writ) (in response to motion to dissolve, the trial court modified; "hearing was held on [defendant-former employee's] motion to dissolve. The parties both agree that as a result of the August 1 hearing, the district court struck the metropolitan areas of Chicago and Miami from the scope of one of the restrictive sections in the injunction. The district court marked through the words Chicago and Miami on the July 3, 1986 temporary injunction and initialed the margin of the injunction beside the change."); see also Kinney v. Barens, 443 S.W.3d 87, 95 (Tex. 2014) ("The traditional rule of Anglo-American law is that equity has no jurisdiction to enjoin defamation") (Internal quotations omitted).

50. *Currie v. Int'l Telecharge, Inc.*, 722 S.W.2d 471, 475 (Tex. App.—Dallas 1986, no writ) (employer obtained injunction against former employee; "trial court did not abuse its discretion by refusing to increase the amount of the temporary injunction bond from $40,000 to $500,000"); *see Maples v. Muscletech, Inc.*, 74 S.W.3d 429, 431 (Tex. App.—Amarillo 2002, no pet.) (per curiam) (affirming denial of motion to increase bond) (citing *Stone v. Griffin Commc'ns. and Sec. Sys., Inc.*, 53 S.W.3d 687, 696 (Tex. App.—Tyler 2001, no pet.)).

51. *Currie, v. Int'l Telecharge, Inc.*, 722 S.W.2d 471, 475 (Tex. App.—Dallas 1986, no writ); *Johnston v. Am. Speedreading Acad., Inc.*, 526 S.W.2d 163, 166 (Tex. Civ. App.—Dallas 1975, no writ) (bond was sufficient in employer's injunction against former employees who formed competing company).

2-15 TEMPORARY INJUNCTION

Applications for a temporary injunction involve many of the requirements to obtain a TRO.[52] For example, TRCP 681 states that "no temporary injunction shall be issued without notice to the adverse party."[53] TRCP 682 commands that a sworn petition is a "prerequisite to a writ of injunction."[54] However, a verified petition for injunction may not be required when a full evidentiary hearing on evidence independent of the petition is held.[55] It may be that TRCP 682 only applies if the insufficiency of a verification is not objected to before evidence is introduced.[56] As stated earlier, requirements of TRCP 680 and 683 are mandatory and must be strictly followed.[57] The practitioner should also take care that all necessary parties are included in the suit. A court has held that is not an abuse of discretion for a court to refuse to grant an injunction where a necessary party (such as a former employee's current employer) is not part of the suit.[58]

---

52. *Indep. Capital Mgmt., L.L.C. v. Collins*, 261 S.W.3d 792, 794-95 (Tex. App.—Dallas 2008, no pet.) ("To be entitled to a temporary injunction, an applicant must plead and prove (1) a cause of action against the defendant; (2) a probable right to the relief sought; and (3) a probable, imminent, and irreparable injury in the interim." (citing *Butnaru v. Ford Motor Co.*, 84 S.W.3d 198, 204 (Tex. 2002)).

53. Tex. R. Civ. P. 681.

54. Tex. R. Civ. P. 682.

55. *See* Tex. R. Civ. P. 682; *Salas v. Chris Christensen Sys.*, 10-11-00107-CV, 2011 WL 4089999, at *5 (Tex. App.—Waco Sept. 14, 2011, no pet.) (mem. op.) ("Generally, applications for injunctive relief are required to be verified, *see* Tex. R. Civ. P. 682; however, the verification requirement of rule 682 can be waived. When a full evidentiary hearing on evidence has been held, a verified petition for injunctive relief is not required."); *see Crystal Media Inc. v. HCI Acquisition Corp.* 773 S.W.2d 732, 734 (Tex. App.—San Antonio 1989, no writ.).

56. *Salas v. Chris Christensen Sys.*, 10-11-00107-CV, 2011 WL 4089999, at *5 (Tex. App.—Waco Sept. 14, 2011, no pet.) (mem. op.) ("Generally, applications for injunctive relief are required to be verified, *see* Tex. R. Civ. P. 682; however, the verification requirement of rule 682 can be waived. When a full evidentiary hearing on evidence has been held, a verified petition for injunctive relief is not required."); *see Crystal Media Inc. v. HCI Acquisition Corp.* 773 S.W.2d 732, 734 (Tex. App.—San Antonio 1989, no writ.).

57. *Int'l BHD. Of ELC. Workers Local Un. v. Becon Constr. Co.*, 104 S.W.3d 239, 243 (Tex. App.—Beaumont 2003, no pet.).

58. *Down Time-South Tex., LLC v. Elps*, 13-13-00495-CV, 2014 WL 1464320, at *8 (Tex. App.—Corpus Christi Mar. 20, 2014, no pet.) (mem. op.).

TROs are not a prerequisite to a temporary injunction. Indeed, many prudent practitioners may choose not to seek a TRO but will use the expedited discovery process to gather evidence to prove their case. The petition contains the same prerequisites as a TRO, except that there can be no *ex parte* relief. Parties are entitled to notice of the temporary injunction, and TRCP 21 requires three days' notice.[59]

2-16 TEMPORARY INJUNCTION HEARING

At hearings for injunctive relief, the issue is preserving the status quo. Even if the defendant fails to show up at the hearing, a temporary injunction may not be granted by default. Courts must hold a full evidentiary hearing, and movants must prove a claim's elements.[60] Courts may limit evidence and reduce a hearing's formality, because the court sits as one in equity. However, hearings must not be so limited as to deprive defendants of their right to a hearing.[61]

2-17 REQUIREMENTS OF THE TEMPORARY INJUNCTION ORDER

The order must recite the specific statements required in Rule 683.[62] If Rule 683 is not followed, then the order can be declared void and dissolved.[63] The order must also state the reasons for

59. Tex. R. Civ. P. 21.

60. *See In re Tex. Natural Res. Conservation Comm'n*, 85 S.W.3d 201, 208 (Tex. 2002) ("a temporary restraining order's purpose is to restrain a party's action only until a full evidentiary hearing on the request for a temporary injunction occurs.").

61. *RRE VIP Borrower, LLC v. Leisure Life Senior Apt. Hous., Ltd.*, 14-09-00923-CV, 2011 WL 1643275, at *2 (Tex. App.—Houston [14th] May 3, 2011, no pet.) (mem. op.) ("In a temporary injunction hearing, the trial court is entitled to reasonably limit the proceedings. However, the trial court may not deprive a party of its right to offer any evidence. The trial court's limitation cannot be arbitrary in its nature or it will be considered an abuse of discretion. The trial court is simply not authorized to enter an order of temporary injunction against a party before that party has had an opportunity to present its defenses and has rested its case.") (citations omitted) (citing *Elliott v. Lewis*, 792 S.W.2d 853, 855 (Tex. App.—Dallas 1990, no writ)).

62. Tex. R. Civ. P. 683.

63. *Reliant Hosp. Partners, LLC v. Cornerstone Healthcare Group Holdings, Inc.*, 374

issuance, define the act to be restrained, include an order setting the case for trial on the merits, and fix the amount of bond. For example, in *Ramirez v. Ignite Holdings, Ltd.*, the defendants (former employees) argued on appeal that a paragraph of the temporary injunction was improper because it did not satisfy Rule 683.[64] The appeals court reversed the injunction in part after finding that the paragraph was not specific and detailed enough to satisfy Rule 683—especially its lack of specificity in defining the term "proprietary information/trade secrets," which failed to give defendants adequate notice of the prohibited acts.[65]

2-17:1 MANDATORY INJUNCTIONS

"Prohibitive Injunctions" maintain the status quo and forbid conduct."[66] "Mandatory Injunctions" require conduct by the restrained party. Issuance of a "temporary mandatory injunction is proper only if a mandatory order is necessary to prevent irreparable injury or extreme hardship."[67] In *Territo,* the Fourteenth Court of Appeals reversed a trial court's mandatory injunction that required the defendant employer to continue issuing

S.W.3d 488, 495 (Tex. App.—Dallas 2012, pet. denied) ("The requirements of [TRCP] 683 are mandatory and must be strictly followed. Even if a sound reason for granting relief appears elsewhere in the record, the Texas Supreme Court has stated in the strongest terms the rule must be followed. If a temporary injunction fails to meet these requirements, it is void.") (citations omitted).

64. *Ramirez v. Ignite Holdings, Ltd.*, 05-12-01024-CV, 2013 WL 4568365, at *3 (Tex. App.—Dallas Aug. 26, 2013, no pet.) (mem. op.).

65. Id. at *3 ("In order to determine whether a particular document relates 'confidential information' or 'proprietary information,' and thus may not be destroyed, appellants would have to infer what those terms encompass. Because paragraph 7(g) forces appellants to infer what conduct is forbidden, that paragraph violates Rule 683 and must be reversed"); *see also Dickerson v. Acadian Cypress & Hardwoods, Inc.*, 09-13-00299-CV, 2014 WL 1400659, at *7 (Tex. App.—Beaumont Apr. 10, 2014, no pet.) (mem. op.) (noncompliance found where parties could be misled by the scope of the order while attempting in good faith to follow it). Heat Shrink Innovations, LLC v. Med. Extrusion Techs.-Texas, Inc., 02-12-00512-CV, 2014 WL 5307191, at *9 (Tex. App. —Fort Worth (Oct. 16, 2014, pet. denied) (injunction lacks specificity and is impermissibly vague when it "prohibits sales to a list of names, but provides no other identifying information.")

66. *See LeFaucheur v. Williams*, 807 S.W.2d 20, 22 (Tex. App.—Austin 1991, no writ).

67. *RP&R Inc. v. Territo*, 32 S.W.3d 396 (Houston [14th Dist.] 2000, no pet.) citing *LeFaucher*, 807 S.W.2d at 22.

paychecks to its former vice president.[68] The Court reasoned, "While granting a mandatory injunction is within the sound discretion of the trial court, the grant should be denied absent a clear and compelling presentation of extreme necessity or hardship.[69]

2-18 DANGER — AGREED TEMPORARY INJUNCTION/ANTI-SLAAP

Often, practitioners agree to a temporary injunction and ignore some of the formalities required by Rule 683 and 684. For example, they may omit the reason for issuance, omit an order setting the trial on the merits, not fix the bond, or try to waive bond. Any of these defects may render the order unenforceable at a contempt hearing.[70] Practitioners should consider getting a permanent injunction or agreement under TRCP 11 because neither contains the same requirements. Moreover, either an agreed temporary injunction or agreed permanent injunction should contain a covenant not to appeal. A court's decision to deny a TRO application or to grant a TRO is not appealable, except when a TRO is "tantamount to a temporary injunction."[71]

---

68. 32 S.W.3d 396 at 402.

69. *Id.* at 401 citing *Rhodia, Inc. v. Harris County*, 470 S.W.2d 415 (Tex. Civ. App.—Houston [1st Dist.] 1971, no writ.).

70. *City of McAllen v. McAllen Police Officers' Union*, No. 13-10-00609-CV, 2011 WL 2175606, at *3, n.7 (Tex. App.—Corpus Christi June 2, 2011, no pet.) (mem. op.) ("whether the [defendant] agreed to the waiver [of Rule 684's bond requirement] is immaterial because the failure of the temporary injunction order to comply with rule 684 renders the order void, and 'a party who agrees to a void order has agreed to nothing.'"); *Chambers v. Rosenberg*, 916 S.W.2d 633, 635 (Tex. App.—Austin 1996, writ denied) ("The [Supreme Court of Texas] has held that temporary orders filed without the bond are void, not merely voidable. Though none of the cited cases explicitly concerns an agreed order, we find the strong theme of literal construction of the rule convinces us that we should construe the rule literally in this case; we are particularly persuaded to do so because the parties here did not explicitly waive the protection of a bond. The temporary injunction was void for lack of a bond.").

71. *Global Natural Res. v. Bear, Stearns & Co.*, 642 S.W.2d 852, 854 (Tex. App.—Dallas 1982, no writ) (TRO was "tantamount to a temporary injunction because the effect of it on the parties went beyond protecting the status quo for a ten-day period"); *c.f.*, Tex. Civ. Prac. & Rem. Code § 51.014(a)(4) ("A person may appeal from an interlocutory order of a district court, county court at law, or county court that . . . grants or refuses a temporary injunction or grants or overrules a motion to dissolve a temporary injunction as provided by Chapter 65 . . . .").

Often a client or employer in a departing employee case may seek to restrict what a former employee can say about the company. Be careful here! That type of relief could potentially give rise to a Texas Anti-SLAPP claim and derail the case. Please see Chapter 8 for a discussion of the statute.

2-19 DEFENSES

Defendants often challenge whether applicants for injunctions followed the TRCP's strict requirements and/or local rules. Also, defendants may argue lack of standing, improper venue, and statute of limitations. Equitable defenses—*e.g.*, laches, unclean hands, waiver—may also be asserted.[72] Accordingly, before applying for injunctive relief against a departing employee, it is imperative to discuss with a client that defenses could be raised. Clients should be advised that (1) the departing employee's response could allege embarrassing facts in an "unclean hands" defense and (2) defenses need to be anticipated so that the injunction request does not overreach.

72. *Sec. Servs., Inc. v. Priest*, 507 S.W.2d 592, 593 (Tex. Civ. App.—Dallas 1974, no writ) ("Defendant contends that the injunction was properly denied because the evidence supports a conclusion by the judge that plaintiff was guilty of unconscionable conduct in discharging defendant without cause after only a short period of employment and after getting the benefit of customer contacts that defendant had developed while working for a previous employer who was in competition with plaintiff. We find that the evidence does support such an inference and, for this and other reasons, we hold that no abuse of discretion is shown."); *Nat'l. Chemsearch Corp. v. Frazier*, 488 S.W.2d 545, 547-48 (Tex. Civ. App.—Waco 1972, no writ) ("Under the 'clean hands' doctrine, an employer may be denied enforcement by injunction of an agreement by an employee not to engage in post-employment competition where the employer has been guilty of a breach of the contract, or other inequitable conduct, that was injurious to the employee. We believe the implied findings of violations by [employer] of its agreements with [employee] justified the application of this rule by the trial court in this case."); *see Vaughan v. Kizer*, 400 S.W.2d 586, 590 (Tex. Civ. App.—Waco 1966, writ ref'd n.r.e.) (employer's "action in reducing [employees'] expense accounts was . . . such wrongful conduct as to render [employer] without clean hands, and precludes him from obtaining injunctive relief against [employees] in a court of equity."); *see also Norris of Houston, Inc. v. Gafas*, 562 S.W.2d 894, 896 (Tex. Civ. App.—Houston [1st Dist.] 1978, writ ref'd n.r.e) ("Although we have found no Texas cases holding that intolerable working conditions make a non-competition covenant unenforceable, that result might obtain if the conditions imposed by management amounted to a breach of the employee's contract or to a wrong done to the employee. We cannot say from the facts in our case, even when taken in the light most favorable to the trial court's order, that [defendant-former employee's] working conditions amounted to a wrong done to her by the appellants.").

An older case discussed the "unclean hands" defense regarding injunctive relief. In *Vaughn v. Kizer*, the Court of Civil Appeals held that in view of the record a period of two years would be ample to protect former employers' goodwill and insurance claims investigating and adjusting business and that any time in excess thereof would be unreasonable, but that the employer's action in reducing claim adjusters' expense accounts was, under facts, such wrongful conduct as to render former employer without clean hands and preclude him from obtaining injunctive relief against adjusters in court of equity.[73] On this same note, injunctive relief may also be denied when a party has failed to show that without injunctive relief she will suffer irreparable injury for which he has no adequate legal remedy.[74]

2-19:1 CAUSES OF ACTION FOR WRONGFUL INJUNCTIONS

There are two separate causes of action for wrongful injunctions: (1) upon the bond ordinarily filed to obtain the injunction and (2) for malicious prosecution.[75] Parties claiming wrongful injunction will likely file in the court that granted the objection.[76]

---

73. *See Vaughn v. Kizer*, 400 S.W.2d 586, 587 (Tex. Civ. App.—Waco 1966, writ ref'd n.r.e.). *See, e.g., Nat'l Chemsearch Corp. v. Frazier*, 488 S.W.2d 545, 546 (Tex. Civ. App.—Waco 1972, no writ).

74. *Parkem Indus. Servs., Inc., v. Garton*, 619 S.W.2d 428, 430–431 (Tex.Civ.App.—Amarillo 1981, no writ).

75. *Sweezy Constr. v. Murray*, 915 S.W.2d 527, 531 (Tex. App.—Corpus Christi 1995, no writ) (citing *DeSantis v. Wackenhut Corp.*, 793 S.W.2d 670, 685 (Tex. 1990)).

76. *Sweezy Constr. v. Murray*, 915 S.W.2d 527, 531-32 (Tex. App.—Corpus Christi 1995, no writ) ("While the first lawsuit remains pending, however, the court having issued the injunction, and which still retains power to issue or refuse further interlocutory relief of that nature, remains the proper forum in which to challenge the propriety of that injunction. An issue concerning the wrongfulness of that injunction is thus inherently interrelated to the underlying injunction proceeding such that both should properly be considered by the same court. It would be inconsistent with the principles of comity for a second court by a separate malicious prosecution action to indirectly judge the propriety of the first court's interlocutory orders while the first court still retains jurisdiction over the underlying lawsuit as a whole.").

2-19:1.1 WRONGFUL INJUNCTION: UPON THE BOND

After a bond is issued—and before such bond is released to plaintiff—defendants may assert a cause of action on the injunction bond.[77] This cause of action is "predicated on a breach of the condition of the bond."[78] Accordingly, claimants must prove that an injunction was issued or perpetuated when it should not have been—and thus such issuance caused damages—and that injunction was later dissolved.[79] Neither malice nor probable cause is required. Recovery is limited to the bond's amount.[80]

2-19:1.2 WRONGFUL INJUNCTION: MALICIOUS PROSECUTION

To succeed on a malicious prosecution claim, movants must "establish that the injunction suit was prosecuted maliciously and without probable cause, was terminated in their favor, and the issuance of the injunction caused them damages."[81]

---

77. *Ameristar Jet Charter, Inc. v. Cobbs*, 184 S.W.3d 369, 377 (Tex. App.—Dallas 2006, no pet.) ("A cause of action for wrongful injunction is predicated on a breach of the injunction bond's condition that the injunction applicant will abide by the court's decision and will pay all sums adjudged against it if the temporary injunction is dissolved in whole or in part. The damages recoverable in an action on an injunction bond are limited to the amount of the bond. Here, it is undisputed that the trial court released the injunction bond at the time it dissolved the temporary injunction. Appellees did not object to the release of the bond. Because there is no injunction bond on which to base appellees' wrongful injunction claim, the trial court did not err in granting a judgment notwithstanding the verdict on this cause of action. In reaching this conclusion, we necessarily reject appellees' contention that the trial court erred in denying their post-trial request to reinstate the bond. Appellees have not provided any authority, nor have we found any, that would support their position.") (citations omitted).

78. *Goodin v. Jolliff*, 257 S.W.3d 341, 353 (Tex. App.—Fort Worth 2008, no pet.) (citing *DeSantis v. Wackenhut Corp.*, 793 S.W.2d 670, 685 (Tex. 1990); *Safeco Ins. Co. of Am. v. Gaubert*, 829 S.W.2d 274, 278 (Tex. App.—Dallas 1992, writ denied).

79. Id.

80. *Energy Transfer Fuel, L.P. v. Head Mgmt., LTD.*, 12-09-00062-CV, 2010 WL 4523767, at *4 (Tex. App.—Tyler Nov. 10, 2010, no pet.) (citing *DeSantis v. Wackenhut Corp.*, 793 S.W.2d 670, 685-86 (Tex. 1990)).

81. *Ameristar Jet Charter, Inc. v. Cobbs*, 184 S.W.3d 369, 375 (Tex. App.—Dallas 2006, no pet.) ("To recover lost profits, the amount of the loss must be shown by competent evidence with reasonable certainty. Given this rule, the injured party must do more than merely show it suffered some lost profits.") (citations omitted).

2-20 POSSIBLE CAUSES OF ACTION TO SUPPORT INJUNCTIVE RELIEF

1. Aiding and abetting and/or conspiracy[82]
2. Breach of contract[83]
3. Breach of duty (*e.g.*, loyalty, fiduciary)[84]
4. Business disparagement[85]
5. Computer Fraud and Abuse Act[86]
6. Conversion[87]

---

82. Tex. Lab. Code § 21.056 ("An employer, labor union, or employment agency commits an unlawful employment practice if the employer, labor union, or employment agency aids, abets, incites, or coerces a person to engage in a discriminatory practice.").

83. *Matuszak v. Houston Oilers, Inc.*, 515 S.W.2d 725, 728 (Tex. Civ. App.—Houston [14th Dist.] 1974, no writ) ("It is the well settled standard of review for temporary injunctions that they may be overturned only where a trial court has clearly abused its discretion. An applicant for a temporary injunction where permanent injunctive relief is sought upon final disposition must show a probable right on final hearing to a permanent injunction. In addition, they must demonstrate that they have no adequate remedy at law. In enforcing negative covenants ancillary to contracts of employment an additional element is required, that is, a determination of whether or not the person against whom relief is sought is a person of 'exceptional and unique knowledge, skill and ability in performing the service called for in the contract.'") (citations omitted).

84. *Kennedy v. Gulf Coast Cancer & Diagnostic Ctr. at Southeast, Inc.*, 326 S.W.3d 352, 359-360 (Tex. App.—Houston [1st Dist.] 2010, no pet.) ("[Former employer's] live pleading asserts causes of action against [former employee] for theft, attempted theft, conversion, actual and constructive fraud, and breach of fiduciary duty. All of these causes of action are grounded in allegations that [former employee] misappropriated funds belonging to [former employer], kept a copy of the memo against [former employer's] wishes, and threatened to disclose the contents of the memo and other sensitive documents that could adversely affect [former employer's] business reputation and potentially expose it to legal liability. [former employer's] request for a temporary injunction details these allegations and asks the court to order [former employee] and others acting in concert with him to return all copies of the memo and to prohibit them from using or disclosing any information contained in the memo. This pleading alleges facts sufficient to put [former employee] on notice of the causes of action against [former employee] that underlie the temporary injunction. As [former employer's] former in-house lawyer, [former employee] owes a fiduciary duty to [former employer] relating to information and advice exchanged in the scope of that employment. A fiduciary relationship exists between attorneys and clients as a matter of law. The attorney-client relationship is thus one of "most abundant good faith," requiring absolute candor, openness and honesty, and prohibiting any concealment or deception. The essence of a claim for breach of fiduciary duty focuses on whether an attorney obtained an improper benefit from representing the client.") (citations omitted).

85. *Swank v. Sverdlin*, 121 S.W.3d 785, 790 (Tex. App.—Houston [1st] 2003, pet. denied).

86. 18 U.S.C.A. § 1030(g) (West 2008).

87. *Jon Scott Salon, Inc. v. Garcia*, 343 S.W.3d 532, 535 (Tex. App.—Dallas 2011,

7. Defamation[88]
8. Fraud[89]
9. Invasion of privacy[90]
10. Misappropriation of trade secrets or name/likeness[91]
11. Texas Trade Secrets Act[92]

---

no pet.) ("even without an enforceable covenant not to compete, an employer may be entitled to an injunction to protect against the disclosure of confidential information and trade secrets. An injunction is the appropriate remedy to prohibit an employee from using confidential information to solicit his former employer's clients. In this case, a portion of appellant's request for an injunction was for this purpose.") (citations omitted).

88. *Morrill v. Cisek*, 226 S.W.3d 545 (Tex. App.—Houston 1st Dist. 2006, no pet.) (Ex-husband was awarded money damages and injunctive relief; "[ex-husband] sued [ex-wife] for defamation and intentional infliction of emotional distress, alleging that [ex-wife] had written several false and defamatory letters to [ex-husband's] employer, Baylor College of Medicine ("Baylor"), and to certain public officials concerning the parties' ongoing dispute over [ex-husband's] child support obligations. In his petitions, [ex-husband] sought recovery of monetary damages, as well as a permanent injunction prohibiting [ex-wife] from contacting any employee or agent of Baylor, other than [ex-husband] himself."); *see Amalgamated Acme Affiliates, Inc. v. Minton*, 33 S.W.3d 387 (Tex. App.—Austin 2004, no pet.); *but see Marketshare Telecom, L.L.C. v. Ericsson, Inc.*, 198 S.W.3d 908, 918 (Tex. App.—Dallas 2006, no pet.) (modifying injunctive relief) ("[D]efamation alone is not a sufficient justification for restraining an individual's right to speak freely.").

89. *See Amalgamated Acme Affiliates, Inc. v. Minton*, 33 S.W.3d 387 (Tex. App.—Austin 2004, no pet.).

90. *Extendacare Health Sys. v. Gisch*, 05-95-00601-CV, 1996 WL 732468, at *7-8 (Tex. App.—Dallas Dec. 16, 1996, pet. denied) (not designated for publication) ("The remedy for an invasion of privacy cause of action may be either injunctive, compensatory, or both. An order granting an injunction 'shall set forth the reasons for its issuance; shall be specific in terms; shall describe in reasonable detail . . . the act or acts sought to be restrained; and is binding only upon the parties to the action, their officers, agents, servants, employees, and attorneys.' The injunction should be capable of reasonable construction, as well as good faith obedience. [Former employee's] invasion of privacy cause of action was based primarily on [former employer's owner] obtaining [former employee's] medical records and [former employer's] refusal to return them to her. The trial court's order for the return of [former employee's] medical records was clear and unambiguous. Moreover, the action ordered by the trial court was within [former employer's] power. Thus, we overrule [former employer's] first point of error concerning the trial court's injunctive order that [former employer] return [former employee's] medical records.") (other judgment reversed in favor of former employer).

91. *Jon Scott Salon, Inc. v. Garcia*, 343 S.W.3d 532, 535 (Tex. App.—Dallas 2011, no pet.) ("even without an enforceable covenant not to compete, an employer may be entitled to an injunction to protect against the disclosure of confidential information and trade secrets. An injunction is the appropriate remedy to prohibit an employee from using confidential information to solicit his former employer's clients. In this case, a portion of appellant's request for an injunction was for this purpose.") (citations omitted).

92. Tex. Civ. Prac. & Rem. Code § 134A.002(6).

12. Tortious interference (with a contractor or prospective business relations)[93]
13. Theft[94]

2-21 BOND — RETURN OR RELEASE

After final judgment, bonds are returned to the bond-issuing party or released to the defendant.[95] Defendants seeking release should plead for such release.[96]

---

93. *FH1 Fin. Servs. v. Debt Settlement Am., Inc.*, 10-06-00167-CV, 2007 WL 2325652, at *3 (Tex. App.—Waco Aug. 15, 2007, no pet.) (mem. op.) ("We modify the temporary injunction against FH1 to prohibit interference with current DSA employees' duty of loyalty."); *see Shuttleworth v. G&A Outsourcing, Inc.*, 01-08-00650-CV, 2009 WL 277052, at *4 (Tex. App.—Houston [1st Dist.] Feb. 5, 2009, no pet.) (mem. op.) ("pleadings reveal that G&A's requests for injunctive relief were merely ancillary to its suit for damages against Shuttleworth and his employers. In reaching this conclusion, we note that G&A's requests for injunctive relief sought to prevent further diversion of G&A's confidential information, as well as to (a) prevent further breaches of the employment agreement and tortious acts by the Shuttleworth Defendants and (b) to preserve evidence for discovery and trial. In addition, the actual damages sought by G&A are substantial, and are in no small part based upon the alleged actual diversion of G&A clients or prospects to the Shuttleworth Defendants. Accordingly, the injunctive relief sought by G&A was not the primary purpose of its suit and section 65.023(a) does not apply.").

94. *See Institutional Secs. Corp. v. Hood*, 390 S.W.3d 680, 684 (Tex. App.—Dallas 2012, no pet.) ("We conclude the trial court's injunction should have extended to all information of clients that were not brought to [former employer] by [former employee] as [former employer's] registered representative and should have extended to the social security numbers and account information of all clients who were brought to [former employer] by [former employee] as a registered representative. We sustain [former employer's] sole issue to the extent it requested protection of that information."); *see also Spring v. Walthall, Sachse & Pipes, Inc.*, 04-05-00228-CV, 2005 WL 2012669, at *2 (Tex. App.—San Antonio Aug. 24, 2005, no pet.) (mem. op.).

95. *Energy Transfer Fuel, L.P. v. Head Mgmt., Ltd.*, 12-09-00062-CV, 2010 WL 4523767, at *5 (Tex. App.—Tyler Nov. 10, 2010, no pet.) ("Initially, we note that we have located no authority supporting the retention, after final judgment, of a bond posted as a condition to the issuance of a TRO." (citing *Lovall v. Yen*, 14-07-00770-CV, 2008 WL 361373, at *2 (Tex. App.—Houston [14th Dist.] Feb. 12, 2008, no pet.) (mem. op.)).

96. *Goodin v. Jolliff*, 257 S.W.3d 341, 353 (Tex. App.—Fort Worth 2008, no pet.) ("The record does not contain any pleading by [former employer's owner] requesting release of the security for damages sustained as a result of the temporary injunction. Moreover, the injunction was entered as part of a rule 11 agreement among the parties; [former employer's owner] agreed to the imposition of the temporary injunction pending trial if the [former employees] would vacate the property within thirty days of any adverse judgment against them becoming final. Accordingly, we conclude and hold that the trial court erred by releasing the security amount to [former employer's owner] in the absence of any pleading or proof that she was damaged by the issuance of the temporary injunction. However, we also conclude and hold that the error was harmless. There is no evidence that the [former employees] superseded the judgment in favor of H.V.G.C. in accordance with rule 24. And the record of the October 6 hearing, along with the trial court's order, shows that the trial court ordered release of the bond in partial execution of the judgment in favor of H.V.G.C. Accordingly, we overrule the [former employees'] fifth issue.") (citations omitted).

Chapter 3
Noncompetition Covenants

Edited by Jason Weber and Mark Shank

3-1 HISTORY AND BACKGROUND OF NONCOMPETITION COVENANTS IN TEXAS

Texas courts consistently hold that noncompetition covenants limit competition and are restraints on trade. Therefore, they are presumed to be invalid unless specifically authorized by statute.[1] The Texas Legislature passed the Covenant Not to Compete Act in 1989 (the "Act").[2] The Act was amended in 1993 and 1999, in part due to tension between the courts and legislature regarding enforcement of noncompetition covenants. Currently, the Act allows the enforceability of noncompetition covenants in certain instances and provides, as a general rule:

> Notwithstanding Section 15.05 of this code, and subject to any applicable provision of Subsection (b), a covenant not to compete is enforceable if it

1. *See, e.g.*, *Hill v. Mobile Auto Trim, Inc.*, 725 S.W.2d 168, 172 (Tex. 1987) ("[C]ovenants not to compete which are primarily designed to limit competition or restrain the right to engage in a common calling are not enforceable." (citing *Robbins v. Finlay*, 645 P.2d 623, 627 (Utah 1982)).

2. Tex. Bus. & Com. Code §§ 15.50–.52.

> is ancillary to or part of an otherwise enforceable agreement at the time the agreement is made to the extent that it contains limitations as to time, geographical area, and scope of activity to be restrained that are reasonable and do not impose a greater restraint than is necessary to protect the goodwill or other business interest of the promisee.[3]

The Act further provides for monetary damages and injunctive relief for breaches of noncompetition covenants.[4] The Act's 1993 amendments make clear that the Act is exclusive as to remedies and that courts may no longer rely on common law theories in addition to the Act when analyzing noncompetition covenants.[5] Since the Act was passed in 1989, however, the Texas Supreme Court's interpretation of it has evolved as set forth below.

In *Light v. Centel Cellular Co. of Tex.*, for example, the Texas Supreme Court set forth a two-pronged test for determining what constitutes an "otherwise enforceable agreement" under Section 15.05 of the Act in the context of at-will employees.[6] The Court held that in order for a noncompetition covenant to be ancillary to an otherwise enforceable agreement between employer and employee:

> (1) the consideration given by the employer in the otherwise enforceable agreement must give rise to the employer's interest in restraining the employee from competing; and
>
> (2) the covenant must be designed to enforce the

---

3. *Id.* § 15.50(a).

4. *Id.*

5. *See id.*

6. 883 S.W.2d 642, 647 (Tex. 1994).

> employee's consideration or return promise in the otherwise enforceable agreement.[7]

This two-pronged test required employers to show a relationship between the noncompetition covenant and the necessity for the restraint on trade to have an enforceable noncompetition agreement.[8] In *Light*, the Court concluded that the promises given by the former employee—(i) 14 days' notice and (ii) an inventory of her property at the time she left employ—had no relationship to the noncompetition covenant at issue and, therefore, the noncompetition covenant was unenforceable.[9] The Court further confirmed that enforceability of a noncompetition covenant is a question of law.[10]

The two-pronged test articulated in *Light* was the law of Texas until the issue was revisited in 2006 by the Texas Supreme Court in *Alex Sheshunoff Mgmt. Servs. v. Johnson*.

In *Sheshunoff*, the Court revisited its holding in *Light* that a unilateral contract could not comply with the Act because the contract was not enforceable at the time it was made.[11] The Court reasoned that a unilateral contract becomes enforceable once it is performed, i.e., by providing the contemplated consideration at a later time.[12] The Supreme Court, therefore, stated:

> We now conclude, contrary to *Light*, that the covenant need only be 'ancillary to or part of' the agreement at the time the agreement is made. Accordingly, a unilateral contract formed when the employer performs a promise, which was

7. *Id.*

8. *Id.*

9. *Id.* at 649.

10. *Id.* at 644.

11. 209 S.W.3d 644, 646 (Tex. 2006).

12. *Id.* at 651.

> illusory when made, can satisfy the requirements of the Act.[13]

In 2009, the Texas Supreme Court took most of the teeth out of *Light* through its holding in *Mann Frankfort Stein & Lipp Advisors, Inc. v. Fielding Mann Frankfort*.[14] In *Mann Frankfort*, the Court explained that, if the nature of employment requires an employer to furnish the employee with confidential information, there is an implied promise to provide confidential information.[15]

In *Mann Frankfort*, the employee challenged the enforceability of the noncompetition agreement on the grounds that it was not supported by consideration because the employer made no express promise to provide confidential information.[16] In that case, the noncompetition covenant contained no express promise to provide access to confidential information, although the former employee promised not to disclose confidential information.[17] The Court held, "[w]hen the nature of the work the employee is hired to perform requires confidential information to be provided for the work to be performed by the employee, the employer impliedly promises confidential information will be provided."[18] The Court further explained, "[w]hen it is clear that performance expressly promised by one party is such that it cannot be accomplished until a second party has first performed, the law will deem the second party to have impliedly promised to perform the necessary action."[19] Thus, the Court held that the noncompetition covenant did not lack consideration.[20]

In 2011, the Texas Supreme Court significantly shifted its attitude

---

13. *Id.*
14. 289 S.W.3d 844, 848–49 (Tex. 2009).
15. *Id.* at 850.
16. *Id.* at 845
17. *Id.*
18. *Id.* at 850.
19. *Id.* at 851.
20. *Id.* at 851–52.

in analyzing noncompetition covenants in *Marsh USA Inc. v. Cook*, and in doing so abrogated its holding in *Light*.[21] In *Marsh*, the Texas Supreme Court addressed whether consideration given to an employee for a noncompetition covenant was required to give rise to the employer's interest in restraining the employee from competing.[22] The Court explained that the Act was intended to expand, rather than restrict, the enforceability of noncompetition covenants.[23] The Court then diluted the "ancillary to" requirement to only require that a covenant be "supplementary" to the agreement (and the consideration given) and need not actually "give rise" to the employer's interest in restraining the individual from competing.[24] Instead, the Court held, the noncompetition covenant need only be "reasonably related" to the employer's interest in protecting its goodwill or other similar interest.[25] The Court held that the "ancillary" requirement was met in *Marsh* "because the business interest being protected (goodwill) [was] reasonably related to the consideration given (stock options)."[26] The Court also addressed whether Texas law requires that the employee receive consideration for the noncompete agreement prior to the time the employer's interest in protecting its goodwill arises.[27] The Court held that Texas law does not require that consideration be given *prior to* the time the employer's interest in protecting its goodwill arises; and, therefore, found that awarding stock options to purchase the employer's stock at a discounted price "provided the required statutory nexus between the noncompete" and the employer's interest in protecting its goodwill.[28]

21. *See* 354 S.W.3d 764, 775 (Tex. 2011).

22. *Id.*

23. *Id.*

24. *Id.* at 774–75.

25. *Id.*

26. *Id.* at 780.

27. *Id.* at 778.

28. *Id.* at 777.

3-2 ELEMENTS OF A CLAIM

To enforce a noncompetition covenant, a movant must prove:

1. A personal services contract that supports the covenant;[29]
2. The covenant was ancillary to or part of an otherwise enforceable agreement;[30]
3. The covenant's limitations are reasonable as to time, geographic area, and scope of activity to be restrained;[31]
4. The covenant does not impose a greater restraint than necessary to protect the employer's business interest;[32] and
5. Breach of the covenant.[33]

Enforcement of a noncompetition covenant is a question of law.[34]

The Act makes a distinction between a contract for personal services and one that is not (e.g., an asset purchase agreement). Specifically, Section 15.51(b) states:

> If the primary purpose of the agreement to which the covenant is ancillary is to obligate the promisor to render personal services, for a term or at will, the promisee has the burden of establishing

29. *See* Tex. Bus. & Com. Code § 15.51(b).

30. *Marsh*, 354 S.W.3d at 771.

31. *Id.*

32. *Id.* at 777.

33. *Shoreline Gas, Inc. v. McGaughey*, No. 13-07-364-CV, 2008 WL 1747624, at *11 (Tex. App.—Corpus Christi Apr. 17, 2008, no pet.) (mem. op.) (Employer "produced no evidence that [defendant] had actually breached or violated any covenant or undertaking contained in the Agreement, or even that [defendant] had threatened to breach or violate any such undertakings." The court noted that the employer's "fear or apprehension of the possibility of injury" was "insufficient to establish a probability of irreparable injury as would support a temporary injunction.").

34. *Mann Frankfort*, 289 S.W.3d at 849; *Martin v. Credit Prot. Ass'n, Inc.*, 793 S.W.2d 667, 668–69 (Tex. 1990).

> that the covenant meets the criteria specified by Section 15.50 of this code. If the agreement has a different primary purpose, the promisor has the burden of establishing that the covenant does not meet those criteria. For the purposes of this subsection, the "burden of establishing" a fact means the burden of persuading the triers of fact that the existence of the fact is more probable than its nonexistence.[35]

3-2:1 PERSONAL SERVICES

Generally, when a contract's primary purpose is *not* to render personal service, that contract involves a sale of a business. This provision, although worded a bit oddly, was seemingly written to make it easier to enforce a covenant given in connection with the sale of a business. For example, in *Heritage Operating, LLP v. Rhine Bros., LLC*, a company's owners sold the company to another company. The sellers/owners, as part of the sale, subsequently signed a noncompetition covenant covering seventy-five miles within prohibited cities for a ten-year period.[36] An appellate court found the ten-year period was not unreasonable when ancillary to a contract for the sale of a business.[37] This case provides an example of courts enforcing and giving deference to covenants connected with the sale of a business, whereas courts may be less likely to enforce a covenant with similar restrictions in a personal services contract. Under Texas law, employment agreements involving sales are treated as agreements to render "personal services."[38]

---

35. Tex. Bus. & Com. Code § 15.51(b).

36. No. 02-10-00474-CV, 2012 WL 2344864, at *2–3 (Tex. App.—Fort Worth June 21, 2012, no pet.) (mem. op.).

37. *Id.* at *18.

38. *See Gomez v. Zamora*, 814 S.W.2d 114, 117 (Tex. App.—Corpus Christi 1991, no writ) (citing *Daytona Grp. of Texas, Inc. v. Smith*, 800 S.W.2d 285, 289 (Tex. App.—Corpus Christi 1990, writ denied)).

3-2:2 ANCILLARY TO

The concept of "otherwise enforceable agreements" has troubled courts analyzing whether noncompetition covenants are enforceable under the Act. Courts have particularly struggled with the illusory nature of employment contracts that are at will.[39] *Sheshunoff* makes clear that an at-will employment agreement can be enforced when there is a unilateral contract that later becomes binding after the employer performs its express or implied promise (*e.g.*, providing its employees with confidential information).[40] To be ancillary to an otherwise enforceable agreement, the consideration must be "reasonably related to an interest worthy of protection" and the covenant must be designed to enforce the employee's consideration for the promise(s) found in the agreement.[41] The term "reasonably related" shows a shift in Texas law. In 2011, the Texas Supreme Court again revisited *Light* and clarified that there is no requirement that consideration for the otherwise enforceable agreement give rise to the interest in restraining the employee from competing.[42] Rather, the Supreme Court held that "[c]onsideration for a noncompete that is reasonably related to an interest worthy of protection, such as trade secrets, confidential information or goodwill, satisfies the statutory nexus."[43]

What constitutes a "protectable interest," remains an issue, even after *Marsh*. An analysis of Texas cases, however, provides insight regarding what constitutes protectable and unprotectable interests. Examples of interests that are *not* protectable, include:

---

39. *See Travel Masters, Inc. v. Star Tours, Inc.*, 827 S.W.2d 830, 832 (Tex. 1991) (where no other promise is made, a contract for at will relationship is illusory).

40. *Alex Sheshunoff, Mgmt. Servs.*, 209 S.W.3d at 649–56.

41. *Marsh USA Inc.*, 354 S.W.3d at 777.

42. *Id.*

43. *Id.*; *CDX Holdings, Inc. v. Heddon*, No. 3:12-CV-126-N, 2012 WL 11019355, *8 (N.D. Tex. Mar. 2, 2012) (explaining *Marsh USA, Inc.*, 354 S.W.3d at 771) (restrictive covenants were ancillary to "stock options, which were consideration for the non-competition; and non-solicitation covenants were reasonably related to [plaintiff] interest in protecting its goodwill.").

(i) general skills and knowledge developed during the course of the employment;[44] (ii) personal goodwill;[45] and (iii) professional referrals.[46] On the other hand, examples of interests that *are* protectable include: (i) trade secrets;[47] (ii) confidential or proprietary information;[48] (iii) business goodwill;[49] and (iv) customer information and customer lists.[50]

In summary, courts since *Light* have held that a promise based upon contingent employment alone is illusory.[51] In *31-W Insulation Company, Inc. v. Dickey*, the Fort Worth Court of Appeals held that an employer's promise to give an employee two-weeks' notice of termination and to compensate him during that two-week period were not promises that gave rise to "an interest worthy of protection by a covenant not to compete."[52] The Austin Court of Appeals in *Pearson v. Visual Innovations Company, Inc.*, however, addressed a seemingly similar set of facts but found that the promises made by the employer were "interests worth of protection by a covenant not to compete." In *Pearson*, the court rejected Pearson's argument that he was merely an at-will employee and that the employer had not made any promises regarding its interests that were worthy of protection.[53]

44. *See Evan's World Travel, Inc. v. Adams*, 978 S.W.2d 225, 231 (Tex. App.—Texarkana 1998, no pet.).

45. *Hill*, 725 S.W.2d at 171–72.

46. *Phillip H. Hunke, D.D.S., M.S.D., Inc. v. Wilcox*, 815 S.W.2d 855, 858 (Tex. App.—Corpus Christi 1991, writ denied).

47. *DeSantis v. Wackenhunt Corp.*, 793 S.W.2d 670, 682 (Tex. 1990).

48. *Gallagher Healthcare*, 312 S.W.3d at 647.

49. *Marsh*, 354 S.W.3d at 777; *Alex Sheshunoff Mgmt. Servs.*, 209 S.W.3d at 649.

50. *Reliant Hosp. Partners, LLC v. Cornerstone Healthcare Grp. Holdings, Inc.*, 374 S.W.3d 488, 499 (Tex. App.—Dallas 2012, pet. filed) ("Customer lists, pricing information, client information, customer preferences, buyer contacts, blueprints, market strategies, and drawings have all been recognized as trade secrets.") (citing *T-N-T Motorsports, Inc. v. Hennessey Motorsports, Inc.*, 965 S.W.2d 18, 22 (Tex. App.—Houston [1st Dist.] 1998, pet. dism'd)).

51. *See Donahue v. Bowles, Troy, Donahue, Johnson, Inc.*, 949 S.W.2d 746, 750–51 (Tex. App.—Dallas 1997, writ denied).

52. 144 S.W.3d 153, 159 (Tex. App.—Fort Worth 2004, no pet.).

53. No. 03-04-00563-CV, 2006 WL 903736, at *4 (Tex. App.—Austin Apr. 6, 2006, pet.

In *Pearson*, the employer could not terminate the employee for six months unless it was determined, in the company's "sole discretion," that his performance was unsatisfactory.[54] Pearson was also supplied confidential information, specialized training, stock options, and other considerations.[55] Thus, the court concluded that the noncompetition covenant was enforceable.

3-2:3 REASONABLENESS

A covenant's reasonableness is a question of law.[56]

3-2:3.1 REASONABLENESS — GEOGRAPHY

The Act requires that the geographical restriction within a noncompetition covenant be reasonable.[57] Often, noncompetition covenants do not contain specific geographic restrictions. For example, a noncompetition covenant may simply state that the former employee may not compete with the employer wherever the employee interacted with customers during the course of employee's employment. In this situation, litigators must ask: First, does this covenant not meet the requirements of the Act because it does not contain a specific geography restriction? Second, if so, can the covenant be "blue penciled" (i.e., reformed after its execution to comply with the reasonableness requirement of the Act)?[58]

---

denied) (mem. op.).

54. *Id.*

55. *Id.* at *18.

56. *See DeSantis*, 793 S.W.2d at 683; *see also Powerhouse Productions, Inc. v. Scott*, 260 S.W.3d 693, 696 (Tex. App.—Dallas 2008, no pet.).

57. Tex. Bus. & Com. Code § 15.50(a).

58. *See id.* at § 15.51(c) (The Act's Section 15.51 "also contains a 'blue pencil' provision, allowing courts to change some, but not all, of a covenant's defects to make the agreement enforceable.); *Marsh* , 354 S.W.3d at 786-787 ("In 2011, overbroad restrictions can strain the gears of an economic engine that has propelled this country so well, and so far. In 2011, terms too severe to be enforced can also escape challenge altogether, instead acting *in terrorem* to freeze an untold number of employees in place rather than allowing human capital to find its highest and best use and thus augment economic and technological growth.") (citing Cynthia L. Estlund, *Between Rights and Contract: Arbitration*

Assuming a geographic territory is specified, courts generally enforce the geographic limitation if it bears a reasonable relationship to the area where the employee worked while employed.[59] In *Curtis v. Ziff Energy Group*, the Houston Court of Appeals noted the general rule:

> Generally, a reasonable area for purposes of a covenant not to compete is considered to be the territory in which the employee worked while in the employment of his employer.[60]

The court in *Curtis* found a reasonable relationship between a former employee's job description and the limitations in the covenant that restricted him from working for any oil and gas company in North America.[61]

Compare the outcome in *Curtis* with the outcome in *Rimkus Consulting Group, Inc. v. Cammarata*, where the geographic restriction in the noncompetition covenant was found to be unreasonable despite the fact that it only covered certain counties

---

Agreements and Non-Compete Covenants as a Hybrid Form of Employment Law, 155 U. Pa. L. Rev. 379, 406 (2006) ("An overbroad non-compete—one that lasts too long or that covers activities that do not threaten the employer's legitimate interests—may deter the employee from quitting and competing even when she has a right to do so, or it may deter a competitor from hiring the employee."). The *in terrorem* effect is magnified in jurisdictions like Texas, where judges simply "blue pencil" overbroad noncompetes to make them enforceable. *See also* Tex. Bus. & Com. Code § 15.51(c); *see e.g., Prod. Action Int'l, Inc. v. Mero*, 277 F. Supp. 2d 919, 931 (S.D. Ind. 2003) ("A current employee may be frozen in his or her job by an unreasonably broad covenant. Even if the employee believes the covenant is too broad, she may be able to test that proposition only through expensive and risky litigation."); *Richard P. Rita Pers. Servs. Int'l., Inc. v. Kot*, 191 S.E.2d 79, 81 (Ga. 1972) ("If severance is generally applied, employers can fashion truly ominous covenants with confidence that they will be pared down and enforced when the facts of a particular case are not unreasonable.").

59. *Property Tax Assocs. v. Staffelt*, 800 S.W.2d 349, 351 (Tex. App.—El Paso 1990, writ denied); *see Curtis v. Ziff Energy Group, Ltd.*, 12 S.W.3d 114, 119 (Tex. App.—Houston [14th Dist.] 1999, no pet.); *see also Zep Mfg. Co. v. Harthcock*, 824 S.W.2d 654, 660-61 (Tex. App.—Dallas 1992, no writ); *AmeriPath, Inc. v. Herbert*, 447 S.W.3d 319, 335 (Tex. App.—Dallas 2014, pet. denied).

60. *Curtis*, 12 S.W.3d at 119 (citing *Zep Mfg. Co. v. Harthcock*, 824 S.W.2d 654 (Tex. App.—Dallas 1992, no writ).

61. *Id.*

in Texas, Mississippi, Alabama, and Florida.[62] The court in *Rimkus* reasoned that the geographic restriction in the noncompetition covenant was unreasonable because the employee primarily worked in Louisiana yet the geographic restriction restricted the employee from working in geographic areas outside Louisiana.[63] Similarly, in *Morrell Masonry Supply, Inc. v. Coddou*, the Houston Court of Appeals held that a noncompetition covenant restricting the employee from working anywhere in the State of Texas was broader than necessary to protect the employer's business interests because the employer provided no evidence that the employee had worked for the employer in any cities other than Houston and Beaumont.[64] Moreover, the court held that there was no evidence that the employer conducted any business in the State of Texas outside of San Antonio, Houston, and Beaumont.[65] In *Cobb v. Caye Publishing*, the Fort Worth Court of Appeals held that the geographic restriction was unreasonable because it restricted the employee from working in areas where the employee never worked for the employer.[66]

Generally, indefinite or unlimited geographic restrictions will be considered unreasonable.[67] In *Sheshunoff*, however, the Texas Supreme Court held that a noncompetition covenant with no defined geographical restriction was reasonable.[68] Similarly, in *Weed Eater, Inc. v. Dowling*, the Houston Court of Appeals found that a noncompetition covenant with no defined geographical restriction was reasonable because the employer's product was sold throughout the United States.[69] Yet, Texas courts have

---

62. 255 F.R.D. 417, 436 (S.D. Tex. 2008).

63. *Id.*

64. No. 01-13-00446-CV, 2014 WL 1778285, at *4 (Tex. App.—Houston [1st Dist.] May 1, 2014, no pet.) (mem. op.).

65. *Id.*

66. 322 S.W.3d 780, 784 (Tex. App.—Fort Worth 2010, no pet.).

67. *Juliet Fowler Homes, Inc. v. Welch Assocs., Inc.*, 793 S.W.2d 660, 663 (Tex. 1990).

68. *Alex Sheshunoff, Mgmt. Servs*, 209 S.W.3d at 667.

69. 562 S.W.2d 898, 902 (Tex. App.—Houston [1st Dist.] 1978, writ ref'd n.r.e.).

held that language such as "existing market area" and "future marketing area of the employer during the employment" are too indefinite to be enforceable.[70] For example, in *Juliet Fowler Homes, Inc. v. Welch Associates, Inc.*, a noncompetition covenant prohibiting employees from entering into service contracts with the employer's clients "wherever they are located" was held to be unreasonable.[71] Most notably on this issue, however, a Houston appellate court explained a "number of courts have held that a [noncompetition covenant] that is limited to the employee's clients is a reasonable alternative to a geographical limit."[72]

3-2:3.2 REASONABLENESS — TIME

The Act requires that the time limitation within a noncompetition covenant be reasonable.[73] Generally, whether a time limitation is reasonable requires courts to balance: (1) the interest to be protected and (2) the hardship to be imposed. As a matter of public policy, courts are reluctant to prevent people from being employed. Thus, courts often balance broader restrictions with shorter time periods. Typically, courts in Texas will uphold non-compete durations ranging from two to five years.[74] However,

70. *Gomez*, 814 S.W.2d at 117–18.

71. *Juliet Fowler Homes*, 793 S.W.2d at 663.

72. *Gallagher Healthcare*, 312 S.W.3d at 654–55 (citing *Stocks v. Banner Am. Corp.*, 599 S.W.2d 665, 666–68 (Tex. App. —Texarkana 1980, no writ) (stating that "[t]he use of a customer list as an alternative to setting a specific geographical limit is a reasonable means of enforcing a covenant not to compete"); *see also Totino v. Alexander & Assocs.*, 01-97-01204-CV, 1998 WL 552818, at *4 (Tex. App. —Houston [1st Dist.] Aug. 20, 1998, no pet.) (relying on *Stocks* and concluding that "trial court did not abuse its discretion in implicitly finding the noncompetition covenants contained a reasonable geographic restriction as written by virtue of their limiting the restriction" to certain clients who were defined in agreement); *Investors Diversified Servs. v. McElroy*, 645 S.W.2d 338, 339 (Tex. App.—Corpus Christi 1982, no writ) (concluding that noncompetition covenant which had one year restraint, and "the restriction was limited to 150 current customers of the [employer], with whom the [employee] had contacted or dealt with" was reasonable).

73. Tex. Bus. & Com. Code § 15.50(c).

74. *Brink's Inc. v. Patrick*, No. 3:14-CV-775-B, 2014 WL 2931824, at *5 (N.D. Tex. June 27, 2014) (citing string of Texas cases enforcing non-compete covenants ranging from two to five years); *Johnson Serv. Group, Inc. v. France,* 763 F.Supp.2d 819, 826 (N.D. Tex. 2011) (noting that "two to five years has repeatedly been held as a reasonable time limitation") (citing *Gallagher Healthcare Ins. Services v. Vogelsang,* 312 S.W.3d

the lack of a fixed time limitation, alone, will not render a non-competition covenant void.[75]

In *Gallagher Healthcare Ins. Services v. Vogelsang*, the Houston Court of Appeals [1st Dist.] held that a two-year time limitation was reasonable, despite the fact that the insurance contracts at issue between the employer and its clients lasted for only one year.[76] An analysis of Texas case law shows that courts have upheld one-year,[77] two-year,[78] three-year,[79] and even five-year restrictions.[80] In contrast, other courts have held that shorter time limitations are unreasonable.[81] Thus, it is clear that the reasonableness of a time limitation is circumstantial and will be decided on a case-by-case basis, yet reasonableness should always be analyzed in the context of how long an employer's interests need protection and the hardship placed on the employee by enforcing the time limitations.

640, 655 (Tex. App.—Houston [1st. Dist.] 2009, pet. denied) (upholding a covenant not to compete as reasonable that imposed a two-year restriction that prohibited a former employee from working with former clients with whom she worked for two years preceding her termination); *Salas v. Chris Christensen Systems Inc.,* No. 10–11–0107–CV, 2011 WL 4089999, at *19 (Tex. App. —Waco Sept. 14, 2011, no pet.) ("we cannot say that the Agreement's five-year restraint is per se unreasonable"); *Amey v. Barrera,* No. 13–01–0130–CV, 2004 WL 63588, at*6 (Tex. App. —Corpus Christ–Edinburgh Jan. 15, 2004, no pet.) (upholding a non-compete agreement that prohibited the defendant from working in "Corpus Christ and surrounding area for 5 years" as reasonable and enforceable).

75. *Arrow Mirror & Glass*, 51 S.W.3d at 793.

76. *Gallagher Healthcare*, 312 S.W.3d at 655.

77. *Investors Diversified Servs.*, 635 S.W.2d at 339.

78. *Gallagher Healthcare*, 312 S.W.3d at 655.

79. *Elec. Data Sys., Corp. v. Powell*, 508 S.W.2d 137, 138–39 (Tex. App.—Dallas 1974, no writ).

80. *Chandler v. Mastercraft Dental Corp. of Tex., Inc.*, 739 S.W.2d 460, 464–65 (Tex. App.—Fort Worth 1987, writ denied).

81. *Bob Pagan Ford, Inc. v. Smith*, 638 S.W.2d 176, 178-79 (Tex. App.—Houston [1st Dist.] 1982, no writ) (three-year covenant was greater restraint than necessary).

3-2:3.3 REASONABLENESS—SCOPE OF ACTIVITY

The Act requires that the scope of activity to be restrained within a noncompetition covenant be reasonable.[82] Courts routinely review a covenant's scope of activity restrictions through the prism of what the former employee's duties were during the employee's former employment.[83] For example, in *Wright v. Sport Supply Group, Inc.*, the Beaumont Court of Appeals explained "a restrictive covenant is unreasonable unless it bears some relation to the activities of the employee."[84] Yet, a noncompetition covenant that contains an industry-wide exclusion from subsequent employment is unenforceable under any circumstances.[85] In another case, a noncompetition covenant prohibiting employees from engaging in a similar business in any area in which the company may enter in the future was unreasonable.[86] In contrast, a covenant prohibiting an employee with knowledge of a former employer's trade secrets from working for the former employer's direct competitors was reasonable,[87] and a limitation against soliciting customers with whom an employee had personal contact during employment is generally reasonable.[88] Similarly, whether a solicitation restriction that prevents a former employee from soliciting existing customers of a former

82. Tex. Bus. & Com. Code § 15.50.

83. *Peat Marwick Main & Co. v. Haass*, 818 S.W.2d 381, 386 (Tex. 1991).

84. *Wright v. Sport Supply Group, Inc.*, 137 S.W.3d 289, 298 (Tex. App.—Beaumont 2004, no pet.).

85. *John R. Ray & Sons, Inc. v. Stroman*, 923 S.W.2d 80, 86 (Tex. App.—Houston [14th Dist.] 1996, no writ).

86. *Weatherford Oil Tool Co. v. Campbell*, 340 S.W.2d 950, 952 (Tex. 1960).

87. *Weed Eater, Inc.*, 562 S.W.2d at 902; *see also Accruent, LLC v. Short*, No. 1:17-CV-858-RP, 2018 WL 297614, at *5 (W.D. Tex. Jan. 4, 2018) ("The Court disagrees with Short that the noncompete must be limited to places where Short did work for Lucernex customers or prospects. Given everything Short knows about Lucernex and its products, customers, and prospects, Short can help a competitor take business from Accruent in any state or country where Lucernex did business. It is therefore reasonable for the noncompete provision to extend to every state or country in which Lucernex did business.").

88. *Investors Diversified Servs.*, 635 S.W.2d at 339.

employer is reasonable depends on whether the former employee interacted with those customers and to what extent.[89]

3-2:3.4 RESTRAINT NOT GREATER THAN NECESSARY

The Act expressly provides that the reasonableness restrictions of time, geographic area, and scope of activity are determined by whether the restraint is greater than necessary.[90] Indeed, to prove a breach of a noncompetition covenant, a movant must meet the Act's requirements.[91] Accordingly, even if a noncompetition covenant is ancillary to an enforceable agreement, if the restrictions within the covenant are broader than necessary, the covenant will be deemed unreasonable. The Act provides, however, that a noncompetition covenant that contains unreasonable limitations as to time, geographic area, or scope of activity to be restrained must be reformed by the court "to the extent necessary to cause the limitations to be reasonable."[92] The Act further provides that if the noncompetition covenant must be reformed, damages may not be awarded until after the covenant is reformed.[93] When, however, a noncompetition covenant is not necessary to protect an employer's legitimate business interest, the covenant cannot be reformed and is, therefore, void.[94]

---

89. *See EMS USA Inc. v. Sharry*, 309 S.W.3d 653, 660 (Tex. App.—Houston [14th Dist.] 2010, no pet.).

90. Tex. Bus. & Com. Code § 15.50(a).

91. *Id.*

92. Tex. Bus. & Com. Code § 15.51(c); *see also Computek Computer & Office Supplies, Inc. v. Walton*, 156 S.W.3d 217, 224 (Tex. App.—Dallas 2005, no pet.) (The Court modified the overly broad permanent injunction to specify which companies: "Removing or destroying any files, or copies of files, including but not limited to Defendants' computer or computer files *relating to OEM*") (emphasis added)).

93. *Tranter, Inc. v. Liss*, No. 02-13-00167-CV, 2014 WL 1257278, at *5 (Tex. App.—Fort Worth Mar. 27, 2014, no pet.) (mem. op.).

94. *Daytona Grp. of Tex.,*, 800 S.W.2d at 290.

Important: The "restraint greater than necessary" argument is often the most effective defense against the enforceability of a restrictive covenant.

3-2:3.5 OTHER DUTIES OF FORMER EMPLOYEES

Although it seems obvious, employees may immediately compete against former employers once their employment ends, absent a valid noncompetition covenant. Of course, employees may not violate other duties, such as the duty of loyalty (e.g., solicit customers or fellow employees while still employed)[95] or take trade secrets[96] or confidential information.[97]

3-2:3.6 BREACH

Typically, breach is not listed as an element of a claim. Breach is treated as an element of a claim, however, because remedies are not available under the Act without showing breach. Many times, proof of breach is simple, particularly within the context of noncompete covenants where a breach is often black and white (whereas the breach of a nonsolicitation covenant, which often requires an affirmative act, can sometimes be less clear). Upon proving breach of a noncompetition covenant, however, courts are required to determine whether the breached covenant is enforceable as written, and if not, whether the breached covenant is enforceable upon reformation (assuming reformation is an option). Other times the question of breach is contested, particularly in situations where the covenant is vague or ambiguous. For this reason, employers should exercise restraint when drafting such covenants to ensure they are no broader than necessary to protect their legitimate business interests. The wisdom of this advice can be seen not only from the prior discussions in this chapter, but also the fact that courts tend to resolve ambiguities

95. *See* discussion *supra* pp. 5–7.

96. *See generally* discussion *supra* p. 5.

97. *See* discussion *supra* pp. 2–3.

within a covenant against the drafter. This is true particularly where the person seeking to enforce the covenant is seeking to restrain trade. In these situations, litigators should consider the following issues: (1) whether a court will accept parol evidence of the parties' intent regarding the allegedly ambiguous terms of the noncompetition covenant; and (2) whether a court will use "surrounding circumstances" or common usage and/or meaning of terms in a particular trade may also come into play (i.e., "terms of art").[98]

Often, noncompetition covenants are drafted so as to prohibit a "threatened" or "future" breach. Courts have generally held that injunctive relief against a "threatened" or "future" breach is not appropriate.[99]

3-2:3.7 WHAT IS A COVENANT NOT TO COMPETE?

Texas's Supreme Court, in *Exxon Mobil Corp. v. Drennen*, opined "[w]hatever it may mean to be a covenant not to compete under Texas law, forfeiture clauses in non-contributory profit sharing plans, like the detrimental-activity provisions in ExxonMobil's Incentive Programs, clearly are not covenants not to compete."[100] Subsequent cases that cite to *Exxon Mobil Corp.* do not elaborate on this position, but rather use *Exxon Mobil Corp.* to guide their choice of law analysis.[101]

To better understand what constitutes a covenant not to compete

---

98. A discussion of parol evidence, terms of art, and other similar contract interpretation issues is beyond the scope of this work.

99. *See Shoreline Gas, Inc.*, 2008 WL 1747624, at *11; *but cf. In re Electro-Motion, Inc.*, 390 B.R. 859 (Bankr. E. D. Tex. 2008); *see also TEXO ABC/AGC, Inc. v. Perez*, No. 3:16-CV-1998-L, 2016 WL 6947911, at *5 (N.D. Tex. Nov. 28, 2016) ("Potential future injury based on unfounded fear and speculation . . . is insufficient to establish a substantial threat that irreparable harm will occur if a preliminary injunction is not granted.")

100. *Exxon Mobil Corp. v. Drennen*, 462 S.W.3d 919, 929 (Tex. 2014).

101. *Cameron Int'l Corp. v. Guillory*, 445 S.W.3d 840, 846–47 (Tex. App.—Houston [1st Dist.] 2014), reh'g *overruled* (Oct. 23, 2014); *Modis, Inc. v. Net Matrix Solutions, Inc.*, No. 14-14-00238-CV, 2015 WL 971292, at *2 (Tex. App.—Houston [14th Dist.] Mar. 3, 2015, no pet.).

we look to the Texas Supreme Court's definition. In *Marsh*, the Supreme Court did not tackle this question directly because the parties agreed the provision at issue in *Marsh* was governed by the Act. The Supreme Court, nonetheless, provided a general definition of what constitutes a covenant not to compete, which it reiterated in *Exxon Mobil Corp.*[102] According to the Court, "[c]ovenants that place limits on former employees' professional mobility or restrict their solicitation of the former employer's customers and employees are restraints on trade and are governed by the Act."[103]

Accordingly, it is prudent for drafters and litigators to first examine the language of purported noncompetition covenants for their relative effect on professional mobility, restraint on solicitation, and restraint on trade to determine whether such covenants are indeed noncompetition covenants to which the Act applies. The prevailing authority appears to be that the Act will apply to covenants that restrict employees from competing with their former employer, soliciting customers of their former employer, and soliciting former co-employees.[104]

3-2:3.8 REMEDIES

3-2:3.8A SECTION 15.52

Section 15.52 of the Act discusses preemptive provisions within noncompetition covenants and provides the exclusive remedies for all breaches of valid noncompetition covenants.[105] The cases below provide examples of how Section 15.52 has been interpreted by Texas courts:

---

102. *Drennen*, 462 S.W.3d at 329 (quoting *Marsh USA, Inc.*, 354 S.W.3d at 768 (holding that the Act did not apply to the detrimental-activities provision at issue because the provision did not "limit" Drennen's professional mobility, per se)).

103. *Id.* at 327; *Marsh USA, Inc.*, 354 S.W3d at 768.

104. *Ally Fin., Inc. v. Gutierrez*, No. 02-13-00108-CV, 2014 WL 261038, at *6 n.5 (Tex. App.—Fort Worth Jan. 23, 2014, no pet.) (mem. op.).

105. Tex. Bus. & Com. Code § 15.52.

1. *Attorneys' Fees.* Courts generally hold that recovery of attorneys' fees is governed by Section 15.52.[106] For example, in *Perez v. Texas Disposal*, the court held that Section 15.52 controls attorneys' fees awards and preempts all other statutes, including the general Texas contract attorneys' fees statute.[107] The claimant in *Perez*, therefore, was not entitled to recover attorneys' fees under Chapter 38 of the Texas Civil Practice and Remedies Code.[108] Compare the holding *Perez*, however, to the holding in *Gage Van Horn & Associates v. Tatom*, where the court held that the claimant could recover attorneys' fees under the Chapter 37 of the Texas Civil Practice and Remedies Code.[109] In *Butler v. Arrow Mirror and Glass, Inc.*, the court did allow the claimant to recover attorneys' fees under Chapter 38, but Section 15.52 of the

---

106. *See Light*, 883 S.W.2d at 642 (the Act was passed to largely supplant common-law).

107. 103 S.W.3d 591 (Tex. App.—San Antonio 2003, pet. denied); *accord Sadler Clinic Ass'n, P.A. v. Hart*, 403 S.W.3d 891, 899–900 (Tex. App.—Beaumont 2013, pet. denied); *Sentinel Integrity Solutions, Inc. v. Mistras Group, Inc.*, 414 S.W.3d 911, 931 (Tex. App.—Houston [1st Dist.] 2013, pet. filed). *See also Rieves v. Buc-ee's Ltd.*, 532 S.W.3d 845, 854 (Tex. App.—Houston [14th Dist.] 2017, no pet.) (finding Section 15.52 preempted the employer's request for attorney fees based on other statute or the underlying agreement); *Ginn v. NCI Bldg. Sys., Inc.*, 472 S.W.3d 802, 827 (Tex. App.—Houston [1st Dist.] 2015, no pet.) ("Because the Act preempts NCI's claim for attorney's fees under section 27.01 and the Act does not allow employers to recover attorney's fees in suits to enforce covenants not to compete, we hold that the trial court did not err in denying NCI's claim for attorney's fees"); *Franlink v. GJMS Unlimited, Inc.*, 401 S.W.3d 705, 712 (Tex. App.—Houston [14th Dist.] 2013, pet. denied) (affirming trial court's denial of employer's request for attorneys' fees because ACT preempts Chapter 38 of the Texas Civil Practice and Remedies Code); *Glatty v. Air Starter Components, Inc.*, 332 S.W.3d 620, 645 (Tex. App.—Houston [1st Dist.] 2010, pet. denied) ("We hold that the trial court properly denied Air Starter's requests for attorney's fees because the Covenants Not to Compete Act does not permit employers to recover their attorney's [fees] in suits to enforce their rights under the Act.").

108. Tex. Civ. Prac. & Rem. Code § 38.001.

109. 26 S.W.3d 730 (Tex. App.—Eastland 2000, pet. denied).

Act was not raised as a defense to the claim for attorneys' fees under Chapter 38.[110]

2. *Injunctive Relief.* Section 15.51 of the Act governs permanent injunctions. It does not replace the common law requirements for grant of a temporary restraining order or a temporary injunction.[111] For further discussion of injunctions, *see supra* Chapter 2.
3. *Release.* At least one Texas appellate court has held that the Act does not preempt the affirmative defense of release.[112]

If some other portion of the agreement between the employer and former employee is breached, such as a nondisclosure agreement, consider seeking attorney's fees under Section 38.001 of the Texas Civil Practice and Remedies Code based upon breach of that provision in the agreement.

3-2:3.8B ATTORNEYS' FEES TO EMPLOYEE

As stated above, normally attorneys' fees in actions to enforce noncompetition covenants are not recoverable. That said, it is possible for an employee to recover attorneys' fees and other costs incurred in defending a suit to enforce an overbroad noncompetition covenant, except as specifically provided in the Act. [113] The Act makes it difficult, however, to prove an overbroad noncompetition covenant. First, employees must prove that when the agreement was executed their employer knew that the covenant's limitations as to time, geographic area, or scope of activity to be

110. *Arrow Mirror and Glass*, 51 S.W.3d at 787 (Tex. App.—Houston [1st Dist.] 2001, no pet.).

111. *NMTC Corp. v. Conarroe*, 99 S.W.3d 865, 867–68 (Tex. App.—Beaumont 2003, no pet.).

112. *Nat'l Cafe Servs., Ltd. v. Podaras*, 148 S.W.3d 194, 200 (Tex. App.—Waco 2004, pet. denied).

113. Tex. Bus. & Com. Code § 15.51(c); *see, e.g., Perez.*, 103 S.W.3d at 591.

restrained were unreasonable, *and* that the covenant's limitations as to time, geographic area, or scope of activity to be restrained imposed greater restraint than necessary to protect the goodwill or other business interests of the employer.[114] Second, employees must prove that their employer tried to enforce the covenant to a greater extent than necessary to protect its goodwill or other business interests.[115] Despite these difficult proof requirements, the court in *Sentinel Integrity Solutions, Inc. v. Mistras Group, Inc.* found there was sufficient evidence to support an award of attorneys' fees to the employee under Section 15.51(c). In *Sentinel*, the court relied on the following evidence to support the award of attorneys' fees: (1) testimony that demonstrated the employer purposefully made the geographic area broad; (2) the covenant's wording revealed a reliance on reformation instead of good-faith attempts to tailor the covenant; and (3) an email response from the employer to the former employee that demonstrated the employer's knowledge of the unreasonableness of the time limitation.[116]

> **An employee seeking to show that a noncompetition covenant is overbroad should examine the employer's track record of enforcing it (e.g., has a court previously found the covenant overbroad) and determine whether the employer has different restrictive covenants for other employees.**

3-2:3.8C MONETARY DAMAGES

Employers may recover damages that are proximately caused by a breach of a noncompetition covenant.[117] The Act does not define the type or measure of damages.[118] Therefore, any

114. Tex. Bus. & Com. Code § 15.51(c); *see Evan's World Travel*, 978 S.W.2d at 234.

115. Tex. Bus. & Com. Code § 15.51(c).

116. *Sentinel Integrity Solutions*, 414 S.W.3d at 924–27.

117. *Strain v. Gansle*, 768 S.W.2d 345, 346–47 (Tex. App.—Corpus Christi 1989, writ denied.).

118. Tex. Bus. & Com. Code § 15.51(c).

provable damages may be recovered. Typically, the recovery is for lost profits.[119] When lost profits are not readily ascertainable, damages may be based upon the wrongdoer's profits.[120] Another measure of damages might include costs associated with remedying a breach, such as lower prices due to competition.

Exemplary damages are not available under the Act.[121] Consequently, a separate intentional tort must be alleged and proved to recover punitive damages.[122]

Damages are often difficult to prove in these types of cases. Your client should understand that even if your client obtains equitable relief, your client may not receive economic damages commensurate with your client's litigation costs—particularly if the covenant has to be reformed.

3-2:3.8D EQUITABLE RELIEF – REMEDIES

As stated above, an employer enforcing a noncompetition covenant may seek a temporary restraining order ("TRO"), a temporary injunction, or a permanent injunction.[123] Section 15.51 governs permanent injunctions, but TROs and temporary injunctions are governed by common law and the applicable rules of civil procedure.[124]

---

119. *Butts Retail, Inc. v. Diversa Foods, Inc.*, 840 S.W.2d 770, 773 (Tex. App.—Beaumont 1992, writ denied.).

120. Morgan v. Stagg, No. 01-87-00027-CV, 1987 WL 18703, at *1, *3 (Tex. App.—Houston [1st Dist.] Oct. 22, 1987, no writ) (awarding damages for breach of a non-compete based on the breaching party's profits).

121. *See* Tex. Bus. Com. Code § 15.51(c).

122. *City Products v. Burman*, 610 S.W.2d 446, 450 (Tex. 1980).

123. *See e.g., EMSL Analytical Inc. v. Younker*, 154 S.W.3d 693, 695 (Tex. App.—Houston [14th Dist.] 2004, no pet.).

124. Tex. Bus. & Com. Code §§ 15.51–52; *EMSL Analytical Inc.*, 154 S.W.3d at 695; *Cardinal Health Staffing Network, Inc. v. Bowen*, 106 S.W.3d 230, 238–39 (Tex. App.—Houston [1st Dist.] 2003, no pet.); *see also* Tex. R. Civ. P. 680–683 (state); Fed. R. Civ. P. 65 (federal).

Consequently, requirements to obtain a permanent injunction are simpler. Employers need only show that a covenant complies with Section 15.50.[125] By contrast, employers seeking temporary injunctions must prove that common law elements such as irreparable injury, no adequate remedy, and a probable right to recover for the injury.[126]

Reformation is also available as an equitable remedy.[127] Courts have broad discretion to reform covenants.[128] Before a court may reform a noncompetition covenant, however, the covenant must be ancillary to an otherwise enforceable agreement and the covenant's limitations as to time, geography, and scope of activity must not impose a greater restraint than necessary. Only then must a court reform a noncompetition covenant to make unreasonable restraints reasonable under the Act.[129] Once reformed, the court must enforce the covenant as reformed.[130] Either the employer or the employee may seek reformation in a specific request. Failure to request reformation is considered waiver of a party's right of reformation under the Act.[131] If your client is attempting to enforce a noncompetition covenant, it is important to seek reformation, if necessary, as soon as possible because

---

125. Tex. Bus. & Com. Code § 15.50; *Cardinal Health Staffing Network v. Bowen*, 106 S.W.3d 230, 239 (Tex. App.—Houston [1st Dist.] 2007, no pet.).

126. *Vaughn v. Intrepid Directional Drilling Specialists LTD*, 288 S.W.3d 931, 936 (Tex. App.—Eastland 2009, no pet.); *Dickerson v. Acadian Cypress & Hardwoods, Inc.*, No. 09-13-00299-CV, 2014 WL 1400659, at *3 (Tex. App.—Beaumont, 2014, Apr. 10, 2014, no pet.); *Argo Grp. US, Inc. v. Levinson*, 468 S.W.3d 698, 702 (Tex. App.—San Antonio 2015, no pet.) ("We join these courts and hold that a plaintiff seeking a temporary Injunction under section 15.51 must show a probable, imminent, and irreparable injury in the interim before trial").

127. Tex. Bus. & Com. Code § 15.51(c).

128. *See Am. Nat'l Ins. Co. v. Cannon*, 86 S.W.3d 801 (Tex. App.—Beaumont, Sept. 16, 2002, no pet.).

129. *Hardy v. Mann Frankfort Stein & Lipp Advisors, Inc.*, 263 S.W.3d 232, 250-51 (Tex. App.—Houston [1st Dist.] 2007) *rev'd on other grounds*, *Mann Frankfort Stein*, 289 S.W.3d at 844.

130. Tex. Bus. & Com. Code § 15.51(c).

131. *Emergicare Sys. Corp. v. Bourdon*, 942 S.W.2d 201, 204 (Tex. App.—Eastland 1997, no writ).

employers cannot recover actual damages until after a covenant is reformed.[132]

When reformation occurs is not always clear. For example, a court may choose to enforce reasonable limitations within a covenant but not all limitations in response to a TRO application. Similarly, a court may, after hearing substantially more evidence, choose to enforce the covenant differently after a temporary injunction hearing. In each case, the court has not actually "reformed the covenant" pursuant to the Act but instead made judgments as to what limitations within the covenant are subject to injunctive relief. For example, the Fifth Circuit holding, in *Calhoun v. Jack Doheny Cos., Inc.*, explained that a court should reform an agreement that will be unenforceable *upon granting a preliminary injunction.*[133]Additionally, in *Lionheart Co., Inc. v. Pgs Onshore Inc.*, the appellate court in Waco upheld the trial court's discretionary grant of an injunction, which was partially based on factual findings that the contract could remain "in the status quo" if reformed partially.[134] It should be stated that the courts in those instances have not "reformed" covenants such

132. Tex. Bus. & Com. Code § 15.51(c); *see, e.g., Compass Bank v. Tex. Cmty. Bank*, No. DR-09-CV-056-AML, 2010 WL 11506745, at *5 (W.D. Tex. Sept. 21, 2010) ("Thus, the Legislature contemplated that a promise of an unreasonable contract not to compete cannot be awarded damages for any pre-reformation breach.").

133. 969 F.3d 232, 235 (5th Cir. 2020), opinion withdrawn and superseded, 973 F.3d 343 (5th Cir. 2020) (While the opinion was withdrawn due to the parties settling prior to the appellate decision, the explanation given by the court remains applicable).); *see also Tranter, Inc. v. Liss*, No. 02-13-00167-CV, 2014 WL 1257278, at *6 (Tex. App.—Fort Worth Mar. 27, 2014, no pet.) (explaining that "the trial court could reform the limitations and enforce the reformed covenant through injunctive relief").

134. No. 10-06-00303-CV, 2007 WL 1704906, at *2 (Tex. App.—Waco June 13, 2007, no pet.) ("The trial court's temporary injunction . . . effectively preserves the status quo under the lease"). Additionally, in Texas, there is currently a circuit split as to whether otherwise unenforceable restrictive covenants can be reformed and enforced before the time of trial. *Compare Cardinal Health Staffing Network, Inc. v. Bowen*, 106 S.W.3d 230, 237–39 (Tex. App.—Houston [1st Dist.] 2003, no pet. (reformation prohibited; *Gray Wireline Service, Inc. v. Cavanna*, 374 S.W.3d 646, 470–71 (Tex. App.—Waco 2011, no pet.) (reformation prohibited) *with Cobb v. Caye Publishing Group, Inc.*, 322 S.W.3d 780, 786 (Tex. App.—Fort Worth 2010, no pet.) (reformation permitted); *Tranter*, 2014 WL 1257278, at *10 (reformation permitted).

that upon a final trial on the merits employers are entitled to damages.[135]

3-2:3.8E LIQUIDATED DAMAGES

Several Texas courts have held that liquidated damages provisions are enforceable under the Act to the extent a noncompetition covenant is enforceable and to the extent that the common law enforcement requirements for liquidated damages provisions are met.[136]

3-2:3.8F DEFENSES

Defending a suit for breach of a noncompetition covenants actually amounts to negating an employer's ability to prove the elements of its claim. Thus, employees typically challenge: (1) whether a covenant is ancillary to an otherwise enforceable agreement; (2) whether the interest of the employer is worthy of protection; (3) the reasonableness of the limitations within the covenant as to geographic area, time, and scope of activity to be restrained; and/or (4) whether the restraint sought is greater than is necessary to protect the employer's goodwill or other legitimate business interest. In addition to the foregoing, typical breach of contract defenses are available in noncompetition covenants actions.[137]

Employees often assert the defense of the employer's "unclean

---

135. In this author's experience as an arbitrator and advocate, the question of whether a reformation occurs appears to be most likely at issue in arbitration. Many employers have arbitration clauses requiring all disputes to go to arbitration. Those arbitration clauses often also have a "carve out" for injunctive relief. So, the district court decides the TRO and temporary injunction and the arbitrator then decides damages and permanent relief, assuming that the court grants some, but not all, of the requested injunctive relief (which almost always occurs). Should the arbitrator find that the covenant has been reformed by the trial court if the injunctive order does not specifically so state?

136. *Pete Marwick Main & Co. v. Haass*, 818 S.W.2d 381, 382 (1991); *Hardy*, 263 S.W.3d at 242.

137. *DeSantis*, 793, S.W.2d at 681 n. 6.

hands."[138] In doing so, employees generally point to a breach of an employment agreement containing the noncompetition covenant. Examples of employees utilizing this defense may occur when employers breach their employment agreement (if applicable) with the employee,[139] fail to pay wages,[140] sexually harass,[141] or commit other inequitable conduct that is injurious to the employee.[142]

The limitations period that applies to breach of contract actions applies to actions to enforce and/or recover damages for breach of a noncompetition covenant.[143] Accordingly, employers seeking to enforce a noncompetition covenant and/or recover damages related thereto must bring their claim within four (4) years.[144] However, as a practical matter, the time period to enforce is often much shorter because of (1) the limited duration of such cove-

---

138. *See Norris of Houston, Inc. v. Gafas*, 562 S.W.2d 894, 896–97 (Tex. App.—Houston [1st Dist.] 1978, writ ref'd, n.r.e.).

139. *See Chapman Air Conditioning, Inc. v. Franks*, 732 S.W.2d 737, 740 (Tex. App.—Dallas 1987, no writ) (employer cannot wrongfully breach a provision of an employment contract that is favorable to the employee, such as reducing wages without consent and without contractual authority to do so, and then go into a court of equity to secure, by injunction, the enforcement of another provision favorable to it.).

140. *See Vaughan v. Kizer*, 400 S.W.2d 586, 590 (Tex. Civ. App.—Waco 1966, writ ref'd n.r.e.) (employer's "action in reducing [employees'] expense accounts was . . . such wrongful conduct as to render [employer] without clean hands, and precludes him from obtaining injunctive relief against [employees] in a court of equity.").

141. *See Norris of Houston,*, 562 S.W.2d at 896 ("Although we have found no Texas cases holding that intolerable working conditions make a non-competition covenant unenforceable, that *result might obtain if the conditions imposed by management amounted to a breach of the employee's contract or to a wrong done to the employee.* We cannot say from the facts in our case, even when taken in the light most favorable to the trial court's order, that [employee's] working conditions amounted to a wrong done to her by the appellants.") (emphasis added).

142. *See National Chemsearch Corp. v. Frazier*, 488 S.W.2d 545, 547-48 (Tex. Civ. App.—Waco 1972, no writ) (employee raised disputes regarding other salesman assigned to his territory and unpaid sales commission; "employer may be denied enforcement by injunction of an agreement by an employee not to engage in post-employment competition where the employer has been guilty of a breach of the contract, or other inequitable conduct, that was injurious to the employee.").

143. *E.g., Oliver v. Rogers*, 976 S.W.2d 792, 802–03 (Tex. App.—Houston [1st Dist.] 1998, pet. denied) (applying the contract statute of limitations to an action brought to enforce a covenant not to compete).

144. Tex. Civ. Prac. & Rem. Code § 16.004.

nants; and (2) an employer's need to act quicky if injunctive relief is indeed necessary.

3-2:3.8G ILLEGALITY

Employers can assert the defense of illegality.[145]

3-3 OTHER ISSUES INVOLVING NONCOMPETITION COVENANTS

3-3:1 CHOICE OF LAW

Historically, courts look unfavorably on choice of law provisions within contracts attempting to be enforced in Texas.[146] If a choice of law provision applies to a noncompetition covenant, Texas courts may disregard the choice of law provision and apply Texas law if:

1. Texas has a more significant relationship to the parties and the transaction;
2. Texas has a materially greater interest in enforcing the covenant than the other state does; and
3. Application of the other state's law would be contrary to the fundamental policy of Texas.[147]

Application of other states' laws to noncompetition covenants, however, is seldom contrary to the fundamental policies in Texas related thereto. Accordingly, Texas courts must thoroughly examine the interests involved to determine whether to enforce

---

145. *Travel Masters*, 827 S.W.2d at 833 n.3.

146. *DeSantis* 793 S.W.2d at 677.

147. *DeSantis*, 793 S.W.2d at 678; *Drennen Exxon Mobil Corp. v. Drennen*, 452 S.W.3d 319, 327 (Tex. 2014).

a choice of law provision or whether to disregard it in favor of Texas law.[148]

3-3:2 CHOICE OF VENUE

Typically, forum selection clauses are routinely enforced in Texas.[149] Consequently, more and more contracts contain a forum selection clause that serves to circumvent Texas's hostility to applying other states' laws.

3-3:2.1 DEPENDENT VS. INDEPENDENT COVENANTS

Courts occasionally determine whether noncompetition covenants are dependent or independent of other promises.[150] Whether covenants are mutually dependent is determined by the intent of the parties at the time the contract was formed, as evidenced by the language of the contract.[151] When covenants are "such an indispensable part of what both parties intended that the contract would not have been made without the covenant, they are mutual conditions and dependent, in the absence of clear

148. *Compare DeSantis*, 793 S.W.2d at 680 (At the time, noncompetition covenants would not be enforced unless found reasonable and unreasonable restraints on trade (including covenants not to compete, are issues of fundamental policy) *with Exxon Mobil Corp. v. Drennen*, 452 S.W.3d 319, 327, 331 (Tex. 2014) (The detrimental-activities provision is not a noncompetition covenant and its application does not rise to the level of fundamental policy) and *Cameron Int'l.*, 445 S.W.3d at 847–48 (The court found "Texas has no overriding interest in protecting an employment relationship [enforcing a covenant not to compete] between a multinational corporation and a resident of another state," and applied Florida law to determine enforceability).

149. *In re AutoNation, Inc.*, 228 S.W.3d 663, 669 (Tex. 2007). However, in order for Texas's mandatory venue provision to apply (*vis-à-vis* a contractual venue provision), the contract must involve a "major transaction." Tex. Civ. Prac. & Rem. Code § 15.020. "'[M]ajor transaction' means a transaction evidenced by a written agreement under which a person pays or receives, or is obligated to pay or entitled to receive, consideration with an aggregate *stated* value equal to or greater than $1 million." *Id.*

150. *See John R. Ray & Sons* 923 S.W.2d at 86.

151. *See id.* (When such intent is unclear, courts "presume the promises are dependent rather than independent.").

indications to the contrary."[152] Courts determine severability as a matter of law.[153]

In the at-will employment context, courts have made it clear that consideration for a noncompetition covenant cannot be dependent on a period of continued employment because such a promise would be illusory.[154] For example, in *Lazer Spot, Inc. v. Hiring Partners, Inc.*, the noncompetition covenant was held to be unenforceable for lack of consideration because the employee was an at-will employee and the only purported consideration made by the employer was continued employment. In *Lazer Spot*, the court's decision was due in large part to the fact that the noncompetition covenant: (1) failed to include a recitation of consideration; (2) failed to identify the confidential, proprietary, or trade secret information to be divulged; and (3) any failed to identify goodwill or specialized training to be provided to the employees.[155]

At-will employment agreements often include promises by the employer to advance some type of consideration in the future.[156] As discussed above, an employer's promise to provide future consideration (e.g., to provide confidential information to the employee at some future, undefined point in time) is considered an illusory promise until the employer actually provides the consideration,

152. *See id.* (Tex. App.—Houston [14th Dist.] 1996, writ denied) ("relevant inquiry is whether or not the parties would have entered into the agreement absent the unenforceable part").

153. *See id.* (Tex. App.—Houston [14th Dist.] 1996, writ denied) ("relevant inquiry is whether or not the parties would have entered into the agreement absent the unenforceable part").

154. *Shoreline Gas, Inc.*, 2008 Tex. App. LEXIS 2760, at *13-14 (citing *Light*, 883 S.W.2d at 645 (promise would be illusory in that it would fail to bind the promisor, who always retains the option of discontinuing employment in lieu of performance); *see also Lazer Spot*, 387 S.W.3d at 49 ("Because the restrictive covenants here were not supported by consideration independent of the simple act of hiring under an at-will agreement, they are not 'ancillary to or part of' an otherwise enforceable agreement under Tex. Bus. & Com. Code § 15.50(a).").

155. 387 S.W.3d 40, 47 (Tex. App.—Texarkana 2012, pet. denied).

156. *Shoreline Gas, Inc.*, 2008 Tex. App. LEXIS 2760, at *14 (mem. op.).

at which time a unilateral contract is formed.[157] In *Shoreline Gas, Inc. v. McGaughey*, an at-will employee promised not to disclose the employer's confidential information.[158] The court held that the "employee's promise not to disclose [the employer's] confidential information, though not enforceable when made, constituted an offer for a unilateral contract which [the employer] had the option to accept."[159] By supplying confidential information, the court held that the employer performed and thus "a unilateral contract was formed under which [the employee] became bound by his promise not to disclose that information."[160] In a similar case, an employer's consideration was its promise to share trade secrets listed in a contract with its employee, and the employee's consideration was her promise not to disclose or use the trade secrets during or after her employment.[161] Courts may distinguish such consideration when employers delay delivery of confidential information.[162]

3-3:2.2 EQUITABLE EXTENSIONS

In some cases, courts may equitably extend the limitations within a noncompetition covenant as geographic area, time, and scope of activity to be restrained. Equitable extensions of noncompetition covenants do not conflict with Texas public policy.[163]

157. *Alex Sheshunoff Mgmt. Servs.*, 209 S.W.3d at 644.

158. *Shoreline Gas, Inc.*, 2008 Tex. App. LEXIS 2760, at *14 (mem. op.).

159. *Shoreline Gas, Inc.*, 2008 Tex. App. LEXIS 2760, at *16–17 (mem. op.).

160. *Id.*

161. *Ireland v. Franklin*, 950 S.W.2d 155, 158 (Tex. App.—San Antonio 1997, no writ).

162. *TMC Worldwide, L.P. v. Gray*, 178 S.W.3d 29, 38-39 (Tex. App.—Houston [1st Dist.] 2005, no pet.) (In support of its argument, TMC relies on the holdings in *Ireland*, 950 S.W.2d at 155 and *Curtis v. Ziff Energy Group, Ltd.*, 12 S.W.3d 114 (Tex. App.—Houston [14th Dist.] 1999, no pet.). ("This reliance is misplaced because neither opinion discusses the issue of whether and to what extent the employer's delay in complying with a promise to deliver confidential information will render the promise illusory. To the extent that these opinions can be read to hold that, in an at-will employment relationship, there is no requirement that the consideration be contemporaneously exchanged to make a promise to provide confidential information not illusory, we decline to follow these opinions.").

163. *Nationsbuilders Ins. Servs.*, 2013 Tex. App. LEXIS 8182, at *17–18 (Tex. App.—

The Fifth Circuit, for example, held that an equitable extension was permissible because of a delay in litigation.[164] Similarly, in *Nationsbuilders Ins. Servs. v. Houston Int'l Ins. Group*, the Dallas Court of Appeals held that limitations within a noncompetition covenant such as geographic area, time, and scope of activity to be restrained may be equitably extended. In that case, the court held that an arbitrator "did not exceed his powers by awarding an equitable extension of the restricted [time] period."[165] In contrast, the Beaumont Court of Appeals declined to grant an equitable extension of the restricted time period where the contract contained a maximum tolling period of no more than eighteen months.[166]

3-3:3 PROVISIONS PREVENTING SOLICITATION OF EMPLOYEES

There is a substantial difference between a contract limiting a former employee's competitive activity and an agreement keeping that former employee from soliciting former co-employees. And in this author's previous experience, courts routinely enforce reasonable employee nonsolicitation provisions without requiring them to comply with the Covenants Not to Compete Act. At least one court of appeals has held that a nonrecruitment covenant is not a contract in restraint of trade or commerce,[167] but contradicting case law exist.[168]

Dallas July 3, 2013, no pet.).

164. *Guy Carpenter & Co. V. Provenzale*, 334 F.3d 459, 464 (5th Cir. Tex. 2003).

165. *Nationsbuilders Ins. Servs.*, 2013 Tex. App. LEXIS 8182, at *19.

166. *Sadler Clinic Ass'n*, , 403 S.W.3d at 898–99.

167. *Totino.*, 1998 Tex. App. LEXIS 5295, at *29-37 (not designated for publication); *see also Nova Consulting Grp., Inc. v. Engineering Consulting Servs., Ltd.*, 2005 WL 2708811 (W.D. Tex. 2005); *see also Beasley v. Hub-City Tex., L.P.*, No. 01-03-00287-CV, 2003 Tex. App. LEXIS 8550 (Tex. App.—Houston [1st Dist.] Sep. 29, 2003, no pet.) (mem. op.).

168. *Miller Paper Co. v. Roberts Paper Co.*, 901 S.W.2d 593, 600 (Tex. App.—Amarillo 1995, no pet.); *Guy Carpenter*, 334 F.3d at 463; *Ally Fin.*, 2014 Tex. App. LEXIS 792, at *24-26.

A recent Texas Court of Appeals cited *Marsh* and held that a covenant not to solicit employees was analyzed under the Covenant Not to Compete Act.[169] Ultimately, the court concluded that the nonsolicitation covenant was unenforceable because it was unreasonable in scope—going beyond what was necessary to protect the goodwill and business interests of the former employer.[170] However, testing the enforceability of nonsolicitation covenants under the covenant not to compete framework is not novel and can be traced back to 1995 and the Amarillo Court of Appeals. To support this budding trend, the court colorfully invoked Plato's "a rose is but a rose; it does not lose its fragrance, or thorns, simply by changing its name" when it analyzed a covenant not to solicit employees or customers against the framework of the Covenant Not to Compete Act; the Court determined, *inter alia*, that "both effectively restrict competition."[171]

It appears that this line of case law is examining the differences between a covenant not to compete and a covenant not to solicit without giving the same depth of treatment to the distinctions between a covenant not to solicit former co-employees and a covenant not to solicit former customers. Moreover, these courts appear to group these covenants together on the basis that they are all a restraint on trade and therefore conclude that they must be applied to the Covenant Not to Compete Act. For example, the Fifth Circuit Court of Appeals, in *Guy Carpenter & Co., Inc. v. Provenzal*, examined the different types of covenants, distinguished nondisclosure covenants from nonsolicitation covenants, but then then concluded that both types of nonsolicitation covenants should fall under the Covenant Not to Compete Act's

169. *Ally Fin.*, 2014 Tex. App. LEXIS 792, *11 n.5 ("Ally fails to state what enforceability test is applicable in the absence of a section 15.50 analysis. Indeed, the purpose of section 15.50 was to return Texas law to the common-law standard for the enforceability of covenants not to compete . . . [f]urther, the more persuasive case law applies section 15.50 to the non-solicitation covenants as well as non-competition covenants.") (emphasis added).

170. *Id.* at *24–26.

171. *Miller Paper Co.*, 901 S.W.2d at 600.

framework because "non-solicitation covenants restrain trade and competition."[172] And since *Guy Carpenter & Co. Inc.*, United States District Courts in Texas have followed the Fifth Circuit.[173]

The Texas Supreme Court's two more recent opinions, *Marsh* and *Exxon Mobil Corp.*, have legitimized this approach. In *Marsh*, the Court's opinion did not explicitly endorse testing the enforceability of a covenant not to solicit employees and customers within the Covenant Not to Compete Act, but it did cite and quote many of the court opinions that have.[174] And while the Court did use the covenant not to compete two-step threshold inquiry test to determine the enforceability of the nonsolicitation covenants, it did not analyze the nonsolicitation covenants for reasonableness as to their geographic area, time, and scope of authority.[175] In *Exxon Mobil Corp.*, the Court reasserted the *Marsh* Court's definition of a covenant not to compete, which included "solicitation of the former employers' customers and employees are restraints on trade and are governed by the Act."[176]

---

172. *See Guy Carpenter*, 334 F.3d at 463–64 ("To the extent that the nonsolicitation provisions constitute a separate covenant, such a nonsolicitation covenant is also a restraint on trade and competition and must meet the criteria of section 15.50 of the Texas Business and Commerce Code to be enforceable").

173. *Rimkus Consulting*, 255 F.R.D. at 439–40 (quoting *Shoreline Gas, Inc.*, 2008 Tex. App. LEXIS 2760, at * (Quoting *Shoreline Gas Inc.*: "non-solicitation agreements are subject to the same analysis as covenants not to compete . . . . A non-solicitation agreement is sufficiently analogous to a covenant not to compete such that the provisions of the Act must apply fully to such agreements") (internal quotations omitted); *see also Premier Polymers, LLC v. Wendt*, CIV.A. H-15-1812, 2015 WL 4434551, at *3 (S.D. Texas July 17, 2015) (The court examined the enforceability of the nonsolicitation of employees covenant with the Covenant Not to Compete Act); *Inter/Nat'l Rental Ins. Services, Inc. v. Albrecht*, 4;11-CV-00853, 2012 U.S. Dist. LEXIS 140635, (E.D. Tex. Mar. 14, 2012), report and recommendation adopted, 4:11-CV-00853, 2012 U.S. Dist. LEXIS 140635, at *3 (E.D. Tex. Sept. 28, 2012) (Quoting *Marsh* and *Exxon Mobil Corp.* "Covenants that place limits on former employees' professional mobility or restrict their solicitation of former employer's customers and employees are restraints on trade and are governed by the Texas Covenants Not to Compete Act").

174. *Marsh USA, Inc.*, 354 S.W.3d at 770 (citing specifically, *Rimkus Consulting Group, Inc. v. Cammarata*, 255 F.R.D. 417 (S.D. Tex. 2008), *Guy Carpenter*, 334 F.3d at 459; *Miller Paper Co. v. Roberts Paper Co.*, 901 S.W.2d 593 (Tex. App.—Amarillo 1995, no pet.)).

175. *Marsh USA, Inc.*, 354 S.W.3d at 773, 788.

176. *See* discussion *supra* Part 3-2:3.6.

Therefore, the prudent practitioner should consider this development when seeking to enforce a covenant not to solicit employees or customers.

3-3:4 COVENANTS INVOLVING PHYSICIANS

Noncompetition covenants involving physicians are addressed separately in the Act.[177] Thus, Section 15.50 provides special limits on the restrictions in noncompetition covenants that affect physicians. These include:

1. Medical records. The physician must have access to a patient's medical records if authorized by the patient.[178]
2. Patient lists. The physician may not be denied access to a list of patients that the physician has seen or treated within one year of termination of the employment.[179]
3. Patient records. The physician must be allowed to obtain patient records for a reasonable fee.[180] The format of the records must be in the same format as they are usually maintained.[181]
4. Buy-out provision. The covenant must allow the physician to buy out the covenant for a reasonable fee.[182]
5. Continuing care. The physician must be allowed to provide continuing care to a

---

177. Tex. Bus. & Com. Code § 15.50(b).

178. *Id.* § 15.50(b)(1)(B).

179. Tex. Bus. & Com. Code § 150.50(b)(1)(A).

180. *Id.* § 15.50(b)(1)(B).

181. *Id.* § 15.50(b)(1)(C).

182. *Id.* § 15.50(b)(2); *Novamed Surgery Ctr. Of Tyler, L.P. v. Bochow*, No. 12-13-00159-CV, 2013 WL 272554, at *3 (Tex. App.—Tyler June 12, 2013, no pet.) (mem. op.).

patient during an acute illness after the employment is terminated.[183]

6. Note that special public policy concerns exist in small communities[184]

A Texas Court of Appeals recently held that the statute requires that the reasonableness of the price in the buy-out provision must (if challenged by either party) be resolved in binding arbitration.[185] Furthermore, arbitration is not precluded even if there is no express reference to arbitration in the covenant because the court presumes the parties knew about the statute's arbitration provision at the time they contracted.[186] However, another court recently held that an arbitrator's role is plainly limited by statute to the reasonable price issue, and he or she cannot create a buyout provision where one is lacking to cure the defect.[187] Tex. Bus. & Com. Code § 15.50(b), the court held, states that the absence of a buy-out provision renders the noncompete covenant unenforceable.[188]

---

183. Tex. Bus. & Com. Code § 15.50(b)(3).

184. *See Nacogdoches Heart Clinic, P.A. v. Pokala*, 2013 Tex. App. LEXIS 1066 (Tex. App.—Tyler, Feb. 6, 2013, pet. filed) (mem. op.) (Appellate court upheld trial court's ruling that noncompetition agreement was unenforceable) ("The trial court determined that the covenant not to compete adversely affects the interest of the public and is therefore unreasonable and unenforceable. The court explained that 'we're a small community' and 'the public interest would be adversely affected, and that being, access to cardiac care.' He noted that [Defendant] testified that he gets up to six calls a night and works eighteen hour days. Noting that the population is aging, the court explained that, unlike large cities where there are 'dozens and dozens of cardiologists,' there is a need for cardiologists in 'this small community.' Further, 'for one doctor to be taken out of the equation hurts the medical care of the people.' The judge also explained that he was considering the fact that Paragraph 19 prohibits [Defendant] from practicing any medicine at all, not just cardiology. Based on the testimony, the court found that the covenant not to compete is unreasonable and therefore unenforceable.") ("An inquiry into the public interest in medical care is not concerned with any damage provision in the covenant. If [the plaintiff-medical clinic] did not want to bear financial consequences from a potential violation of the covenant not to compete, it was incumbent upon it to draft a covenant that did not violate public policy.").

185. *Sadler Clinic Ass'n*, 403 S.W.3d at 898.

186. *Id.*

187. *LasikPlus of Texas, P.C. v. Mattioli*, 418 S.W.3d 210, 220 (Tex. App.—Houston [14th Dist.] 2013, no pet.).

188. *Id.*

Chapter 4
Arbitration[1]

Edited by Mark Shank

4-1 INTRODUCTION

With increasing frequency, practitioners encounter an arbitration clause that facially covers a dispute with a departing employee. Typically, the arbitration clause is broad and attempts to reach any and all disputes between the employee and employer that touch upon the employment relationship, including post-employment disputes. In Texas, courts routinely send these types of cases to arbitration.[2] Another typical arbitration provision is one that contains a "carve-out," which allows the employer to obtain injunctive relief at the courthouse and then proceed to arbitration for the remainder of the case.[3] In this chapter, we will deal first with the developing body of law concerning the enforceability of

1. The author gratefully acknowledges the substantive and organizational assistance provided by Scott McElhaney in his paper of March 19, 2012, entitled "Enforcing and Avoiding Arbitration Clauses Under Texas Law."

2. *In re H.E. Butt Grocery Co.*, 17 S.W.3d 360, 378 (Tex. App.—Houston [14th Dist.] 2000, no pet.) (directing trial court to vacate its order denying the defendant's motion to compel arbitration).

3. *See BossCorp, Inc. v. Donegal, Inc.*, 370 S.W.3d 68, 76 (Tex. App.—Houston [14th Dist.] 2012, no pet.) ("Where an arbitration agreement contains carve-outs and exceptions providing judicial remedies for disputes, something more than mere reference to the AAA Rules for the conduct of the arbitration is needed to show that the parties clearly and unmistakably intended to delegate arbitrability to the arbitrator instead of the court.").

an arbitration provision and then discuss tactics and remedies in arbitration.

4-2 ENFORCEABILITY OF AN ARBITRATION PROVISION

4-2:1 THE FEDERAL ARBITRATION ACT

Although courts have historically resisted enforcing arbitration agreements, the passage of the Federal Arbitration Act (FAA)[4] and the Texas General Arbitration Act (TAA) altered that trend.[5] Since the passage of the statutes, parties frequently invoke the FAA, which courts regularly use to enforce arbitration agreements.[6]

Courts normally analyze an arbitration agreement under the requirements of a particular state's general contract law.[7] Congress intended the FAA to "exercise Congress' commerce power to the full[est]."[8] Initially, there were some arguments that the language of FAA § 1 precluded the FAA from covering employment contracts,[9] but the Supreme Court held that this exception narrowly applies only to "workers actually engaged in the movement of goods in interstate commerce."[10]

The FAA requires a court to order a party to arbitrate its claims when there is an arbitration agreement to that effect.[11] Indeed, the

---

4. 9 U.S.C. § 1.

5. Tex. Civ. Prac. & Rem. Code § 171.001.

6. *See, e.g., Thomas Petroleum, Inc. v. Morris*, 355 S.W.3d 94, 97 (Tex. App.—Houston [1st Dist.] 2011, pet. denied) (a party waived any objection to arbitration by invoking the FAA in court); *Ancor Holdings, LLC v. Peterson, Goldman & Villani, Inc.*, 294 S.W.3d 818, 829 (Tex. App.—Dallas 2009, no pet.) (parties pursued arbitration according to terms that expressly invoked the FAA).

7. *See, e.g., In re AdvancePCS Health L.P.*, 172 S.W.3d 603, 606 (Tex. 2005).

8. *Allied-Bruce Terminix Cos. v. Dobson*, 513 U.S. 265, 277 (1995).

9. FAA § 1 excluded coverage of "contracts of employment of Seaman, Railroad employees, or any other class of workers engaged in foreign or interstate commerce."

10. *Circuit City Stores, Inc. v. Adams*, 532 U.S. 105, 112 (2001).

11. 9 U.S.C. § 4.

FAA mandates a stay of a case until the arbitration has been completed.[12] Additionally, a court may not delay arbitration pending discovery or pending mediation.[13] However, a court may issue a preliminary injunction to preserve the status quo before the court determines that the issue can be referred to arbitration.[14]

Because arbitration requires only that an agreement "involves commerce," seldom will the FAA not be invoked.[15] The parties can choose to arbitrate under state arbitral rules alone,[16] but a reference to adoption of Texas substantive law in an arbitration clause does not preclude application of the FAA.[17] Moreover, when the parties specifically adopt the FAA in their agreement, no additional showing is necessary.[18] If the arbitration agreement refers to the TAA alone, then the FAA probably is excluded.[19] But, if the arbitration agreement does not specify, then both the TAA and the FAA apply.[20]

---

12. 9 U.S.C. § 3.

13. *In re Champion Techs., Inc.*, 173 S.W.3d 595, 599 (Tex. App.—Eastland 2005, pet. denied); *In re Heritage Bldg. Sys., Inc.*, 185 S.W.3d 539, 542 (Tex. App.—Beaumont 2006, no pet.).

14. *See Fisher v. Carlile*, 2017 WL 2774486, at *5 (Tex. App.—Houston [1st Dist.] 2017) (holding that "seeking injunctive relief in the court does not waive an arbitration clause if its purpose is to simply preserve the status quo."). *See also Janvey v. Alguire*, 647 F.3d 585, 595 (5th Cir. 2011) ("'[C]ongressional desire to enforce arbitration agreements would frequently be frustrated if the courts were precluded from issuing preliminary injunctive relief to preserve the status quo pending arbitration and, *ipso facto*, the meaningfulness of the arbitration process.'").

15. *See Lost Creek Mun. Util. Dist. v. Travis Indus. Painters, Inc.*, 827 S.W.2d 103, 105 (Tex. App.—Austin 1992, writ denied) (the court here deciding to interpret the FAA broadly); *Mesa Operating Ltd., P'ship v. La. Intrastate Gas Corp.*, 797 F.2d 238, 243-44 (5th Cir. 1986) (holding that "the existence of commerce under the FAA is dispositive with respect to the law which governs arbitrability even where the parties contemplated state law governance").

16. *See Volt Info. Scis., Inc. v. Bd. of Trs. of Leland Stanford Junior Univ.*, 489 U.S. 468, 479 (1989).

17. *Mesa Operating, L.P. v. Louisiana Intrastate Gas Corp.*, 797 F.2d 238, 243-44 (5th Cir. 1986).

18. *In re AdvancePCS Health L.P.*, 172 S.W.3d 603, 606 n. 3 (Tex. 2005).

19. *Atlas Gulf-Coast, Inc. v. Stanford*, 299 S.W.3d 356, 358 (Tex. App.—Houston [14th Dist.] 2009, no pet.).

20. *In re Devon Energy Corp.*, 332 S.W.3d 543, 547 (Tex. App.—Houston [1st Dist.] 2009, orig. proceeding).

4-2:2 THE TEXAS GENERAL ARBITRATION ACT

The TAA mirrors most of the substantive parts of the FAA[21]; however, the TAA excludes collective bargaining agreements as well as claims for workers' compensation benefits.[22] Because of the supremacy clause, the FAA, which does not contain these exclusions will preempt the TAA.[23] Further, the TAA requires enforcement of arbitration agreements,[24] and the trial court may not refuse to order arbitration.[25] Unlike under the FAA, where an arbitration award may not be subject to additional contractual appellate review,[26] in Texas, the parties can contract for appellate review of an arbitrator's decision.[27] However, both the FAA and the TAA specifically exclude immediate appellate review of orders compelling arbitration, and when review is permissible the appellant must show that they lack an adequate appellate remedy.[28] Moreover, before appellate review is granted, a court must address all defenses raised opposing arbitration.[29]

---

21. *See generally* Tex. Civ. Prac. & Rem. Code § 171; 9 U.S.C. § 1.

22. Tex. Civ. Prac. & Rem. Code § 171.002(a).

23. *In re Nexion Health at Humble, Inc.*, 173 S.W.3d 67, 69 (Tex. 2005).

24. *See* Tex. Civ. Prac. & Rem. Code § 171.021.

25. *See In re MHI P'ship, Ltd.*, 7 S.W.3d 918, 923 (Tex. App.—Houston [1st Dist.] 1999, no pet.) (holding that the "trial judge had no discretion to defer his ruling until after discovery").

26. *Hall St. Assocs., L.L.C. v. Mattel, Inc.*, 552 U.S. 576, 590 (2008).

27. *Compare Nafta Traders, Inc. v. Quinn*, 339 S.W.3d 84, 93 (Tex. 2011) (express authorization for appellate review), *with Forest Oil Corp. v. El Rucio Land & Cattle Co., Inc.*, 446 S.W.3d 58, 87 (Tex. App. —Houston [1st Dist.] 2014), *order withdrawn* (Dec. 2, 2016), *aff'd*, 518 S.W.3d 422 (Tex. 2017) ("Arbitration provision here does not show a clear agreement by the parties to provide courts with the authority to review. . . . Without clear language in the arbitration agreement, we have no authority to conduct expanded judicial review").

28. *Frontera Generation Ltd. P'ship v. Mission Pipeline Co.*, 400 S.W.3d 102, 113 (Tex. App.—Corpus Christi 2012, no pet.) (Mandamus relief is "generally not available to review orders compelling arbitration" except upon a showing that "the district court did not have the discretion to stay the proceedings pending arbitration" or if the order compelling arbitration also "dismisses the entire case and is therefore a final rather than interlocutory, order.").

29. *Cardwell v. Whataburger Restaurants, LLC*, 484 S.W.3d 426, 428 (Tex. 2016) (holding that "the court of appeals could not order arbitration without either addressing all the employee's arguments or remanding to the trial court to address them").

4-2:3 ENFORCEABILITY OF ARBITRATION AGREEMENTS

In general, courts favor arbitration agreements[30] and address the validity of such agreements.[31] The trial court has the power to determine "gateway" issues such as whether an arbitration agreement exists or is enforceable.[32] After conducting the gateway inquiry, if the trial court determines that an arbitration clause broadly incorporates gateway issues within the scope of the agreement, and there is evidence that both parties agreed to the covenants, then the trial court should compel arbitration and leave issues of validity and enforceability to the arbitrator.[33] Therefore, the trial court determines arbitrability of an arbitration agreement. [34] Moreover, a trial court may vacate awards when the arbitrator exceeds his power by acting contrary to express contractual provisions.[35]

By comparison, in a case involving the enforceability of a noncompetition agreement, the U.S. Supreme Court confirmed the general rule that attacks on the validity of a contract, as opposed to attacks on the validity of an arbitration clause, should be presented to and decided by the arbitrator rather than the courts.[36] Texas law also provides that an arbitrator must decide an attack on the validity

30. *See In re Olshan Found. Repair Co.*, 328 S.W.3d 883, 893 (Tex. 2010) (stating that arbitration is "an effective alternative to litigation"); *Valero Energy Corp. v. Teco Pipeline Co.*, 2 S.W.3d 576, 590 (Tex. App.—Houston [14th Dist.] 1999, no pet.).

31. *See Rent-A-Center W., Inc. v. Jackson*, 561 U.S. 63, 70 (2010); *Forest Oil Corp. v. McAllen*, 268 S.W.3d 51, 61 (Tex. 2008).

32. *Lucchese Boot Co. v. Rodriguez*, 473 S.W.3d 373, 381-82 (Tex. App—El Paso 2015, no pet.).

33. *Id.* at 382.

34. *Southwinds Express Constr., L.L.C. v. D.H. Griffin of Tex., Inc.*, 513 S.W.3d 66, 72-73 (Tex. App.—Houston [14th Dist.] 2016).

35. *BNSF R. Co. v. Alston Transp., Inc.*, 777 F.3d 785, 788 (5th Cir. 2015); *PoolRe Ins. Corp. v. Organizational Strategies, Inc.*, 783 F.3d 256, 262 (5th Cir. 2015) (ruling that "the power and authority of arbitrators in an arbitration proceeding is dependent on the provisions under which the arbitrators were appointed").

36. *Nitro-Lift Techs., L.L.C. v. Howard*, 568 U.S. 17, 20-21 (2012).

of a contract and not just an arbitration clause.[37] The parties may waive this rule by express provision in their arbitration agreement or by adoption of an arbitration rule to the same effect.[38]

Ordinarily, the first step in an arbitral proceeding is to determine whether the parties agreed to arbitrate a particular dispute. No specific language is required as long as the parties and court generally understand the arbitration obligation.[39] Neither do the parties need to sign the agreement if they have evidence of assent.[40] However, the Texas Supreme Court has repeatedly held that an arbitration agreement must be in writing and agreed to by the parties.[41] An arbitration agreement does not need to be in the same contract that is at issue in the dispute; it can be incorporated by reference.[42]

From time to time, the issue of mutuality of obligation arises. For example, an employer's right to modify or alter an arbitration agreement retroactively is not enforceable,[43] but an arbitration clause that reserves only a forward-looking right to amend is enforceable.[44] The Texas Supreme Court also has held that an arbitration "policy" is binding on employees when it is published and when the employees continue to work after being given notice; therefore, the employee is required to follow the

---

37. *In re Labatt Food Serv., L.P.*, 279 S.W.3d 640, 648 (Tex. 2009).

38. *See, e.g.*, AAA Commercial Arbitration Rules & Mediation Procedures, ¶ R-7 (2013).

39. *Belmont Constructors v. Lyondell Petrochemical Co.*, 896 S.W.2d 352, 356 (Tex. App.—Houston [1st Dist.] 1995, no writ).

40. *See In re AdvancePCS Health L.P.*, 172 S.W.3d 603, 606 (Tex. 2005); *Glass Producing Co., Inc. v. Jared Res., Ltd.*, 422 S.W.3d 68, 80-81 (Tex. App. —Texarkana 2014, no pet.) (Theories binding nonsignatories to "an arbitration clause [are]: '(1) incorporation by reference; (2) assumption; (3) agency; (4) alter ego; (5) equitable estoppel, and (6) third-party beneficiary'").

41. *Wright v. Hernandez*, 469 S.W.3d 744, 757 (Tex. App---El Paso, 2015).

42. *See In re AdvancePCS Health L.P.*, 172 S.W.3d at 606.

43. *J.M. Davidson, Inc. v. Webster*, 128 S.W.3d 223, 238-39 (Tex. 2003) (Smith, J., dissenting).

44. *In re Odyssey Healthcare, Inc.*, 310 S.W.3d 419, 421, 424 (Tex. 2010).

program.[45] Texas courts have further elaborated that "merely posting an arbitration policy on an intranet site is insufficient to give employees notice."[46]

General contract defenses are available for arbitration agreements. These defenses, such as fraud, misrepresentation, or deceit, may invalidate an arbitration agreement.[47] A court will rule on these issues. To illustrate, whether a party lacked mental capacity to assent to an arbitration contract was for the court to decide,[48] as opposed to an arbitrator deciding whether the entire agreement was unenforceable.[49] Moreover, a material breach of an arbitration agreement can excuse a party from obligations under an arbitration clause.[50] A Texas court emphasized this point when it found a party's interference with an accounting firm hired under an arbitration agreement to perform an accounting of production on a national gas project amounted to a material breach, which justified the vacation of an arbitration award and the refusal to reorder arbitration.[51]

Additionally, a party may waive the right to compel arbitration if it "substantially invokes" the judicial process prior to seeking an order compelling arbitration,[52] although the courts tend to be quite forgiving of parties who take multiple steps at the courthouse before invoking arbitration. For instance, filing a motion to transfer venue, mediating a case, engaging in written discovery, and conducting depositions when discovery was available in

---

45. *In re Halliburton Co.*, 80 S.W.3d 566, 568-69 (Tex. 2002).

46. *Doe v. Columbia N. Hills Hosp. Subsidiary, L.P.*, 521 S.W.3d 76, 82 (Tex. App.—Ft. Worth 2017, pet. denied).

47. *In re McKinney*, 167 S.W.3d 833, 835 (Tex. 2005).

48. *In re Morgan Stanley & Co., Inc.*, 293 S.W.3d 182, 190 (Tex. 2009).

49. *Will-Drill Res., Inc. v. Samson Res. Co.*, 352 F.3d 211, 212 (5th Cir. 2003).

50. *See Hooters of Am., Inc. v. Phillips*, 173 F.3d 933, 940 (4th Cir. 1999) (holding that rescission of an agreement is a proper remedy for a material breach).

51. *Tri-Star Petroleum Co. v. Tipperary Corp.*, 107 S.W.3d 607, 614-15 (Tex. App.—El Paso 2003, pet. denied).

52. *In re Serv. Corp. Int'l*, 85 S.W.3d 171, 174 (Tex. 2002); *Structured Capital Res. Corp. v. Arctic Cold Storage, LLC*, 237 S.W.3d 890, 894 (Tex. App.--Tyler 2007, no pet.).

the arbitral forum did not waive arbitration.[53] To the contrary, moving for summary judgment or taking any other step to seek final resolution of the dispute constituted substantially invoking the judicial process to preclude compelling arbitration.[54]

Lastly, burdensome costs may invalidate an arbitration agreement. Courts have grappled with arbitration clauses that put substantial costs on an employee or former employee. The U.S. Supreme Court noted that requiring a current or former employee to pay substantial arbitration costs may invalidate an arbitration agreement.[55] Under Fifth Circuit law, the court determines the arbitration cost issue on a case-by-case basis that must be established upon an affirmative showing that the costs would prevent the litigant from having a full opportunity to pursue his or her claim.[56] The Texas Supreme Court has adopted a similar approach.[57]

4-3 LITIGATION OF DISPUTES IN ARBITRATION

4-3:1 INSTITUTING AN ARBITRATION PROCEEDING

Once one or more of the parties to a dispute determines that a matter should be arbitrated, an arbitration proceeding must be instituted. There are three ways to commence the arbitration process: (1) submission, (2) initiation by demand or notice, and (3) court order.

---

53. *Granite Constr. Co. v. Beaty*, 130 S.W.3d 362, 367 (Tex. App.—Beaumont 2004, no pet.).

54. *Williams Indus., Inc. v. Earth Dev. Sys. Corp.*, 110 S.W.3d 131, 134, 139-40 (Tex. App.—Houston [1st Dist.] 2003, no pet.).

55. *Green Tree Fin. Corp. v. Randolph*, 531 U.S. 79, 90-91 (2000).

56. *Williams v. Cigna Fin. Advisors, Inc.*, 197 F.3d 752, 763 (5th Cir. 1999).

57. *In re FirstMerit Bank, N.A.*, 52 S.W.3d 749, 756 (Tex. 2001).

4-3:1.1 SUBMISSION

This usually occurs when there is no prior agreement to arbitrate. Essentially, the parties' counsel determine the "recipe" for the arbitration process. Recipe factors to consider include:

1. The scope of the arbitration;
2. Whether other parties will need to be included;
3. Whether the entire dispute should be arbitrated;
4. Whether and how the arbitration will be administered;
5. The number of arbitrators that will compose the arbitral panel;
6. Whether the parties will want to select the arbitrators before arbitration or will agree on a process for arbitrator selection;
7. How the costs of arbitration will be determined and allocated;
8. Whether the parties will want to limit discovery, motions, or any other procedures;
9. Whether arbitrator authority will be limited; and
10. Whether remedies will be limited.

The submission agreement that outlines the determined arbitration process can be detailed or it can be simple by relying upon the rules of the administrative authority. The more detailed the document, the more difficult the submission by arbitration because the parties probably are already embroiled in a dispute.

4-3:1.2 INITIATION BY DEMAND OR NOTICE

Arbitration most commonly begins by this method. One party provides a demand or notice to the other in accordance with an arbitration clause. The demand generally looks like a scaled-down petition or complaint, establishing the subject matter of the dispute and giving notice to the arbitral institution. Either the demand or the institution will determine the applicable rules, the arbitrators who will preside over the dispute, and the location for the proceeding. Common practice is to prepare the arbitration demand consistent with a contract's arbitration clause and applicable rules and to request the arbitrator to order a remedy. The opposing party may submit an answer or answering statement to the demand and may also make a counterclaim. An answer, while not always required, is usually filed, especially if the opposing party chooses to raise specific defenses other than a general denial. It is beneficial to set out in detail the issues in dispute in the demand and answer (and counterclaim), which frame the dispute.

Arbitral institutions allow for expedited procedures[58] in certain matters, which regularly involve amounts in controversy below a specific threshold.[59] Even in larger arbitrations, the parties can agree to expedited procedures.[60] Indeed, some arbitration clauses specify that an arbitration award must be granted within days of the initial submission to arbitration.

After the demand is filed, the administrating authority sets an administrative conference for the parties and the selected arbitrator(s) to plan a scheduling order. The arbitrator(s) then issues an order that outlines in fairly great detail all time limitations, the amount of discovery to be taken, the form of the award, and various other matters.

58. *See, e.g.*, AAA Commercial Rules, ¶¶ E-1 – E-10.

59. *See, e.g.*, AAA Commercial Rules, ¶ E-2.

60. *Id.*

4-3:1.3 COURT ORDER

If the court order is a result of a motion to compel arbitration, then the court will order one party to make a demand for arbitration. When the arbitration is court-annexed or court-mandated, the court initiates the arbitration by an order that includes decisions concerning arbitrator selection, location, and rules. Depending on the circumstances, court-annexed arbitration may or may not be binding.

4-4 SELECTION OF THE ARBITRATOR

One of the greatest benefits of arbitration is that you can choose the arbitrator(s). Arbitrator selection is crucial because the arbitrator is the judge of both the law and the facts. Except in very limited instances, absent prejudicial misconduct that justifies vacatur of the award, the arbitrator's decision is largely immune from judicial supervision or review. The most common method of arbitrator selection comes with the help of an administrative body. The American Arbitration Association (AAA) outlines the traditional and best-known arbitrator selection process. The AAA assembles a list of five to ten appropriate arbitrators from a larger pool of qualified panelists and provides the parties with the arbitrators' biographical information.[61] Then the parties select from that list the arbitrators to sit on their panel. The parties can choose to alternatively "strike" a panelist until only one remains or to select certain panelists and, to the extent their selections overlap, allow the administrator to choose an arbitrator acceptable to both parties.[62] A third selection method is for each party to rank the arbitrators in order of preference, after which the administrator chooses the highest-ranked panelists that overlap each list.

In the case of three panelists, often the parties' arbitration agreement requires two "party-appointed" arbitrators, one selected

61. *See, e.g., AAA Commercial Rules, ¶ R-12.*

62. *Id. at ¶ R-12(b).*

by each side, and one jointly selected "neutral arbitrator"—a process that is unnecessary, expensive, and cumbersome. In the past, particularly in labor arbitrations, the party-appointed arbitrator would maintain contact with the parties throughout the arbitration process, but this is now the exception rather than the rule.[63] Today, the most common practice is for the "party-appointed arbitrator" to communicate with the appointing party only until the jointly-appointed "neutral" is selected, after which all three arbitrators become "neutral."[64]

Cooperation between counsel about arbitration selection varies. Each party communicates almost entirely with the case manager and designates respective preferences according to the applicable process. Occasionally, counsel may give additional input to the case administrator concerning attributes of a neutral arbitrator that they would find most acceptable. In some instances, adverse counsel may even agree on arbitrator selection.

Once a particular candidate is suggested or a list is provided, diligent counsel engages in collecting information about the potential arbitrators. Paradoxically, the more first-hand knowledge that counsel or one of the parties has about an arbitrator, the more likely that arbitral prospect will be stricken as unsuitable. The ability to obtain information about arbitral candidates is limited only by the creativity of counsel. Below is a list of common sources of information.

Spend the necessary time on arbitrator selection. Choice of arbitrator is often the single most important decision you will make in your case.

4-4:1 BIOGRAPHICAL RESUMES

All arbitrators provide biographical information, usually in the form of a resume. The resumes are detailed and specific,

63. *See, e.g., id.* at ¶ R-17.

64. *See, e.g., id.* at ¶ R-18.

particularly given the burden that current case law places upon arbitrators regarding disclosure.[65] Under recent AAA practices, arbitrators' biographies have become even more detailed and elaborate. Additionally, each time arbitrators are appointed, their biographies are furnished to the parties, and they must certify that their information is current. Certainly, the parties should not limit themselves to the biographical information furnished by the AAA. Other sources, such as directories, may provide additional biographical information. The internet hosts a wealth of information, such as the biographies of alternative dispute resolutions professionals posted on personal, organizational, and other professional webpages. Counsel should also search for biographical information in professional or general social media or other databases.

4-4:2 BOOKS AND ARTICLES

Any books, articles, or CLE papers given by a candidate may contain personal information about that candidate. These writings may indicate an arbitrator's understanding of certain subject matters and potentially provide insight into an arbitrator's approach to and views about the arbitral process or the subject matter at hand.

4-4:3 WORD OF MOUTH

A time-honored method for determining whether an arbitrator is suitable is "word of mouth." Inquiries to members of one's firm, members of former firms where the arbitrator has served, professional friends and colleagues, and anyone who practiced in front of the arbitrator often provide the richest information. Occasionally, firms or services may provide copies of opinions or other information about the arbitrators. As in all cases, the

65. *See, e.g., Blue Cross Blue Shield v. Juneau*, 114 S.W.3d 126, 132-133 (Tex. App.—Austin 2003, no pet.); *see also Karlseng v. Cooke*, 346 S.W.3d 85, 91 (Tex. App.—Dallas 2011, no pet.).

sources must be evaluated for reliability and relevancy, with more recent arbitral experience likely being the most reliable.

Concerning the qualities one should expect from an arbitrator, the foremost is fairness. An arbitrator should be a person of integrity and sound judgment and, if possible, should have expertise or specialized knowledge in the involved subject matter. The arbitrator should be completely impartial, having no interest in the outcome. Accordingly, before selection, each candidate must disclose any potential conflicts of interest after reviewing a list of the parties, counsel, witnesses, and other relevant information.[66] Arbitrators have a duty to provide supplemental disclosures at any time appropriate, particularly when new parties or potential witnesses are added, or if information comes to mind that was not considered previously.[67]

The arbitrator should avoid any appearance of impropriety. For that reason, arbitrators may not engage in any direct communication with the parties or their counsel after neutral arbitration selection (except when the opposition is present).[68] An advantage of an arbitral administrator is that communications can be made through the administrator to create a buffer. Additionally, counsel first sends filings to the administrator, although some procedures allow for direct submission to the arbitrator with copies sent to the administrator. The foregoing procedures are important and valuable in maintaining arbitrator neutrality.

4-5 EXPEDITED PROCEDURES

In the case of a claim for injunction, time is extraordinarily important to the prosecuting party. It is imperative to make the administrative body aware that a party is seeking expedited relief for a claim.

66. *See, e.g.*, AAA Commercial Rules, ¶ R-18.

67. *See, e.g., id. at ¶ R-17.*

68. *Id. at ¶ R-19.*

Courts do not address specifically the actions parties and their counsel should take when there is a broad-based arbitration clause with no carve-out; however, the AAA Commercial Arbitration Rules do address this issue. Rule 37(a) states: "the arbitrator may take whatever interim measures he or she deems necessary, including injunctive relief and measures for the protection or conservation of property and the disposition of perishable goods."[69] Rule 37(c) also states: "[The] request for interim measures addressed by a party to a judicial authority shall not be deemed incompatible with the agreement to arbitrate or a waiver of the right to arbitrate."[70]

You will often want to use expedited procedures in departing employee cases. Know the rules, and be firm (but polite) with your case administrator about taking advantage of them.

4-6 EMERGENCY ARBITRATION

4-6:1 APPOINTMENT OF EMERGENCY ARBITRATOR

After a party who needs emergency protection notifies the AAA and other pertinent parties in writing of the relief's nature and the reasons that the relief needs to be emergent, then, within one business day of receipt, the AAA will appoint a single emergency arbitrator from a designated panel that rules on emergency applications.[71] Immediately after being selected, the arbitrator will then divulge any circumstances that might affect his or her objectivity. Any challenge to the selection of the emergency arbitrator must be stated within one business day from the time the AAA discloses their choice.[72]

---

69. *Id. at ¶ 37(a).*

70. *Id. at ¶ 37(c).*

71. *See, e.g.*, AAA Emp't Arbitration Rules & Mediation Procedures, ¶ O-2.

72. *See, e.g., id.*

4-6:2 SCHEDULE

Within two business days (at the very latest), the emergency arbitrator must create a schedule for consideration of the application for emergency relief.[73] In the schedule, all parties must be given a reasonable opportunity to be heard. However, telephone and written communications may be allowed as an alternative to formal hearings.[74]

4-6:3 INTERIM AWARD

Once the arbitrator is persuaded that instant and irreparable damage will occur without granting the seeking, entitled party emergency relief, the arbitrator is able to grant an interim award that gives the necessary party the emergency relief and reveals to both parties the reasoning behind the grant.[75]

4-6:4 CONSTITUTION OF THE PANEL

While a party may apply to the emergency arbitrator, the panel is the body that will act and rule on an application for the modification of an interim reward. The only power an emergency arbitrator has over the modification is if he or she is included on the panel.[76]

4-6:5 SECURITY

The AAA Employment Arbitration Rules and Mediation Procedure states that "[a]ny interim award of emergency relief may be conditioned on provision by the party seeking such relief of appropriate security."[77]

---

73. *See, e.g.*, *id.* at ¶ O-3.

74. *See, e.g.*, *id.*

75. *See, e.g.*, *id.* at ¶ O-4.

76. *See, e.g.*, AAA Emp't Arbitration Rules & Mediation Procedures, ¶ O-5.

77. *Id.* at ¶ O-6.

4-6:6 SPECIAL MASTER

The agreement (or waiver of the right) to arbitrate and a request for interim actions that a party asks of the court shall not be deemed irreconcilable. If the court directs the AAA to nominate a special master to contemplate the request, the AAA will act in accordance with Section O-1 of these rules.[78]

4-7 THE MANAGEMENT CONFERENCE

Regardless of a need for expedited relief, an arbitrator will arrange for a management conference during which the parties discuss with the arbitrator their preferred procedures and timelines for the arbitration hearing. The items decided at a management conference include:

1. The date of the hearing;
2. The length of the hearing;
3. The damages amounts from any claims and counterclaims;
4. Any discovery to be provided and deadlines for submission;
5. The deadlines for exchange of witness lists with outlines of testimonies;
6. The deadlines for exchange of expert designations and exchange of expert witness reports;
7. Whether any other discovery should be had, such as document production and interrogatories;
8. The location of the hearing;
9. Whether briefs will be exchanged before or after the hearing;

78. *Id.* at ¶ O-7.

10. The deadline for exchange of trial exhibits;
11. The deadline for stipulation of uncontested facts;
12. The type of award to be rendered by the arbitrator;
13. The deadlines for dispositive motions, if any; and
14. A possible date for additional preliminary hearings or pretrial hearings prior to arbitration.[79]

Most often, this hearing is held via telephone conference. It is wise for the parties to confer and agree on as many deadlines as possible before the management conference.

4-8 DISCOVERY AND DEADLINES

Arbitrators do not provide discovery as a matter of right as under most rules of civil procedure. Usually, the arbitrator and counsel agree to conduct limited discovery, which often involves stipulating limitations on the number of hours for deposition, the number of requests for production or interrogatories, and some type of preliminary exchange of information (such as under Fed. R. Civ. P. 26 and the like). An arbitrator then includes these limitations in the order prescribed by the management conference. Sometimes, the arbitration procedure will set forth the manner and method of conducting discovery, which the arbitrator will follow unless the parties otherwise agree.

One advantage of arbitration is that the arbitrator can resolve discovery disputes in short order. Arbitrators generally can make themselves available within a day or two of a discovery dispute arising, and they commonly schedule discovery conferences via telephone to resolve the dispute without need of further motions

79. *See, e.g.*, AAA Commercial Rules, ¶ R-22; In this context, "pretrial" means before the final arbitral hearing.

or paperwork. Of course, if the dispute is more complicated and not remediable by such procedure, an arbitrator will set a rapid briefing schedule to address outstanding disputes. As a result, many parties find that arbitrators deal quickly with discovery disputes that would otherwise slow down a case.

4-9 TYPE OF AWARD

An arbitrator has the option to grant one of three types of awards: (1) the standard award, (2) the reasoned award, and (3) findings of fact and conclusions of law. The standard award is very short and simply states the result: who wins, who loses, and the damages or other remedies granted. A reasoned award is the most common and is similar to a *per curiam* opinion, generally containing a summary of the facts and the arbitrator's line of reasoning. Findings of fact and conclusions of law mirror that of a judge entering judgment with detailed findings of all facts and conclusions of law.

4-10 PROTECTIVE ORDERS

A party may request a protective order to protect confidential documents or witness testimony. Then, counsel will confer and propose a protective order to the arbitrator, which arbitrators routinely sign. In the rare instance where the parties cannot agree, they can request a hearing with the arbitrator to determine an appropriate protective order.

4-11 SUBPOENAS

Arbitrators also routinely sign subpoenas prepared on forms provided by the arbitral authority staff. What few involved in arbitration fully understand is the limited power of arbitrators to enforce subpoenas. In fact, enforcement of a subpoena requires judicial intervention.

Arbitral subpoenas are usually only an issue when they are

directed at a nonparty. The question then becomes whether an arbitrator has the power to subpoena a nonparty to appear at a hearing as a witness or to bring requested documents. The arbitral subpoena power can be found in the Federal Arbitration Act (FAA), which states:

> The arbitrators selected either as prescribed in this title or otherwise, or a majority of them, may summon in writing any person to attend before them or any of them as a witness and in a proper case to bring with him or them any book, record, document, or paper which may be deemed material as evidence in the case. The fees for such attendance shall be the same as the fees of witnesses before masters of the United States courts. Said summons shall issue in the name of the arbitrator or arbitrators, or a majority of them, and shall be signed by the arbitrators, or a majority of them, and shall be directed to the said person and shall be served in the same manner as subpoenas to appear and testify before the court; if any person or persons so summoned to testify shall refuse or neglect to obey said summons, upon petition the United States district court for the district in which such arbitrators, or a majority of them, are sitting may compel the attendance of such person or persons before said arbitrator or arbitrators, or punish said person or persons for contempt in the same manner provided by law for securing the attendance of witnesses or their punishment for neglect or refusal to attend in the courts of the United States.[80]

Additionally, Rule 31(d) of the AAA Commercial Rules states:

> "[a]n arbitrator or other person authorized by law

80. 9 U.S.C. § 7.

> to subpoena witnesses or documents may do so upon the request of any party or independently."[81]

Courts are split as to whether a nonparty must comply with an arbitrator's prehearing document subpoena. The Eighth Circuit,[82] in *In re Sec. Life Ins. Co. of Am.*, held that the arbitrators had "implicit" power to subpoena relevant documents for review by a nonparty prior to the hearing, since they had power to subpoena relevant documents for production at the hearing. The Third Circuit, however, has taken a contrary position.[83] There, the court found that, in an arbitration governed by the FAA, arbitrators did not have the authority to issue discovery subpoenas for documents to nonparties.[84] Alternatively, the Fourth Circuit[85] in *COMSAT Corp. v. National Science Foundation*, held it would enforce the arbitral orders for prehearing discovery of nonparties only upon a showing of "special need." In addition to its holding regarding the subpoena power, the Eighth Circuit[86] has also found that, implicit in an arbitration panel's power to subpoena relevant documents for production at a hearing, is the power to order the production of relevant documents for review by a party before the hearing.

Judge Fitzwater has eloquently articulated what will be the likely result in Texas Federal Courts:

> The court adopts the reasoning of the Third and Second Circuits and holds that § 7 of the FAA does not authorize arbitrators to compel production of documents from a non-party, unless they

---

81. AAA Commercial Rules, ¶ R-31(d).

82. *In Re Sec. Life Ins. Co. of Am.*, 228 F.3d 865, 870-71 (8th Cir. 2000).

83. *See Hay Group, Inc. v. E.B.S. Acquisition Corp.*, 360 F.3d 404, 408 (3d Cir. 2004) (elaborating that the intent of the drafters showed that subpoena power was not conferred by implication).

84. *Id.*

85. *COMSAT Corp. v. Nat'l Sci. Found.*, 190 F.3d 269, 278 (4th Cir. 1999).

86. *In Re Sec. Life Ins. Co. of Am.*, 228 F.3d 865, 870-71 (8th Cir. 2000).

> are doing so in connection with the non-party's attendance at an arbitration hearing. As the Third Circuit reasoned, the text of § 7 mentions only orders to produce documents when brought with a witness to a hearing. *Hay Group*, 360 F.3d at 407. The text is "straightforward and unambiguous." *Life Receivables*, 549 F.3d at 216. Further, the section is similar to a previous version of Fed. R. Civ. P. 45, which before 1991 did not allow pre-hearing subpoenas of documents from non-parties. See *Hay Group*, 360 F.3d at 407; *Life Receivables*, 549 F.3d at 216 ("The FAA was enacted in a time when pre-hearing discovery in civil litigation was generally not permitted."). Finally, the court declines to read greater powers into the text of § 7 despite policy preferences favoring arbitration efficiency, because the court's policy preferences cannot override the clear text of the statute. *See Hay Group*, 360 F.3d at 406 (citing *Eaves v. County of Cap May*, 239 F.3d 527, 531-32 (3d Cir. 2000)).[87]

Section 7 of the FAA clearly grants power to the district court in the districts in which the arbitrator is sitting to enforce arbitral subpoenas directed to parties as well as nonparties. The Federal Rules of Civil Procedure require that an order seeking enforcement of a subpoena of a nonparty must be made in the district where the discovery is being or is to be taken.[88] Moreover, an arbitrator has the authority to require nonparties to be witnesses and to produce documents at a hearing.[89]

The Texas Arbitration Act allows prehearing discovery in

---

87. *Empire Fin. Group, Inc., v. Pension Fin. Services, Inc.*, Civil Action No. 3:09-CV-2155-D, 2010 U.S. Dist. LEXIS 18782, 285-86 (N.D. Tex. 2010) (mem. op.)

88. Fed. R. Civ. P. 37(a)(1).

89. 9 U.S.C. § 7.

arbitration.[90] Of course, when the witness is more than 150 miles from the arbitration location, discovery from that witness may be difficult to obtain.[91] To subpoena a witness outside the 150 mile radius, counsel must file an ancillary action in the Texas district where the witness resides (that supports the arbitrator-issued subpoena) and then serve a subpoena with that caption. Should the witness be from another state that will not enforce the subpoena of the arbitrator, then likely the best course is for counsel is to file an ancillary action where the arbitration is pending, request a commission (or whatever the other state requires), and comply with the additional requirements of that state.

Many practitioners overlook the difficulty in procuring testimony from a reluctant nonparty witness. If applicable, this is something that should be considered early in the process.

4-12 ALTERNATIVE METHODS OF PROCURING TESTIMONY

Another benefit of arbitration is an arbitrator's flexibility in presentation. For example, arbitrators routinely take witnesses out of order for the parties' or witnesses' convenience, and they may take witness testimony by video conference, livestreamed video, telephone conference, or any other effective method of communication. Arbitrators can take testimony by deposition and review the testimony at a time when the parties are not present. Occasionally, arbitrators take affidavit testimony, which is considered by most arbitrators to be unpersuasive as to any contested issue. Arbitrators often dispense with prove-up of documents via records custodians, instead requesting or requiring the parties' stipulation to the authenticity of documents, unless authenticity is genuinely at issue.

---

90. Tex. Civ. Prac. & Rem. Code § 171.051.

91. Tex. R. Civ. P. 176.3(a).

4-13 CONTINUANCE

Arbitrators view the processes as driven by the parties and will generally grant continuances or postponements, provided that the parties agree. However, many are reluctant to grant continuances because of the perceived benefit of expedited resolution through arbitration. Therefore, arbitrators often require the attorneys' clients either to sign off on a motion for continuance or to be present at any hearing at which a party requests a continuance.

4-14 CONFIDENTIALITY

Arbitrations are private. Uniformly among all arbitral authorities, no outsiders may be involved in an arbitral process absent consent from both parties agreeing to arbitration. Any person who attends arbitration must have a direct interest in the case—as a party or party representative, witness, or attorney. Beyond that, others may attend only if the parties agree and the arbitrator grants permission.

4-15 COURT REPORTERS

Under the rules of most arbitral authorities, court reporters are optional. Indeed, many arbitrators discourage court reporters as an unnecessary, additional cost. Typically, the rules require the party requesting the transcript to pay for it and to provide a copy to the opposing party.[92] Certainly, a transcript assists the arbitrator in any situations where the prior testimony was unclear. But, in general, arbitrators take sufficient notes and have adequate recollection, making a transcript unnecessary.

92. *See AAA Commercial Rules, ¶ R-28.*

4-16 THE FINAL HEARING

4-16:1 OPENING STATEMENTS

Arbitrators usually request opening statements of the parties, which tend to be rather brief.[93] An effective opening statement provides the arbitrator with a road map of what the advocate intends to prove throughout the case. Most arbitrators are not interested in long or argumentative opening statements.

4-16:2 THE RULE

Almost all arbitral authorities provide in their rules the ability to invoke the "Rule."[94] The parties may waive invocation of the Rule.

4-16:3 EVIDENCE

Unless the arbitration agreement provides otherwise, most arbitration agreements provide a relaxed version of the rules of evidence. In almost all cases, arbitrators will admit any reasonable evidence proffered by a party. Objections to evidence are frequently met by an arbitral response that the evidence will be admitted for "what it is worth." This is, in part, because under the FAA and the TAA an arbitral decision cannot be overturned for admitting evidence but might be overturned for refusing to admit evidence.[95]

4-16:4 WITNESS PRESENTATION

As stated earlier, arbitrators regularly accommodate witness schedules by allowing witnesses to be taken out of order. An arbitrator has great flexibility in the manner and method of witness

---

93. *See AAA Commercial Rules, ¶ R-32.*

94. The "Rule" is sequestration of witnesses to avoid one witness testimony influencing another testimony.

95. *See* 9 USCS § 10(a)(3); *see also* Tex. Civ. Prac. & Rem. Code § 171.047.

presentation, such as videotaped depositions, video conferencing, livestreamed video communications, and telephonic witness examinations.[96]

4-16:5 CLOSING ARGUMENTS

It is very common for an arbitrator to allow the parties to present closing statements, which often take the form of a summary of the evidence followed by a question and answer session with the arbitrator.[97] Counsel should always be attentive to an arbitrator's questions because they provide much insight into areas with which the advocate may assist the arbitrator in reaching a favorable decision.

---

96. AAA Commercial Rules, ¶ R-32.

97. *See AAA Commercial Rules, ¶ R-39.*

Chapter 5
Other Causes of Action

Edited by Pat Maher

5-1 BREACH OF CONTRACTS AND VIOLATION OF COVENANTS

5-1:1 BREACH OF CONTRACT

In departing employee cases, breach of contract is among the claims available to a former employer. Breach of contract claims involve various promises or covenants, such as a covenant defining confidential information, the scope of confidentiality, and the return of such information when employment ends; a covenant not to solicit or to hire employees from the former employer; a restrictive covenant prohibiting solicitation of former customers; or a covenant not to compete.[1]

The elements of an action for breach of contract are:

1. a valid and enforceable contract;
2. that the plaintiff is the proper party to sue;
3. that the plaintiff performed or was excused from performance;

1. *See* discussion on covenants not to compete in Chapter 3.

4. that the defendant breached the contract; and
5. that the breach caused the plaintiff injury.

5-1:1.1 VALID AND ENFORCEABLE CONTRACT

Typically in the departing employee context, proof of an enforceable contract is not an issue. Occasionally, however, the fact of signature may be. Texas has adopted the Uniform Electronic Transactions Act (UETA), which recognizes the increasing use of electronic signatures and electronic records relations to electronic transactions.[2] The UETA applies to any electronic signature "created, generated, sent, communicated, received, or stored on or after January 1, 2002."[3] However, it applies only to transactions that the parties have agreed to conduct electronically.[4] A signature cannot be denied legal effect simply because it is in electronic form.[5] Neither is a contract unenforceable merely because an electronic record was used,[6] as an electronic record satisfies the legal requirement for a written record and for a signature.[7] In fact, an electronic signature is attributable to a person if the

---

2. Tex. Bus. & Comm. Code Ann. § 322.003(a).

3. Tex. Bus. & Comm. Code Ann. § 322.004.

4. Tex. Bus. & Comm. Code Ann. § 322.005(b). *See, e.g., Fries Rest. Mgmt., LLC v. Silva,* No. 13-18-00596-CV, 2020 Tex. App. LEXIS 5970 (Tex. App. Corpus Christi July 30, 2020)(employer entitled to an order compelling arbitration because its evidence of a paperless system and an online application with an arbitration agreement conclusively disproved an employee's testimony claiming to have completed a paper application with no arbitration agreement); *Wal-Mart Stores, Inc. v. Constantine,* No. 05-17-00694-CV, 2018 Tex. App. LEXIS 3023 (Tex. App. Dallas Apr. 30, 2018)(where the employee was required to log in by entering a confidential employee identification number and password, accessed an employer's benefit form, clicked through it where required, and acknowledged completion by clicking an acknowledgement button, the requirements of Tex. Bus. & Com. Code Ann. § 322.005(b) were met by the employer's evidence of the context and surrounding circumstances, including the parties' conduct.).

5. Tex. Bus. & Comm. Code Ann. § 322.007(a).

6. Tex. Bus. & Comm. Code Ann. § 322.007(b).

7. Tex. Bus. & Comm. Code Ann. § 322.007(c)-(d. *See Khoury v. Tomlinson,* 518 S.W.3d 568 (Tex. App. Houston 1st Dist. Mar. 30, 2017, no pet.)(the corporate officer's signature block in an email performed the same authenticating function as a "from" field and satisfies the statute of frauds).

person made the signature,[8] proof of which can be determined from the context and surrounding circumstances at the time it was made.[9] The signature may not be excluded from evidence solely because of its electronic form.[10] The UETA also states when an electronic signature is deemed sent or received. Basically, an electronic signature is sent or received when it is properly addressed electronically in a form capable of being processed.[11]

When several documents, e.g., an offer letter acceptance and accompanying documents, such as a nondisclosure agreement, are executed during the same transaction and for the same purpose, the documents are construed together as a single instrument.[12] In addition, if only one party signs the agreement, the other party may accept by his or her acts, conduct, or acquiescence in the terms of the contract.[13]

5-1:1.2 PROPER PARTY

Proper parties to contracts are:

1. direct parties to the contract;
2. assignees of parties to the contract;
3. agents entitled to sue on behalf of the parties to the contract; and
4. intended third-party beneficiaries to the contract.

8. Tex. Bus. & Comm. Code Ann. § 322.009(a).

9. Tex. Bus. & Comm. Code Ann. § 322.009(b).

10. Tex. Bus. & Comm. Code Ann. § 322.013.

11. Tex. Bus. & Comm. Code Ann. § 322.015(a)-(b).

12. *Sanders v. Future Com, Ltd.*, No. 02-15-00077-CV, 2017 Tex. App. LEXIS 4575, slip op. at *3 (Tex. App.—Fort Worth May 18, 2017).

13. *Id.*

Courts will often enforce an arbitration clause against a nonsignatory to the underlying arbitration agreement under the third-party beneficiary doctrine.[14] A forum selection clause may also be enforced on behalf of a nonsignatory defendant in a case brought by a signatory plaintiff under the direct benefit beneficiary doctrine.[15] Under this doctrine, if the plaintiff is relying on a contract that contains the forum selection clause to support the plaintiff's claim against the nonsignatory, the plaintiff may be bound by the forum selection clause in the underlying contract.[16]

Because of mergers, often the entity suing is not the entity with whom the employee contracted, so counsel should determine the proper plaintiff. Note that "all contracts are freely assignable" under Texas law unless the parties otherwise agree.[17] An employee, however, is not a party to a contract between the employer and a third party.[18]

5-1:1.3 PERFORMANCE

A plaintiff must establish that he or she fully or substantially performed contractual obligations under a contract or was excused from performance to recover for breach.[19] A plaintiff may be excused from performing those obligations when the opposing

---

14. *See In re Palm Harbor Homes, Inc.*, 195 S.W.3d 672, 677-678 (Tex. 2006) (citing *In re Vesta Ins.*, 192 S.W.3d 759, 761 (Tex. 2006) (per curiam) ("if the parties to the contract intended to secure a benefit to that third party and entered into the contract directly for the third party's benefit" and "the controversy arises from a contract containing an arbitration clause," the nonsignatory third-party may enforce the arbitration provision), *cited in Cielo Prop. Grp. LLC v. Mulcahy*, 2019 Tex. App. LEXIS 5789 *6 (Tex. App. – Austin, July 11, 2019) (enforcing arbitration clause against former employee and in favor of customer of former employer).

15. *Smith v. Kenda Capital, LLC.*, 451 S.W.3d 453, 458-59 (Tex. App. – Houston [14th Dist.], no pet.).

16. *Id.*

17. *Vaughn v. DAP Fin. Servs., Inc.*, 982 S.W.2d 1, 7 (Tex. App.—Houston [1st Dist.] 1997, no pet.).

18. *Downhole Tech., LLC v. Silver Creek Servs., Inc.*, No. H-17-0020, 2017 U.S. Dist. LEXIS 70056, slip op. at *3 (S.D. Tex. May 8, 2017).

19. *Weitzul Constr., Inc. v. Outdoor Environs*, 849 S.W.2d 359, 363 (Tex. App.—Dallas 1993, writ denied).

party materially breached the contract, repudiated the contract, prevented performance, or waived performance.[20] Additionally, a plaintiff should allege that "all conditions precedent have been performed or have occurred,"[21] although it is not necessary to prove compliance with any conditions precedent unless defendant specifically denies them.[22] Moreover, a plaintiff who does not make this allegation may obtain a favorable judgment by proving performance of all conditions precedent.[23] Accordingly, counsel should carefully question the client about performance, particularly about unpaid compensation to the former employee because these are the areas where a former employee usually claims his or her former employer failed to perform.

5-1:1.4 BREACH

To recover under a contract, a plaintiff must demonstrate that the defendant breached the contract by failing to perform an act that the defendant expressly or impliedly promised to perform.[24]

5-1:1.5 RESULTING INJURY

The breach must cause damage to meet the requirements for a breach of contract claim. In most cases, the remedy for breach is recovery of money damages for the loss or harm incurred.[25] Damages recoverable in an action for breach consist of direct (or general) damages and consequential (or special) damages.[26] Direct

---

20. *Mustang Pipeline Co. v. Driver Pipeline Co.*, 134 S.W.3d 195, 196 (Tex. 2004) (per curiam) (breach); *Another Attic, Ltd. v. Plains Builders, Inc.*, 07-08-0312-CV, 2010 Tex. App. LEXIS 9620, at *8 (Tex. App.—Amarillo Dec. 6, 2010, no pet.) (repudiation); *Daneshjou Co. v. Bullock*, No. 03-05-00106-CV, 2009 Tex. App. LEXIS 2001, at *43 (Tex. App.—Austin Mar. 27, 2009, pet. granted) (prevention).

21. Tex. R. Civ. P. 54.

22. *Id.*

23. *Grimm v. Grimm*, 864 S.W.2d 160, 162 (Tex. App.—Houston [14th Dist.] 1993, no writ).

24. *Gaspar v. Lawnpro, Inc.*, 372 S.W.3d 754, 757 (Tex. App.—Dallas 2012, no pet.).

25. Aquaplex, Inc. v. Rancho La Valencia, Inc., 297 S.W.3d 768, 774 (Tex. 2009).

26. *DaimlerChrysler Motors Co., LLC v. Manuel*, 362 S.W.3d 160, 179-80 (Tex. App.—

damages compensate for harm that naturally and necessarily results from the failure to perform the promise.[27] Consequential damages compensate for losses that are foreseeable but that do not necessarily result from the breaching party's acts.[28]

5-1:2 ATTORNEYS' FEES AND COURT COSTS

Under Texas law, parties are entitled to reasonable attorneys' fees in a breach of contract action.[29] The contract itself may provide for attorneys' fees.[30] Parties must exercise reasonable care to minimize their damages where they can be reasonably avoided.[31] Interest and court costs are recoverable.

In the context of noncompetition litigation, however, a number of courts have interpreted Texas Business and Professions Code §§ 15.51-15.52, as limiting the award of attorneys' fees to defendants who establish the underlying noncompetition agreement was overbroad and unenforceable. Employers who prove the defendant breached a valid and enforceable noncompetition agreement, therefore, have been found not entitled to attorneys' fees that would otherwise be awardable under Texas Civil Practice and Remedies Code § 38.001.[32]

Fort Worth 2012, no pet.).

27. *Id.*

28. *Stuart v. Bayless*, 964 S.W.2d. 920, 921 (Tex. 1998).

29. Tex. Civ. Prac. & Rem. Code Ann. § 38.001.

30. *See Bullet Concrete Materials Inc. v. Texoga Techs. Corp.*, No. 09-11-00162-CV, 2012 Tex. App. LEXIS 1347, at *4 (Tex. App.—Beaumont Feb. 23, 2012, no pet.) (mem. op.).

31. *Walker v. Salt Flat Water Co.*, 96 S.W.2d 231, 232 (Tex. 1936).

32. *See, e.g. Rieves v. Buc-ee's Ltd.*, 532 S.W.3d 845, 854 (Tex. App. Houston [14th Dist.] 2015, no pet.) *see also Ginn v. NCI Bldg. Sys., Inc.*, 472 S.W3d 802, 827 (Tex. App.—Houston [1st Dist.] 2015, no pet.) (affirming trial court's denial of employer's request for attorneys' fees because Covenants Not to Compete Act does not authorize award of attorneys' fees to employers); *Franlink v. GJMS Unlimited, Inc.*, 401 S.W.3d 705, 712 (Tex. App.—Houston [14th Dist.] 2013, pet. denied) (affirming trial court's denial of employer's request for attorneys' fees because Covenants Not to Compete Act preempts Civil Practices & Remedies Code Chapter 38); *Perez v. Texas Disposal Sys., Inc.*, 103 S.W.3d 591, 594 (Tex. App.—San Antonio 2003, pet. denied) (holding Covenants Not to Compete Act controls award of attorney's fees and preempts award of fees under any other law).

5-1:3 BREACH OF NONDISCLOSURE AGREEMENT OR COVENANT OF CONFIDENTIALITY

Contracting parties can agree by contract that information rising to the level of trade secrets will be maintained as confidential, proprietary information. Generally, nondisclosure agreements and covenants of confidentiality are enforceable. Notably, confidentiality covenants often contain a long list of information, not all of which is confidential under close scrutiny. Therefore, counsel should exercise care to take a realistic approach in drafting such agreements. One constant is the issue regarding whether information that is generally confidential is *kept* confidential. Courts will consider whether a party took some or all of the following steps to preserve confidentiality:

1. documents stamped confidential;
2. use of computer passwords;
3. use of locked cabinets with limited access;
4. limited access to confidential information with receipts for those acquiring the information;
5. login and logout system for files, prospect guards, customer lists, and similar items;
6. training about confidential information; and
7. checklist for return of confidential information.

5-1:4 REMEDIES

Remedies are available, both in equity and in law, for breach of restrictive covenants.[33] With respect to injunctive relief, one court recently held that the plaintiff did not need to establish "irreparable harm" (i.e., one of the general elements required for

33. *See generally* discussion on equitable relief in Chapter 2.

injunctive relief) at the permanent injunction stage.[34] Subsequent courts, however, have continued to require proof of irreparable harm at least at the temporary injunction stage.[35]

Do not overlook your breach of contract claims based upon provisions in the contract other than the restrictive covenants.

5-2 TEXAS UNIFORM TRADE SECRETS ACT (TEXAS UTSA)

Texas Governor Rick Perry signed the Texas UTSA into law on May 2, 2013. The Texas UTSA brought Texas in line with other states by adopting a version of the model Uniform Trade Secrets Act (model UTSA). This should bring more predictability as to when information will be classified as trade secrets. While the Texas UTSA will not end the facts-specific nature of trade secret analysis, it should provide more specificity, guidance, and greater protection of information. The Texas UTSA became effective on September 1, 2013 for acts commencing on or after that date.[36]

5-2:1 OVERVIEW OF THE TEXAS UTSA

The Texas UTSA applies to any misappropriation claims that began on or after September 1, 2013.[37] It provides a broader definition of trade secret, expressly including financial data and lists

34. *Sanders v. Future Com, Ltd.*, No. 02-15-00077-CV, 2017 Tex. App. LEXIS 4575, slip op. at *10 (Tex. App.—Fort Worth May 18, 2017), citing Tex. Bus. & Com. Code Ann. § 15.51(a).

35. *Equine Sports Med. & Surgery Weatherford Div., PLLC v. Tipton,* 2020 Tex. App. LEXIS 8343, slip op. at *10 n. 7 (Tex. App. – Fort Worth, Oct. 22, 2020, no pet. h.) (distinguishing permanent and temporary injunction stages for purposes of irreparable injury requirement), *see also Thomas v. A*Amed Mgmt.,* 2020 Tex. App. LEXIS 7185, slip op. at ** 12-13 (Tex. App. – Houston [1st Dist.] Sept. 3, 2020, no pet. h.) (temporary injunction properly granted on evidence of loss of customers due to violation of nonsolicitation agreement).

36. *See ZeniMax Media, Inc. v. Oculus VR LLV*, 166 F. Supp. 3d 697, 703-4 (N.D. Tex. 2015) (common law misappropriation claim based on alleged misappropriation commencing before and continuing after enactment of the Texas UTSA not preempted).

37. S.B. 953, 83rd Leg., Reg. Sess. (Tex. 2013).

of actual or potential customers or suppliers, which better reflects current business practices and technologies. The Texas UTSA also limits trade secrets in some ways. For example, information acquired through reverse engineering will generally not become a trade secret.[38] Whether or not information is a *bona fide* trade secret is typically a question of fact.[39]

On May 19, 2017, Texas amended the Texas UTSA by defining the "clear and convincing" standard of proof and the meaning of a "willful and malicious misappropriation" for exemplary damage purposes.[40] Texas also more closely harmonized the definitions of an "owner" of a trade secret and "trade secret" with the definitions in the federal Defend Trade Secrets Act.[41]

The 2017 amendments added to the definition of an "Actual or threatened" misappropriation of trade secrets subject to injunction "An injunction cannot prohibit a person from using general knowledge, skill, and experience that person acquired during employment."[42]

Finally, the 2017 amendments provided a seven-factor balancing test for when a court can exclude a party representative from proceedings in which trade secrets may be disclosed, i.e., an evaluation of (1) the value of the trade secret, (2) the potential competitive harm from disclosure, (3) whether the party allegedly already has possession of the trade secret, (4) whether the party representative is a competitive decision maker, (5) the potential limitation on the party's ability to defend itself, (6) whether the party representative has specialized knowledge unavailable to an expert witness,

38. Tex. Civ. Prac. & Rem. Code Ann. § 134A.002(4).

39. *See, e.g., A.M. Castle & Co. v. Byrne*, 123 F. Supp. 3d 909 (S.D. Tex. 2015).

40. An Act relating to the Texas Uniform Trade Secrets Act, H.B. 1995, 2017 Tex. Sess. Law Serv. Ch. 37 (Vernon's), § 1 (May 19, 2017), *amending* Tex. Civ. Prac. & Rem. Code Ann. § 134A.002.

41. *Id.*

42. *Id.*

and (7) the state of the litigation.[43] This balancing test is largely derived from a Texas Supreme Court decision in 2016.[44]

The Texas UTSA allows for injunction for "actual or threatened misappropriation."[45] Because the injunctive relief includes threatened misappropriation, courts may interpret such language to include "inevitable disclosure," which so far Texas has not adopted.[46] The Texas UTSA does requires termination of an injunction when a trade secret no longer exists, except to the extent reasonable and necessary to ensure the opposing party does not obtain a commercial advantage through misappropriation.[47] The Texas UTSA also encourages protective orders to preserve the integrity of trade secrets during litigation and allows courts to seal documents and limit disclosure of information solely to lawyers working on the case.[48]

Perhaps the biggest change brought by TUTSA is the permitted recovery of attorney's fees. There is currently no basis for recovery of attorney's fees in Texas for misappropriation of trade secrets unless authorized by a separate cause of action, such as breach of a confidentiality agreement or recovery under the Texas Theft Liability Act (TTLA).[49] The ability to recover attorney's fees in trade secrets cases is significant. Often, it is very challenging to prove actual damages because it is difficult to place a value on the misappropriated trade secret or on the benefit of what the competitor obtained. In that case, a wronged competitor may spend a significant amount of money in litigation but obtain no damages—only an injunction prohibiting the behavior in the future. A misappropriation claim that includes attorney's

43. *Id.*

44. *In re M-I L.L.C.*, 505 S.W.3d 569, 575-76 (Tex. 2016) (remanding for application of balancing test to exclude corporate representative at temporary injunction hearing).

45. Tex. Civ. Prac. & Rem. Code Ann. § 134A.003(a).

46. *See* discussion on inevitable disclosure in § 5-3.

47. Tex. Civ. Prac. & Rem. Code Ann. § 134A.003(a).

48. Tex. Civ. Prac. & Rem. Code Ann. § 134A.006.

49. *See* discussion of the Texas Theft Liability Act in § 5-4.

fees will "up the ante" by allowing the claimant to recover what is often hundreds of thousands of dollars in attorney's fees. The recovery of attorney's fees is limited to bad faith claims and to willful and malicious misappropriation.[50] Nonetheless, the possibility of attorney's fees for the prevailing party may incentivize former employers to pursue claims that they would not otherwise pursue.

5-2:1 MISAPPROPRIATION OF TRADE SECRETS

The four common law elements of a claim for misappropriation of trade secrets are:

1. existence of a trade secret;
2. obtaining the trade secret through a confidential relationship or by other improper means;
3. unauthorized use or disclosure of the trade secret; and
4. damage caused to the owner of the trade secret by its use.[51]

Cases prior to the Texas UTSA defined trade secrets as any formula, pattern, device, or compilation used in business that provides an advantage over competitors who do not know or use it.[52] The Texas UTSA now governs the existence of a trade secret, which is defined as:

a formula, pattern, compilation, program, device, method, technique, process, financial data, or list of actual or potential customers or suppliers, that:

---

50. Tex. Civ. Prac. & Rem. Code Ann. § 134A.005(1)-(3).

51. *General Universal Sys., Inc. v. Lee*, 379 F.3d 131, 149-50 (5th Cir. 2004) (applying Texas law); *Avera v. Clark Moulding*, 791 S.W.2d 144, 145 (Tex. App.—Dallas 1990, no writ); *see also K & G Oil Tool & Serv. Co. v. G & G Fishing Tool Serv.*, 314 S.W.2d 782, 793 (Tex. 1958).

52. *Evan's World Travel, Inc. v. Adams*, 978 S.W.2d 225, 231 (Tex. App.—Texarkana 1998, pet. denied); *see also Hyde Corp. v. Huffines*, 314 S.W.2d 763, 776 (Tex. 1958).

(A) derives independent economic value, actual or potential, from not being generally known to, and not being readily ascertainable by proper means by, other persons who can obtain economic value from its disclosure or use; and

(B) is the subject of efforts that are reasonable under the circumstances to maintain its secrecy.[53]

A trade secret must not be "generally known or readily ascertainable by independent investigation." *Marek Bros. Syst., Inc. v. Enriquez.*[54] In *Marek,* the defendant, a construction project manager, had allegedly emailed extensive customer information to himself before starting his own competitive construction company. The court held that, at least for purposes of a temporary restraining order, the plaintiff had not adequately shown that the customer information was, in fact, secret or could not be readily discovered through due diligence.[55]

The alleged trade secret information must be kept secret with access restricted.[56] Consequently, anyone claiming a trade secret must prove that he or she has taken adequate measures to keep it secret from others who are not required to maintain secrecy.[57] In one case, however, a court rejected the argument that the alleged

53. Tex. Civ. Prac. & Rem. Code Ann. § 134A.002(6).

54. 2019 WL 3322162, slip op. at *4 (N.D. Tex. July 24, 2019), *quoting Trilogy Software, Inc.*, 143 S.W.3d 452, 467 (Tex. App. – Austin 2004, pet. denied).

55. *Id.*

56. *Furr's, Inc. v. United Specialty Advert. Co.*, 385 S.W.2d 456, 459 (Tex. Civ. App.—El Paso 1964, writ ref'd n.r.e.).

57. *See, e.g., Vest Safety Medical Services, LLC v. Arbor Environmental, LLC,* 2020 WL 4003642, slip op. at **3-4 (S.D. Tex. July 15, 2020); *Baxter & Assocs., L.L.C. v. D&D Elevators, Inc.*, 2017 Tex. App. LEXIS 1352, ** 27-29 (Tex. App. – Dallas, Feb. 15, 2017, no pet.)(although customer list was on password protected computer system, no evidence it was encrypted or labelled confidential or inaccessible to former employees with prior passwords, therefore not sufficiently protected under Texas UTSA); *Wissman v. Boucher*, 240 S.W.2d 278, 280 (Tex. 1951); *See* Tex. Civ. Prac. & Rem. Code Ann. § 134A.002(6)(B).

disclosure of the claimed trade secrets in trial exhibits stripped the information's trade secret status with respect to a misappropriation that had occurred more than a year before trial.[58]

Pay careful attention to the definition of trade secret. It requires more than just confidential information.

Additionally, the Texas UTSA defines misappropriation as:

> (A) acquisition of a trade secret of another by a person who knows or has reason to know that the trade secret was acquired by improper means; or
>
> (B) disclosure or use of a trade secret of another without express or implied consent by a person who:
>
> > (i) used improper means to acquire knowledge of the trade secret;
> >
> > (ii) at the time of disclosure or use, knew or had reason to know that the person's knowledge of the trade secret was:
> >
> > > (a) derived from or through a person who had utilized improper means to acquire it;
> > >
> > > (b) acquired under circumstances giving rise to a duty to maintain its secrecy or limit its use; or
> > >
> > > (c) derived from or through a person who owed a duty to the person seeking relief to maintain its secrecy or limit its use; or
> >
> > (iii) before a material change of the person's

58. *Title Source, Inc. v. HouseCanary, Inc.*, 2020 Tex. App. LEXIS 6835, slip op. at *23 (Tex. App. – San Antonio, Aug. 26, 2020, pet. filed).

> position, knew or had reason to know that it was a trade secret and that knowledge of it had been acquired by accident or mistake.[59]

Prior misappropriation definitions seem generally in accord with this definition. Misappropriation occurs when trade secrets are acquired through breach of a confidential relationship or by other improper means, including theft, wiretapping, and even aerial espionage.[60]

The most common misappropriation case involves the confidential relationship between an employer and an employee and the subsequent use or disclosure of a trade secret by the former employee. Employees may not use confidential or proprietary or trade secret information acquired during their employment against their former employer.[61] The law imposes a duty on the employee not to disclose confidential information acquired during employment when the employee knows the information is secret.[62] This duty applies regardless of whether the employee signed a nondisclosure agreement, but certainly a nondisclosure agreement notifies the employee of this duty.[63]

A new employer of a former employee also may be liable for trade secret misappropriation. One who discloses or uses another's

59. Tex. Civ. Prac. & Rem. Code Ann. § 134A.002(3).

60. *E.I. DuPont de Nemours & Co. v. Christopher*, 431 F.2d 1012, 1016 (5th Cir. 1970).

61. *T-N-T Motorsports, Inc. v. Hennessey Motorsports, Inc.*, 965 S.W.2d 18, 21-22 (Tex. App.—Houston [1st Dist.] 1998, pet. dismissed); *M. N. Dannenbaum, Inc. v. Brummerhop*, 840 S.W.2d 624, 632 (Tex. App.—Houston [14th Dist.] 1992, writ denied); *Reading & Bates Constr. Co. v. O'Donnell*, 627 S.W.2d 239, 242-43 (Tex. Civ. App.—Corpus Christi 1982, writ ref'd n.r.e.); *Jeter v. Associated Rack Corp.*, 607 S.W.2d 272, 276 (Tex. Civ. App.—Texarkana 1980, writ ref'd n.r.e.); *Johnston v. Am. Speedreading Acad., Inc.*, 526 S.W.2d 163, 166 (Tex. Civ. App.—Dallas 1975, no writ); *Crouch v. Swing Mach. Co.*, 468 S.W.2d 604, 607 (Tex. Civ. App.—San Antonio, 1971, no writ); *Welex Jet Servs., Inc. v. Owen*, 325 S.W.2d 856, 858 (Tex. Civ. App.—Fort Worth 1959, writ ref'd n.r.e.).

62. *Lamons Metal Gasket Co. v. Traylor*, 361 S.W.2d 211, 213 (Tex. Civ. App.—Houston 1962, writ ref'd n.r.e.).

63. *Miller Paper Co. v. Roberts Paper Co.*, 901 S.W.2d 593, 600 (Tex. App.—Amarillo 1995, no writ).

trade secret after discovering it by "improper means" or after learning that it was wrongfully disclosed may be liable for misappropriation.[64] Thus, if a company is aware that the trade secrets have been wrongfully misappropriated, but still exercises dominion or control over that trade secret, it may be liable for misappropriation.[65] Other courts indicate that the company must seek to profit from use of the information.[66]

The Texas UTSA defines "improper means" to include "theft, bribery, misrepresentation, breach or inducement of a breach of a duty to maintain secrecy, to limit use, or to prohibit discovery of a trade secret, or espionage through electronic or other means."[67] Conversely, the statute defines "proper means" as "discovery by independent development, reverse engineering (unless prohibited), or any other means that is not improper."[68] And one court has already had to determine the effect of TUTSA definitions of "improper means" and "acquired" versus their common law definitions. In *Education Management Services, LLC v. Tracey*, the defendant moved, *inter alia,* under Fed. R. Civ. P. 12(b)(6) to dismiss the Plaintiff's misappropriation claim.[69] The Court ultimately dismissed the claim because the Plaintiff failed to "allege that the Defendant acquired the trade secrets at issue through an improper means," which is required under both TUTSA and common law.[70] The court concluded that:

64. *Wellogix, Inc. v. Accenture, L.L.P.*, No. 11-20816, 2013 U.S. App. LEXIS 9758, at *11-12 (5th Cir. May 15, 2013); *Computer Assocs. Int'l v. Altai, Inc.*, 982 F.2d 693, 718 (2d Cir. 1992); *Metallurgical Indus., Inc. v. Fourtek, Inc.*, 790 F.2d 1195, 1204 (5th Cir. 1986).

65. *See Garth v. Staktek Corp.*, 876 S.W.2d 545, 548 (Tex. App.—Austin 1994, writ dismissed w.o.j.) (noting that liability for trade secret misappropriation requires commercial use, defined as any misappropriation followed by an exercise of dominion or control).

66. *Atlantic Richfield Co. v. Misty Prods., Inc.*, 820 S.W.2d 414, 422 (Tex. App.—Houston [14th Dist.] 1991, writ denied).

67. Tex. Civ. Prac. & Rem. Code Ann. § 134A.002(2); *see also Wellogix, Inc. v. Accenture, L.L.P.*, No. 11-20816, 2013 U.S. App. LEXIS 9758, at *11-12 (5th Cir. May 15, 2013).

68. Tex. Civ. Prac. & Rem. Code Ann. § 134A.002(4).

69. *Education Mgmt. Servs., LLC v. Tracey*, 102 F. Supp. 3d 906, 909 (W.D. Tex. 2015).

70. *Id.*

Plaintiff has not alleged that defendant *acquired* the trade secrets through a breach of the Contractor Agreements. Rather, Plaintiff admits that it willingly disclosed trade secrets to the Defendant pursuant to those Agreements. The fact that Defendant later allegedly breached the confidentiality provisions of the agreement is irrelevant to the method by which he obtained access to the trade secrets in the first instance. Thus, under the plain language of the TUTSA, Plaintiff has failed to state a claim for misappropriation of trade secrets.[71]

Ultimately, the Plaintiff's attempts to graft the Texas common law of misappropriation of Trade Secrets were unpersuasive because the "TUTSA specifically provides that it displaces conflicting tort [law]" of this state when providing civil remedies for misappropriation.[72]

More recent federal court decisions in Texas, however, have rejected *Education Management Services*' narrower definition of "improper means." Surveying a split of authority concerning the application of the Uniform Trade Secrets Act, as well as Texas legislative history and policy considerations, the court in *His Co., Inc. v Stover* provided a detailed analysis of both the common law misappropriation standards and the Texas UTSA text. The court concluded that actionable misappropriation can be established under the Texas UTSA by showing either (1) the trade secrets were improperly acquired *ab initio*· or (2) although properly acquired, were subsequently wrongfully disclosed or used in violation of a duty to maintain confidentiality.[73]

One recent case emphasized the importance of clearly tracking the misappropriation theory actually supported by the evidence

71. *Id.*

72. *Id.*

73. *His Co., Inc. v Stover*, 202 F. Supp. 3d 685, 691-95 (S.D. Tex. 2016), *vacated as moot, after settlement*; *see also Lifesize, Inc. v. Chimene*, No. 1:16-CV-1109-RP, 2017 U.S. Dist. LEXIS 64033, slip op. at *8-9 (W.D. Tex. Apr. 26, 2017), and *360 Mortg. Grp., LLC v. HomeBridge Fin. Servs., Inc.*, No. A-14-CA-00847-SS, 2016 U.S. Dist. LEXIS 25652, slip op. at *5 (W.D. Tex. Mar. 2, 2016).

in the jury charge. In *Title Source, Inc. v. HouseCanary, Inc.*,[74] the court of appeals acknowledged that a Texas UTSA claim could be established either by improper acquisition *ab initio* or improper disclosure or use by a person that had the obligation not to disclose, but reversed a multimillion dollar verdict because the jury charge included both of those alternative means of misappropriation when the evidence only supported one of those means. A petition for review has been filed, however, so the ultimate outcome of that case is uncertain.

Misappropriation under the Texas UTSA specifically requires "disclosure or use of a trade secret."[75] Thus, this element appears to be retained after passage of the Texas UTSA. Generally, "use" means commercial use, which has been defined as use from which a party seeks to profit.[76] In fact, most courts will not impose liability for misappropriation without evidence that the actor attempted to obtain financial profit from trade secret use.[77] While use is profiting from another's trade secret, disclosure is destroying the value of the secret by making something public or known.[78] The use or disclosure in the context of a contract breach can be the basis for a trade secret misappropriation claim.[79] In fact, to prove an action for trade secret misappropriation at common law, a

74. 2020 Tex. App. LEXIS 6835 (Tex. App. – San Antonio, Aug. 26, 2020, pet. filed).

75. Tex. Civ. Prac. & Rem. Code Ann. § 134A.002(3)(B).

76. *Trilogy Software, Inc. v. Callidus Software, Inc.*, 143 S.W.3d 452, 464 (Tex. App.—Austin 2004, pet. denied).

77. *Atlantic Richfield Co.*, 820 S.W.2d 414, 422 (Tex. App.—Houston [14th Dist.] 1991, writ denied); *see also Daily Int'l Sales Corp. v. Eastman Whipstock, Inc.*, 662 S.W.2d 60, 64 (Tex. App.—Houston [1st Dist.] 1983, no writ).

78. *Precision Plating & Metal Finishing, Inc. v. Martin-Marietta Corp.*, 435 F.2d 1262, 1263 (5th Cir. 1970) (finding that the defendant made the plaintiff's secret process public, thus destroying the value of secrecy).

79. *K & G Oil Tool & Serv. Co. v. G & G Fishing Tool Serv.*, 314 S.W.2d 782, 787 (Tex. 1958).

plaintiff must establish that it sustained an injury[80] by demonstrating causation between the actions and injuries.[81]

However, it long has been Texas law that former employees may use their general knowledge, skills, and experiences acquired during their prior employment, even to compete with their former employers and to conduct business with customers of their former employers because they do not constitute trade secrets and thus belong to the employees.[82] If employees on their own initiative create the subject matter of the alleged trade, they have an interest in that matter at least equal to that of the employers. Consequently, employees who take nothing from their former employers other than their memory may be in a better position to defend against trade secret misappropriation claims.

The Texas UTSA provides for injunctive relief as follows:

> (a) Actual or threatened misappropriation may be enjoined. On application to the court, an injunction shall be terminated when the trade secret has ceased to exist, but the injunction may be continued for an additional reasonable period of time in order to eliminate commercial advantage that otherwise would be derived from the misappropriation.
>
> (b) In exceptional circumstances, an injunction may condition future use upon payment of a reasonable royalty for no longer than

80. *IBP, Inc. v. Klumpe*, 101 S.W.3d 461, 476-77 (Tex. App.—Amarillo 2001, pet. denied).

81. *Houston Mercantile Exch. Corp. v. Dailey Pet. Corp.*, 930 S.W.2d 242, 248 (Tex. App.—Houston [14th Dist.] 1996, no pet.) (explaining that to recover any type of damages, a plaintiff must plead and prove a direct causal link between a defendant's actions, injury suffered, and damages awarded).

82. *Global Supply Chain Sols, LLC v. Riverwood Sols., Inc.*, 2019 Tex. App. LEXIS 7261, slip op. at *48 (Tex. App. – Dallas, Aug. 16, 2019, no pet.); *Reliant Hosp. Partners, LLC v. Cornerstone Healthcare Grp. Holdings*, 374 S.W.3d 488, 499 (Tex. App.—Dallas 2012, pet. filed).

the period of time for which use could have been prohibited. Exceptional circumstances include a material and prejudicial change of position before acquiring knowledge or reason to know of misappropriation that renders a prohibitive injunction inequitable.

(c) In appropriate circumstances, affirmative acts to protect a trade secret may be compelled by court order.[83]

Thus, injunctive relief is available for actual or threatened misappropriation and may condition future use on payment of a reasonable royalty. Moreover, a prohibitive injunction to protect a trade secret is expressly authorized. However, one United States District Court denied a preliminary injunction after it concluded that the plaintiff failed to show a substantial likelihood of success and that a greater harm would occur if the injunction was not granted.[84] During its analysis, the Court called into question the Plaintiff's ability to identify the specific trade secret, identify who owned the trade secret, show improper means of acquisition, and if actual or threatened disclosure occurred.[85] However, when injunctions are granted under TUTSA they should be definite, clear, precise as possible, and inform the defendant of the acts being constrained.[86]

Injunctive relief though is still quite powerful under TUTSA. In *Haliburton Energy Services, Inc.*, the Court held that the trial court abused its discretion when it failed order a perpetual injunction against the Defendant after the jury found there was a misappropriation of trade secrets because "the burden is on the defendant to show at trial that an injunction for a period of time

---

83. Tex. Civ. Prac. & Rem. Code Ann. § 134A.003(a)-(c).

84. *St Jude Med. S.C., Inc. v. Janseen-Counottee*, No. A-14-CA-877-SS, 2014 WL 7237411, at *14-17 (W.D. Tex. Dec. 17, 2014).

85. *Id.*

86. *Haliburton Energy Servs., Inc. v. Axis Techs., LLC*, 444 S.W.3d 251, 261 (Tex. App— Dallas 2014, no pet.).

less than perpetual will be adequate to protect the rights for the injured plaintiff."[87]

The Texas UTSA also provides specific language regarding available damages as follows:

> (a) In addition to or in lieu of injunctive relief, a claimant is entitled to recover damages for misappropriation. Damages can include both the actual loss caused by misappropriation and the unjust enrichment caused by misappropriation that is not taken into account in computing actual loss. In lieu of damages measured by any other methods, the damages caused by misappropriation may be measured by imposition of liability for a reasonable royalty for a misappropriator's unauthorized disclosure or use of a trade secret.
>
> (b) If willful and malicious misappropriation exists, the court may award exemplary damages in an amount not exceeding twice any award made under Subsection (a).[88]

As stated above, damages include "actual loss," "unjust enrichment," or a "reasonable royalty." The statute also expressly authorizes exemplary damages not exceeding twice the actual damage for "willful and malicious misappropriation."

This statute is consistent with past case law that authorizes the value lost by the claimant, as a result of the misappropriation, usually measured in terms of lost profits.[89] Case law also provides damages based on the value of what the misappropriator has

87. *Haliburton Energy Servs., Inc. v. Axis Techs., LLC*, 444 S.W.3d 251, 261 (Tex. App— Dallas 2014, no pet.).

88. Tex. Civ. Prac. & Rem. Code Ann. § 134A.004(a)-(b).

89. *Jackson v. Fontaine's Clinics, Inc.*, 499 S.W.2d 87, 90 (Tex. 1973); *Elcor Chem. Corp. v. Agri-Sul, Inc.*, 494 S.W.2d 204, 214 (Tex. App.—Dallas 1973, writ ref'd n.r.e.).

gained as a result of the bad acts. Typically, these damages are measured by the defendant's profits from the use or disclosure.[90] Third, the damages also may be calculated by a reasonable royalty.[91] The measure is the total value of the secret to the plaintiff, comprising developmental costs and the importance of the secret to the plaintiff's business.[92] The actual damages include the value that an investor would have paid for the secret.[93] The Texas UTSA grants attorney's fees that previously were not authorized under the common law trade secret misappropriation doctrine. The statute states:

The court may award reasonable attorney's fees to the prevailing party if:

> (1) a claim of misappropriation is made in bad faith;
>
> (2) a motion to terminate an injunction is made or resisted in bad faith; or
>
> (3) willful and malicious misappropriation exists.[94]

The statute also makes clear that it does *not* affect:

> (1) contractual remedies, whether or not based upon misappropriation of a trade secret;
>
> (2) other civil remedies that are not based upon misappropriation of a trade secret; or

---

90. *Calce v. Dorado Expl., Inc.*, 309 S.W.3d 719, 738 (Tex. App.—Dallas 2010, no pet.).

91. *Calce v. Dorado Expl., Inc.*, 309 S.W.3d 719, 738 (Tex. App.—Dallas 2010, no pet.); *Elcor Chem. Corp. v. Agri-Sul, Inc.*, 494 S.W.2d 204, 214 (Tex. App.—Dallas 1973, writ ref'd n.r.e.).

92. *Calce v. Dorado Expl., Inc.*, 309 S.W.3d 719, 738 (Tex. App.—Dallas 2010, no pet.).

93. *Precision Plating & Metal Finishing, Inc. v. Martin-Marietta Corp.*, 435 F.2d 1262, 1263-64 (5th Cir. 1970).

94. Tex. Civ. Prac. & Rem. Code Ann. § 134A.005(1)-(3).

(3) criminal remedies, whether or not based upon misappropriation of a trade secret.[95]

The possible recovery of attorneys' fees is an important change in the Texas UTSA.

A novel twist to Texas UTSA analysis occurred In *Elite Auto Body LLC v. Autocraft Bodywerks, Inc*.[96] In that case, the Austin Court of Appeals held that the Texas Citizens Participation Act (TCPA)[97] applied to a Texas UTSA claim. The defendants alleged that the alleged misappropriation claims in *Elite* related to their own free association and free speech rights and, therefore, granted defendants a right to a summary dismissal unless the plaintiff could provide "clear and convincing" evidence establishing all elements of the misappropriation claim in response to a TCPA motion to dismiss. The Austin Court of Appeals agreed, at least in part. It held that all claims based on communications and associations between the defendants were subject to the TCPA. However, claims independent of communication and association allegations (e.g., copying trade secret documents) were not subject to the TCPA.[98]

The Austin Court of Appeals *Elite Auto Body* case, however, would appear to be undermined by the Texas Supreme Court in *Creative Oil & Gas, LLC v. Lona Hills Ranch, LLC*.[99] In that case, the Court noted that "not every communication related

95. Tex. Civ. Prac. & Rem. Code Ann. § 134A.007(b)(1)-(3).

96. *Elite Auto Body LLC v. Autocraft Bodywerks, Inc.* No. 03-15-00064-CV, 2017 WL 1833495, at *1 (Tex. App.—Austin May 5, 2017, no pet. h.) (Texas Citizens Participation Act applied to a motion for expedited dismissal of a TUTSA claim; plaintiff required to have "clear and convincing" evidence of misappropriation at the very outset of case to survive dismissal.).

97. Tex. Civ. Prac. & Rem. Code Ann. §§ 27.001-011.

98. *Elite Auto Body LLC v. Autocraft Bodywerks, Inc.* No. 03-15-00064-CV, 2017 WL 1833495, at *3-9 (Tex. App.—Austin May 5, 2017, no pet. h.) (Texas Citizens Participation Act applied to a motion for expedited dismissal of a TUTSA claim; plaintiff required to have "clear and convincing" evidence of misappropriation at the very outset of case to survive dismissal.).

99. 591 S.W.3d 127 (Tex. 2019).

somehow to one of the broad categories set out in section 27.001(7) always regards a matter of public concern."[100] The term "a good, product, or service in the marketplace" must be interpreted considering the common meaning of a "matter of public concern," which does not include "purely private matters."[101] Therefore, a communication regarding "a good, product, or service in the marketplace" does not constitute a "matter of public concern" unless the communication has "some relevance to a public audience of potential buyers or sellers."[102]

Relying in part on *Creative Oil & Gas*, the Houston Court of Appeals has held that communications between former employees related to the employees' alleged misappropriation, sharing, and use of the plaintiff's confidential information did not constitute an exercise of their free-speech rights because these communications "had no potential impact on the wider community or a public audience of potential buyers or sellers. In short, the communications [*16] had no public relevance beyond the pecuniary interests of the private parties."[103]

Finally, courts are beginning to explore the scope of Texas UTSA's preemptive effect. Texas UTSA expressly "displaces conflicting tort, restitutionary, and other law of this state providing civil remedies for misappropriation of trade secrets."[104] It, however, does not preempt claims based on contract or in which the remedies "are not based upon misappropriation of a trade secret."[105]

In *360 Mortgage Group v. HomeBridge Financial Services, Inc.*, the federal court found that claims for conversion, unjust

---

100. *Id.* at 137.

101. *Id.* at 135.

102. Id.

103. *Gaskamp v. WSP USA, Inc.*, 596 S.W.3d 457, 477 (Tex. App.—Houston [1st Dist.] 2020, pet. filed) (en banc).

104. Tex. Civ. Prac. & Rem. Code Ann. § 134A.007(a).

105. Tex. Civ. Prac. & Rem. Code Ann. § 134A.007(b)(1) and (2).

enrichment, and constructive trust were preempted, but not claims for breach of contract, breach of fiduciary duty, tortious interference, and conspiracy.[106] In contrast, in *Downhole Technology LLC v. Silver Creek Services Inc.*[107] and *Amid, Inc. v. Medic Alert Foundation United States, Inc.*,[108] federal courts found that a plaintiff could plead tort claims (e.g., breach of fiduciary duty, tortious interference, and unjust enrichment) in the alternative in case plaintiff could only establish the information was confidential, but not a trade secret. Finally, in *BHL Boresight, Inc. v. Geo Steering Solutions, Inc.*˒ the court discussed at length the differences and interrelationship between Texas UTSA, common law misappropriation, TTLA civil theft, and TTLA misappropriation of trade secrets claims.[109] In sum, the preemptive effect of the Texas UTSA remains a developing area of law.

5-3 INEVITABLE DISCLOSURE

Practitioners disagree about whether the doctrine of inevitable disclosure has been adopted in Texas. The Seventh Circuit's decision in *PepsiCo v. Redmond* is probably the most famous case involving this doctrine.[110] Arguably, the doctrine has been a part of Texas law since 1975 when the Dallas Court of Appeals stated:

Even in the best of good faith, a former technical or "creative" employee such as Powell working for a competitor such as SRI can hardly prevent his knowledge of his former employer's confidential methods from showing up in his work. . . . If Powell is permitted to work for SIR in the same area as that in which he

106. *360 Mortg. Grp., LLC v. HomeBridge Fin. Servs., Inc.*, No. A-14-CA-00847-SS, 2016 U.S. Dist. LEXIS 25652, slip op. at *6-8 (W.D. Tex. Mar. 2, 2016).

107. *Downhole Tech., LLC v. Silver Creek Servs., Inc.*, No. H-17-0020, 2017 U.S. Dist. LEXIS 70056, slip op. at *3 (S.D. Tex. May 8, 2017).

108. *Amid, Inc. v. Medic Alert Found. U.S., Inc.*, No. H-16-1137, 2017 U.S. Dist. LEXIS 37699, at *27 (S.D. Tex. Mar. 16, 2017).

109. *BHLBoresight, Inc. v. Geo-Steering Sols., Inc.*, No. 4:15-CV-00627, 2016 U.S. Dist. LEXIS 44729, slip op. at * 11-3 (S.D. Tex. Mar. 29, 2016).

110. *PepsiCo, Inc. v. Redmond*, 54 F.3d 1262, 1268-69 (7th Cir. 1995).

was trained by EDS, injunctive relief limited to restraint of imparting such special knowledge as prepayment utilization review, is likely to prove insufficient. The mere rendition of service in the same area would almost necessarily impart some knowledge to some degree in his subsequent employment. Powell cannot be loyal both to his promise to his former employer, EDS, and to his new obligation to his present employer, SRI. In these circumstances, the most effective protective device is to restrain Powell from working in the computer field in which he was associated while employed by EDS.[111]

Two Houston cases have adopted a similar rationale, noting:

> Texas courts clearly recognize the right of an employer to insist that the non-disclosure provisions of his contract with an employee be specifically enforced. . . . Proof that trade secrets will be used by the employee in competition against his former employer afford support for an injunction specifically enforcing the non-competition covenant. This is usually the only way use of a secret by the former employee can be prevented.[112]

Typically, the inevitable disclosure cases involve situations where the former employee's new job is so similar to the former job that the former employee cannot prevent his knowledge of the "former employer's confidential methods from showing up in his work."[113] Similarly, the Conley court enjoined a former employee

111. *Electronic Data Sys. Corp. v. Powell*, 524 S.W.2d 393, 398 (Tex. Civ. App.—Dallas 1975, writ ref'd n.r.e.).

112. *Williams v. Compressor Eng'g Corp.*, 704 S.W.2d 469, 471-72 (Tex. App.—Houston [14th Dist.] 1986, writ ref'd n.r.e.); *see Weed Eater, Inc. v. Dowling*, 562 S.W.2d 898, 901 (Tex. Civ. App.—Houston [1st Dist.] 1978, writ ref'd n.r.e.).

113. *Electronic Data Sys. Corp. v. Powell*, 524 S.W.2d 393, 398 (Tex. Civ. App.—Dallas 1975, writ ref'd n.r.e.); *see also T-N-T Motorsports, Inc. v. Hennessey Motorsports, Inc.*, 965 S.W.2d 18, 17 (Tex. App.—Houston [1st Dist.] 1998, pet. dismissed) (ruling that a former employee's possessing an employer's confidential information and being in a position to use that information in direct competition with the employer amount to a

based on inevitable disclosure, although the court did not call it by name.[114] Importantly, the Uniform Trade Secrets Act's explicit sanction of forward-looking injunctions may signify that Texas has adopted the inevitable disclosure doctrine, at least implicitly.

Some courts have recognized the need for injunctive relief in situations where employees, who possesses trade secrets, accept similar employment with competitors of their former employers because those employees will have difficulty preventing the knowledge from infiltrating their work—even if they are acting in good faith.[115] Of course, this standard is met when the former employee is actively disclosing confidential and trade secret information to aid the new employer in competition against the former employer.[116]

Furthermore, under the inevitable disclosure doctrine, the former employer does not necessarily have to demonstrate that the former employee and/or competitor has used the trade secret information. Rather, it might be sufficient for an employer to simply demonstrate that the former employee and/or competitor *could have used* the trade secrets to their "tremendous

likelihood that the former employee will use the information, also known as inevitable disclosure); *Rugen v. Interactive Bus. Sys., Inc.*, 864 S.W.2d 548, 552 (Tex. App.—Dallas 1993, no writ) (finding that a former employee's possession of her former employer's confidential information coupled with her direct competition with the former employer resulted in a probability that the employee would use that information to her benefit and her former employer's detriment).

114. *Conley v. DSC Commc'ns Corp.*, No. 05-98-01051-CV, 1999 Tex. App. LEXIS 1321, at *10 (Tex. App.—Dallas Feb. 24, 1999) (not designated for publication). *But see Conley v. DSC Commc'ns Corp.*, No. 05-98-01051-CV, 1999 Tex. App. LEXIS 1321, at *31-32 (Tex. App.—Dallas Feb. 24, 1999, no pet.) (not designated for publication) (dissenting and arguing that Texas law does not or should not recognize inevitable disclosure).

115. *Daily Instruments Corp. v. Heidt*, No. H-13-2189, 2014 U.S. Dist. LEXIS 21766, at *38-39 (S.D. Tex. Feb. 21, 2014); *see also Tranter, Inc. v. Liss*, No. 02-13-00167-CV, 2014 Tex. App. LEXIS 3398, at *27 (Tex. App.—Fort Worth Mar. 27, 2014, no pet. h.) (mem. op.) ("While there was evidence that [the former employee] was not actively trying to use Tranter's confidential information, there was no evidence rebutting the presumption that [the former employee] would have extreme difficulty in not indirectly applying some of that confidential knowledge in his position at PMC.").

116. *Daily Instruments Corp. v. Heidt*, No. H-13-2189, 2014 U.S. Dist. LEXIS 21766 (S.D. Tex. Feb. 21, 2014).

advantage." The Fifth Circuit affirmed a finding of trade-secret misappropriation where a former employer demonstrated such possibility, coupled with the adverse-inference jury instructions resulting from the former employee's refusal to answer questions pertaining to pricing calculators and the deletion of information from his laptop's hard drive.[117]

The applicability of the inevitable disclosure doctrine in Texas, however, is far from settled. More recent Texas courts have acknowledged that Texas courts have yet to explicitly recognize the inevitable disclosure doctrine.[118] In *Cardoni v. Prosperity Bank*, the Fifth Circuit[119] concluded that Texas had not adopted the inevitable disclosure doctrine outside of the context of potential misappropriation of specific manufacturing processes.[120] Most recently, a Texas court joined the Fifth Circuit in rejecting the notion that Texas had adopted a broad inevitable disclosure doctrine.[121]

It might also be noted that, while some may argue that the "threatened" misappropriation prong of the Texas UTSA may support the application of the inevitable disclosure doctrine, in drafting the Defend Trade Secrets Act, Congress appears to have deliberately foreclosed that doctrine under that Act, at least. That Act limits injunctions to "threatened misappropriations and not

117. *Aspen Tech., Inc. v. M3 Tech., Inc.*, No. 12-20388 cons. with No. 13-20268, 2014 U.S. App. LEXIS 9916 (5th Cir. May 29, 2014) (per curiam) (not for publication). Indirect support for the inevitable disclosure doctrine may also be found in *In re M-I L.L.C.*, 505 S.W.3d 569 (Tex. 2016) in which the Texas Supreme Court recognized as one of the factors in determining whether to exclude a corporate representative from a temporary injunction hearing the fact that, if the representative was a decision-maker and exposed to the opposing party's trade secrets, he may not be able to "resist acting on what he may learn." *In re M-I L.L.C.*, 505 S.W.3d 569, 575 (Tex. 2016).

118. *Cardinal Health Staffing Network. v. Bowen*, 106 S.W.3d 230, 242-43 (Tex. App.—Houston [1st Dist.] 2003, no pet. h.); *M-I LLC v. Stelly*, No. H-09-cv-01552, 2009 U.S. Dist. LEXIS 65866, at *7 (S.D. Tex. July 30, 2009).

119. *Cardoni v. Prosperity Bank*, 805 F.3d 573, 589-90 (5th Cir. 2013).

120. *Id.*

121. *DGM Servs. v. Figueroa*, No. 01-16-00186-CV, 2016 Tex. App. LEXIS 13808, slip op. at *5 (Tex. App.—Houston [1st Dist.] Dec. 29, 2016, no pet. h.) (mem. op.).

merely on the information the person knows."[122] This language would appear to require more than an assumption that a person's knowledge from a prior employer cannot be contained. Moreover, in *Global Supply Chain Sols, LLC v. Riverwood Sols., Inc*,[123] a court rejected the contention that, under the Texas UTSA's threatened injury provision, the inevitable disclosure doctrine could create at least a material issue of fact sufficient to defeat a summary judgment on the merits due to the lack of damage evidence.

5-4 TEXAS THEFT LIABILITY ACT

The Texas Theft Liability Act (TTLA) was enacted in 1989 at the request of the Texas Retailers Association to create a civil remedy for the crime of theft.[124] The Texas Retailers Association was concerned principally with shoplifting, but the TTLA extends beyond this area and even covers theft of trade secrets.[125] Prior to the passage of the TTLA, the Texas Penal Code prohibited trade secret theft but did not allow for a private cause of action for civil liability.[126] Consequently, the TTLA augmented the previous existing remedies for theft of trade secrets through a misappropriation claim or through a breach of contract claim, if a contract between the employer and the employee prohibits competition, disclosure, or taking of trade secrets or confidential information.[127] The statutory intent of the TTLA is to create a

122. 18 U.S.C. § 1836(b)(3)(A)(I).

123. 2019 Tex. App. LEXIS 7261, slip op. at ** 20-23 (Tex. App. – Dallas, Aug. 16, 2019, no pet.)

124. Tex. Civ. Prac. & Rem. Code Ann. § 134; H.R. Comm. Research Org. Daily Floor Rep., S.B. 269, 70th Leg., Reg. Sess. (Tex. 1987).

125. *See* Tex. Civ. Prac. & Rem. Code Ann. § 134.002(2): less theft of trade secrets under Tex. Penal Code Ann. § 31.05 as an action for theft under the TTLA.

126. *See Auguilar v. Chastain*, 923 S.W.2d 740, 745 (Tex. App.—Tyler 1996, writ denied).

127. *See* discussion on breach of contract in § 5-1.

civil remedy for enumerated acts prohibited by the Texas Penal Code—one of which is theft of trade secrets.[128]

The TTLA defines "theft" as "unlawfully appropriating property or unlawfully obtaining services [including] as described by . . . Section 31.05 . . . Penal Code."[129] Texas Penal Code Ann. Section 31.5 provides that a person commits a felony offense if, without the effective consent of the owner, the person knowingly:

1. steals a trade secret;
2. communicates a copy of an article representing a trade secret; or
3. communicates or transmits a trade secret.

In comparison, Texas common law lists four factors in analyzing a trade secret misappropriation claim:

1. existence of a trade secret;
2. breach of confidentiality or improper discovery of the trade secret;
3. use; and
4. resulting damages.[130]

Further, the Penal Code defines trade secrets to mean:

> . . . the whole or any part of any scientific or technical information, design, process, procedure, formula, or improvement that has value and that the owner has taken measures to prevent from becoming available to persons other than those selected by the owner to have access for limited purposes.[131]

---

128. H.R. Comm. Research Org. Daily Floor Rep., S.B. 269, 70th Leg., Reg. Sess. (Tex. 1987).

129. Tex. Civ. Prac. & Rem. Code Ann. § 134.002(2).

130. *SP Midtown, Ltd. v. Urban Storage, L.P.*, No. 14-07-00717-CV, 2008 Tex. App. LEXIS 3364, at *12 (Tex. App.—Houston [14th Dist.] May 8, 2008, pet. denied).

131. Tex. Penal Code Ann. § 31.05(a)(4); *see* Tex. Civ. Prac. & Rem. Code Ann. §

Courts have held that the TTLA definition of trade secrets is consistent with the Texas common law definition.[132] Indeed, as explained in one case, "the statutory definition of trade secret comports with the definition used when tort and contract trade secret law is considered."[133] It remains to be seen how courts will treat this issue since the passing of the Texas UTSA,[134] but it is unlikely there will be much concern about changes as there are not major differences between the definitions.

As with common law claims, the burden of proof under the TTLA is a preponderance of the evidence.[135] The cases to date seem fairly uniform in applying the following six-factor common law trade secret analysis to determine whether a trade secret exists under the TTLA:

1. the extent to which the information is known outside the claimant's business;
2. the extent to which the information is known by employees and others involved in the claimant's business;
3. the extent of the measures taken by the claimant to guard the secrecy of the information;
4. the value of the information to the claimant and to its competitors;
5. the amount of effort or money expended by the claimant in developing the information; and
6. the ease or difficulty with which the

134.002(2) (incorporating definitions from the Penal Code).

132. *SP Midtown, Ltd. v. Urban Storage, L.P.*, No. 14-07-00717-CV, 2008 Tex. App. LEXIS 3364, at *15 n.6 (Tex. App.—Houston [14th Dist.] May 8, 2008, pet. denied).

133. *IBP, Inc. v. Klumpe*, 101 S.W.3d 461, 472 (Tex. App.—Amarillo 2001, pet. denied).

134. *See* discussion of the Texas Uniform Trade Secrets Act *in* § 5-2.

135. *Powers v. Caremark, Inc.*, 261 Fed. Appx. 719, 721 (5th Cir. 2008).

> information could be properly acquired or duplicated by others.[136]

Presumably, to the extent the courts adjust their analysis due to the passage of the Texas UTSA, TTLA cases will make similar changes.

The parties to a TTLA suit can include almost any person or entity, such as an individual, an association, a corporation, a partnership, or any other group.[137] The claimant must prove: (1) that he or she was the owner of the property, (2) the defendant unlawfully appropriated, secured, or stole the property, (3) the unlawful taking was with intent to deprive plaintiff of the property or avoid payment for services, and (4) the plaintiff sustained damages as a result. Under the penal code, an owner means anyone having a possessory interest in the property.[138] Thus, anyone who has title or a right to possession of the property qualifies as an owner.[139] An "owner" merely needs to have a greater right of possession than an alleged thief.[140] The penal code defines property as real property and any tangible or intangible personal property.[141] Trade secrets specifically are included as a type of personal property.[142] A person can appropriate property either by obtaining title or acquiring or exercising control over the personal property.[143] Note that innocently taking property cannot be a basis for a claim under the TTLA because the TTLA requires intent to deprive someone of property.[144]

---

136. *Texas Integrated Conveyor Sys., Inc. v. Innovative Conveyor Concepts, Inc.*, 300 S.W.3d 348, 370 (Tex. App.—Dallas 2009, pet. denied).

137. Tex. Civ. Prac. & Rem. Code Ann. § 134.002(1).

138. *Freeman v. State*, 707 S.W.2d 597, 603 (Tex. Crim. App. 1986); *see* Tex. Penal Code Ann. § 31.03(a).

139. Tex. Penal Code Ann. § 107(a)(35)(A).

140. *Id.*

141. Tex. Penal Code Ann. § 31.01(5)(A)-(B).

142. Tex. Penal Code Ann. § 31.05.

143. Tex. Penal Code Ann. § 31.01(4)(A).

144. *Cf.* discussion on conversion for which intent is not an element *in* § 5-8.

Normally, when trade secret misappropriation is alleged, consent is not at issue. When consent is alleged, consent must be either with the owner's actual consent or where the consent is not rendered ineffective. Examples when consent is ineffective are when it was obtained by coercion or deception,[145] or when the person was not authorized to act, did not have the capacity to act, or was given authority solely to detect the commission of an offense.[146] The intent to deprive, which means withholding property permanently or for such an extended amount of time that the owner loses the value and enjoyment of the property, returning the property only in exchange for payment of award or other compensation, or disposing of the property and making the owner's recovery unlikely.[147]

A person who commits a theft punishable under the TTLA is liable for resulting damages.[148] The TTLA provides as a remedy actual damages plus $1,000.[149] The TTLA is one of the few causes of action in the Texas that carries with it a clause awarding court costs and reasonable attorney's fees to the prevailing party clause.[150] It is not surprising that this clause has been hotly contested. TTLA cases have applied the *Intercontinental* decision, which essentially held that awarded damages or other relief is a prerequisite to becoming a "prevailing party" under the TTLA.[151] However, other cases, *Johns v. Ram-Forwarding, Inc.*, hold that becoming a prevailing party depends on success on the merits and not on whether damages were awarded.[152] The U.S. Supreme

145. Tex. Penal Code Ann. § 31.01(3)(A).

146. Tex. Penal Code Ann. § 31.01(3)(B)-(E).

147. Tex. Penal Code Ann. § 31.01(2).

148. Tex. Civ. Prac. & Rem. Code Ann. § 134.004(a).

149. Tex. Civ. Prac. & Rem. Code Ann. § 134.005(a)(1).

150. Tex. Civ. Prac. & Rem. Code Ann. § 134.005(b).

151. Intercontinental Grp. P'ship v. KB Home Lone Star L.P., 295 S.W.3d 650, 655 (Tex. 2009).

152. *Johns v. Ram-Forwarding, Inc.*, 29 S.W.3d 635, 638 (Tex. App.—Houston [1st Dist.] 2000, no pet.) (awarding the plaintiff attorneys' fees even though he did not recover damages because he was successful on the merits of his claim).

Court held similarly in *Lefemine v. Wideman*, ruling that even injunctions and declaratory judgments can support a prevailing party finding.[153]

Two subsequent cases have wrestled with *Ram-Forwarding* in light of the *Intercontinental* case. In an unpublished opinion, the Fifth Circuit stated that a claimant does not need to prove damages to be entitled to attorneys' fees under the TTLA.[154] It is important to note that there was another basis for fees under Texas law in the form of a breach of contract claim, which could have provided a basis for finding the claimant to be a prevailing party. Contrast this result with *Glattly v. Air Starter Components, Inc.*, where the plaintiff Air Starter sued a rival company, along with shareholders and members of its sales force, for violating the TTLA, specifically for theft of trade secrets.[155] The jury found a TTLA violation, but it did not award any damages.[156] As a result, the court refused to grant Air Starter attorney's fees, disapproving of the *Ram-Forwarding* case by stating that a party cannot "prevail" under the TTLA simply by winning an injunction.[157] Because Air Started received no actual damages—and actual damages are the only relief specifically provided for in the TLLA—Air Starter did not "prevail" under the TLLA.[158]

Because the TTLA is a prevailing *party* statute, a defendant is also entitled to reasonable and necessary attorney's fees by

---

153. *Lefemine v. Wideman* 133 S. Ct. 9, 11 (2012) (ruling that a party prevails when he or she receives actual relief on the merits of a claim, which materially alters "the legal relationship between" the parties by "modifying the [non-prevailing party's] behavior in a way that directly benefits the [prevailing party]," and which includes injunctions and declaratory judgments).

154. *Always at Mkt., Inc. v. Giradi*, 365 Fed. Appx. 603, 608 (5th Cir. 2010).

155. *Glattly v. Air Starter Components, Inc.*, 332 S.W.3d 620, 625-26 (Tex. App.—Houston [1st Dist.] 2010, pet. denied).

156. *Id.* at 629-30.

157. *Agar Corp., Inc. v. Electro Circuits Int'l, LLC*, 580 S.W.3d 136, 148 (Tex. 2019)); *Glattly v. Air Starter Components, Inc.*, 332 S.W.3d 620, 641-42 (Tex. App.—Houston [1st Dist.] 2010, pet. denied).

158. *Glattly v. Air Starter Components, Inc.*, 332 S.W.3d 620, 641 (Tex. App.—Houston [1st Dist.] 2010, pet. denied).

prevailing.[159] The TTLA is unusual in this regard because there is no requirement that the defendant prove that the TTLA claim was brought in bad faith or is frivolous or groundless.[160] Consequently, a plaintiff under the TTLA should determine carefully whether there is sufficient value added to bringing a TTLA claim to offset the risk of a successful defensive attorney's fees claim made. Defendants likely must plead for attorney's fees in order to recover them.[161]

Finally, a federal district court has found that the Texas UTSA preempts the TTLA civil claims, at least to the extent the claim is based solely on the misappropriation of trade secrets.[162] As noted above, the precise preemptive effect of the Texas UTSA remains unsettled despite the express preemptive language in the statute.[163]

5-5 COMPUTER FRAUD AND ABUSE ACT

The Computer Fraud and Abuse Act of 1984 (CFAA) covers primarily criminal acts involving computers used in interstate and foreign commerce.[164] As will be described more fully below, it also contains a private right of action.

Over time, the CFAA has evolved to provide a private right of action for any person who suffers damage or loss because of a CFAA violation. Employers have increasingly taken advantage of the CFAA's civil remedies to obtain injunctive and monetary relief

---

159. *See Air Routing Int'l Corp. v. Britannia Airways, Ltd.*, 150 S.W.3d 682, 686 (Tex. App.—Houston [14th Dist.] 2004, no pet.).

160. *Air Routing Int'l Corp. v. Britannia Airways, Ltd.*, 150 S.W.3d 682, 686 (Tex. App.— Houston [14th Dist.] 2004, no pet.); *Arrow Marble, LLC v. Estate of Killion*, 441 S.W.3d 702 (Tex. App.—Houston [1st Dist.] 2010, pet. denied).

161. *Prize Energy Res, L.P. v. Cliff Hoskins, Inc.*, 345 S.W.3d 537, 569 (Tex. App.—San Antonio, 2011, pet. denied).

162. *His Co., Inc. v. Stover*, 202 F. Supp. 3d 685, 691 (S.D. Tex. 2016), vacated as moot, after settlement.

163. *See* discussion in § 5-2:2.

164. 18 U.S.C. § 1030(a)(1). This section takes much of its language from the Espionage Act of 1917.

against employees. Understandably, this federal statute is growing in significance in non-compete and trade secrets litigation.

The elements of a civil claim under the CFAA include:

1. knowingly and with the intent to defraud;
2. accessed a protected computer;
3. without authorization or in excess of authorization; and
4. resulting in damage or loss of at least $5,000.[165]

As a threshold matter, a CFAA violation must involve misconduct prohibited by the CFAA, particularly:

1. damage to a protected computer that results in a loss of at least $5,000;
2. impairment of a medical examination, diagnosis, treatment or care of an individual;
3. physical injury to a person; and
4. threats to public health or safety.[166]

In order for there to be coverage under the CFAA, the alleged unauthorized access must involve a protected computer, which is any computer used in "interstate or foreign commerce or communication," including any computer connected to the Internet.[167]

Under the right circumstances, a claim under the CFAA may be an effective way to attach liability to departing employees.

---

165. 18 U.S.C. § 1030(a)(4); *see also Pacific Aerospace & Elecs., Inc. v. Taylor*, 295 F. Supp. 2d 1188, 1195 (E.D. Wash. 2003).

166. 18 U.S.C. § 1030(c)(4)(i)(I)-(IV).

167. 18 U.S.C. § 1030(e)(2)(B); *see Continental Grp., Inc. v. KW Prop. Mgmt. LLC*, 622 F. Supp. 2d 1357, 1370 (S.D. Fla. 2009) (holding that connection to the Internet is "affecting interstate commerce or communication" and thus, computers connected to the Internet are protected under CFAA).

5-5:1 UNAUTHORIZED ACCESS

Often the most hotly contested element to a CFAA claim is whether or not the employee had unauthorized access to the computer or computer system. An employee may respond that access was never revoked.[168] The courts have wrestled over the question of whether an employee exceeds the authorized access so that the CFAA becomes implicated.[169] For example, the Fourth Circuit considered whether the CFAA applies to disloyal employees who access the employer's workplace computers to misappropriate, copy, or otherwise transfer corporate data.[170] There, WEC provided Miller "with a laptop computer and cell phone, and authorized his access to the company's intranet and computer servers."[171] During his employment, Miller had unrestricted "access to numerous confidential and trade secret documents . . . including pricing terms, pending projects, and the technical capabilities of WEC."[172] WEC alleged that, prior to departing, Miller emailed this confidential information to personal email accounts and a personal computer in violation of employment policies.[173] The Fourth Circuit observed "two schools of thought" when it interpreted the CFAA.[174]

The first school comes from a court ruling that, when employees access computer information to further their own interests rather than those of their employers, the agency relationship terminates and they loses all authority to access the computers or

168. *See LVRC Holdings LLC v. Brekka*, 581 F.3d 1127, 1135 (9th Cir. 2009) (finding that an employee uses a computer "without authorization" when that employee has not received permission "to use the computer for any purpose . . . or when the employer has rescinded permission to access the computer and the [employee] uses the computer anyway").

169. Shortly before this book was completed, the Supreme Court of the United States narrowed the applicability of CFAA regarding whether an employee "exceeds authorized access" under CFAA. *Van Buren v. United States*, 141 S. Ct. 1648, 1649 (2021).

170. *WEC Carolina Energy Sols. LLC v. Miller*, 687 F.3d 199, 203 (4th Cir. 2012).

171. *Id.*

172. *Id.*

173. *Id.*

174. *Id.*

any information on them.[175] The Fourth Circuit in *WEC* adopted a second, narrower interpretation of the words "without authorization" to mean that, at the time an individual accesses a computer's information, that individual is on a computer without permission.[176] The court found that Congress's intent was to target hackers, and it would not "transform" the statute to "imput[e] liability to workers who access computers or information in bad faith, or who disregard a use policy."[177]

Another ruling similar to *WEC* is that an employer cannot make a CFAA claim where an employee's "access ha[s] not been revoked."[178] The *Werner-Matsuda* court followed the line of reasoning that the CFAA was not intended to penalize disloyal employees who have the right to access their employer's computer system but rather computer hackers.[179] Similarly in *Bridal Expo*' the court found that former employees did not copy the information from the company's computers "without authorization," even though they downloaded their former employer's database and used the information for improper purposes, because there was no confidentiality agreement or other agreement restricting access to the files.[180] Likewise, the Ninth Circuit found that a former employee did not violate the CFAA despite emailing his employer's documents to himself and his wife to assist his own competing business.[181] The Ninth Circuit rejected the notion that

---

175. *WEC Carolina Energy Sols. LLC v. Miller*, 687 F.3d 199, 203 (4th Cir. 2012) (citing *International Airport Ctrs., LLC v. Citrin*, 440 F.3d 418, 420-21 (7th Cir. 2006)).

176. *WEC Carolina Energy Sols. LLC v. Miller*, 687 F.3d 199, 206 (4th Cir. 2012) (adopting *LVRC Holdings LLC v. Brekka*, 581 F.3d 1127, 1134-35 (9th Cir. 2009), holding that "without authorization" or "exceeds authorization" narrowly apply only when an individual accesses a computer without permission or obtains or alters information on a computer without permission to so obtain or alter).

177. *WEC Carolina Energy Sols. LLC v. Miller*, 687 F.3d 199, 207 (4th Cir. 2012).

178. *International Ass'n of Machinists & Aerospace Workers v. Werner-Matsuda*, 390 F. Supp. 2d 479, 499 (D. Md. 2005).

179. *Id.*

180. *Bridal Expo, Inc. v. Van Florestein*, No. 4:08-cv-03777, 2009 U.S. Dist. LEXIS 7388, at *33-34 (S.D. Tex. 2009).

181. *LVRC Holdings LLC v. Brekka*, 581 F.3d 1127, 1129 (9th Cir. 2009).

authorization to use a computer ceases when the employee starts to use the computer contrary to the employer's interest and instead focused on whether the former employee used the computer with permission for any purpose or whether the employer revoked permission to access the computer and the employee used it anyway.[182]

There are cases that reject the Fourth Circuit's view of "without authorization" and follow the Seventh Circuit approach, such as the decision in *United States v. John* that employees violate their duty of loyalty when they access computers or information on computers to further interests that are adverse to their employers'.[183] At such point, he terminates his agency relationship and loses any authority to access the computer or any of its stored information.[184] This latter, broader interpretation continues to be applied by federal courts in Texas.[185]

The United States Supreme Court had the opportunity to resolve this circuit split, when a party filed a petition for writ of certiorari seeking review of the Fourth Circuit's opinion in the *WEC Energy*, but the Court dismissed the petition on January 2, 2013.[186]

Relatedly, in at least one case, a company could not prove that its employee accessed the computer system without authorization or in excess of authorization.[187] Significantly, the employer had not

---

182. *LVRC Holdings LLC v. Brekka*, 581 F.3d 1127, 1135 (9th Cir. 2009); *see also Shamrock Foods Co. v. Gast*, 535 F. Supp. 2d 962, 967-68 (D. Ariz. 2008) (employee's acquisition of employer's confidential information prior to resigning and joining with employer's competitor was not "without authorization" or in matter that "exceeded authorized access" where employee was permitted to view specific files he allegedly emailed himself).

183. *United States v. John*, 597 F.3d 263, 273 (5th Cir. 2010).

184. *International Airport Ctrs., LLC v. Citrin*, 440 F.3d 418, 420-21 (7th Cir. 2006).

185. *BHLBoresight, Inc. v. Geo-Steering Sols., Inc.*, No. 4:15-CV-00627, 2016 U.S. Dist. LEXIS 44729, slip op. at *17 (S.D. Tex. Mar. 29, 2016); *Merritt Hawkins & Assoc. LLC v. Gresham*, 79 F. Supp. 3d 625, 634, 637 (N.D. Tex. 2015).

186. WEC Energy Sols. LLC v. Miller, 133 S. Ct. 831 (2013).

187. *LVRC Holdings LLC v. Brekka*, 581 F.3d 1127, 1136-37 (9th Cir. 2009) (CFAA claim against employee failed because of contradictory evidence between the employer's own witness and expert evidence).

promulgated a policy distinguishing between proper and unauthorized use of the information.[188] Because the CFAA is largely a criminal statute, the employee would need notice of what constitutes prohibitive conduct.[189] Thus, employers should be aware of the importance of a policy or practice prohibiting employees from accessing confidential information for improper purposes.

5-5:2 DAMAGES OR LOSS

To bring a successful CFAA claim, the former employer must plead and prove that the offensive conduct caused $5,000 or more in damage or loss to the employer.[190] Loss means expenses relating to restoring data, repairing any damage to a computer system, and modifying the computer system to preclude further unauthorized data transfer.[191] Loss also includes expenses incurred to investigate the unauthorized computer access.[192] The plaintiff, however, must adequately plead losses in excess of the $5,000 threshold amount.[193]

The CFAA also covers losses resulting from the unauthorized deletion of information on a computer system. In *IberiaBank*

---

188. *Id.* at 1129.

189. *Id.* at 1134-35.

190. *Pearl Invs. LLC v. Standard I/O, Inc.*, 257 F. Supp. 2d 326, 349 (D. Me. 2003).

191. *See Lasco Foods, Inc. v. Hall & Shaw Sales, Mktg. & Consulting, LLC*, 600 F. Supp. 2d 1045, 1052 (E.D. Mo. 2009) ("[C]ourts have consistently interpreted loss . . . to mean a cost of investigating or remedying damage to a computer, or a cost incurred because the computer's service was interrupted."); *Forge Indus. Staffing, Inc. v. De La Fuente*, No. 06 C 3848, 2006 U.S. Dist. LEXIS 75286, at *19-20 (N.D. Ill. Oct. 16, 2006) (explaining that loss includes the cost of hiring a forensic computer expert to recover destroyed data in addition to actual damages to computer system); *see also Matter of Doubleclick, Inc. Privacy Litig.*, 154 F. Supp. 2d 497, 521 (S.D.N.Y. 2001) ("Congress intended the term 'loss' to target remedial expenses borne by victims that could not properly be considered direct damage caused by a computer hacker."); 18 U.S.C. § 1030(e)(11) (loss is defined as "any reasonable cost to any victim, including the cost of responding to an offense, conducting a damage assessment and restoring the data, program, system or information to its condition prior to the offense, and any revenue lost, cost incurred or other consequential damages incurred because of interruption of service.").

192. *Vest Safety Medical Services, LLC v. Arbor Environmental, LLC*, 2020 WL 4003642, slip op. at **2-3 (S.D. Tex. July 15, 2020).

193. *Id.*

v. Broussard, an executive unhappy with the acquisition of his long-time employer bank deleted information off of his own designated drive before quitting and joining a competitor bank. The plaintiff established that this resulted in more than $6,000 in damages. The Fifth Circuit sustained the trial court's finding of a CFAA violation.[194]

It is unclear whether consequential damages, such as a loss of trade secrets or a competitive advantage, meet the CFAA definition of loss. For example, using the computer to take trade secrets did not, standing alone, meet the "damage" requirement under the CFAA in *Garelli Wong*.[195] On the other hand, taking misappropriated property, a former employer suffering loss of good will, and investigative costs are sufficient to meet the "loss" requirement.[196] Still other courts have determined that non-computer costs, even if associated with investigations of a violation, are not within the ambit of the CFAA.[197]

Importantly, a party must show damage independent of loss. Damage is "any impairment to the integrity or availability of data, a program, a system, or information."[198] The question becomes whether damage is shown merely by misappropriation of trade secrets or must there be other harm. For one court, damage occurred where data had not been erased or changed but the misappropriation amounted to an impairment of the integrity

194. *IberiaBank*, 907 F.3d 826, 837-38 (5th Cir. 2018); *compare U.S. v. Thomas*, 877 F.3d 591 (5th Cir. 2017)(sustaining a criminal conviction for such damages).

195. *Garelli Wong & Assocs., Inc. v. Nichols*, 551 F. Supp. 2d 704, 709-10 (N.D. Ill. 2008).

196. *Continental Grp., Inc. v. KW Prop. Mgmt. LLC*, 622 F. Supp. 2d 1357, 1370-71 (S.D. Fla. 2009).

197. *BHLBoresight, Inc. v. Geo-Steering Sols., Inc.*, No. 4:15-CV-00627, 2016 U.S. Dist. LEXIS 44729, slip op. at *18 (S.D. Tex. Mar. 29, 2016); *Donohue v. Tokyo Electron Am., Inc.*, 42 F. Supp. 3d 829, 844 (W.D. Tex. 2014); *Continental Grp., Inc. v. KW Prop. Mgmt. LLC*, 622 F. Supp. 2d 1357, 1370-71 (S.D. Fla. 2009).

198. 18 U.S.C. § 1030(e)(8).

of that data.[199] However, most courts hold that misappropriation of trade secrets alone does not amount to damages.[200]

Employers sometimes attempt to use the CFAA to acquire federal jurisdiction in trade secret cases. Defendants challenge federal jurisdiction, usually at the remand stage, by arguing that the CFAA is a criminal statute and deserves narrow construction. At the outset, they also challenge whether the plaintiff met the element of accessing a computer "without authorization" or "exceeding authorization,"[201] as well as the element of $5,000 or more in loss or damages. To illustrate how the courts analyze these issues, consider a case where a company alleged its former employees misappropriated trade secrets using confidential information from contracts, customer lists, schedules, employee files, and driver files to steal business from the company.[202] The plaintiff employer pled multiple causes of action, including a CFAA violation.[203] The defendants removed the action to the Northern District of Texas, alleging federal jurisdiction.[204] Initially, the court remanded the case back to the state court, but, on a motion for reconsideration, it retained jurisdiction.[205] In its ruling on a motion to remand, the court explained:

> Ennis's original petition avers Defendants accessed Ennis's confidential information by exceeding Defendants' authority without authorization. . . . Ennis continues to allege that it has consequently

---

199. *Shurgard Storage Ctrs., Inc. v. Safeguard Self Storage, Inc.*, 119 F. Supp. 2d 1121, 1126-27 (W.D. Wash. 2000); *see also* 18 U.S.C. § 1030(e)(8)(A) (2000).

200. *Donohue v. Tokyo Electron Am., Inc.*, 42 F. Supp. 3d 829, 844 (W.D. Tex. 2014); *Andritz v. S. Maint. Corp.*, 626 F. Supp. 2d 1264, 1266-67 (M.D. Ga. 2009); *Sam's Wines & Liquors, Inc. v. Hartig*, No. 08 C 570, 2008 WL 4394962, at *8 (N.D. Ill. Sept. 24, 2008).

201. *See* discussion on unauthorized access *in* § 5-5:1.

202. *Ennis Transp. Co., Inc. v. Richter*, No. 3:08-CV-2206-B, 2009 U.S. Dist. LEXIS 15585, at *1-2 (N.D. Tex. Feb. 24, 2009).

203. *Id.* at *2.

204. *Id.*

205. *Id.* at *3.

> 'suffered losses and damages by reason of the violations in excess of the statutory limits of the [CFAA] in less than a one year period of time.' . . . The Court accordingly finds that it has subject matter jurisdiction over Ennis's CFAA claim. See 18 U.S.C. §§ 1030(a)(4); 1030(c)(4)(A)(i)(I).
>
> Whether Ennis's claim would satisfy a motion for failure to state a claim upon which relief can be granted is not before the Court, and is therefore reserved for another day. This Court is further vested with jurisdiction over Ennis's state law causes of action by virtue of its supplemental jurisdiction. *See* 28 U.S.C. § 1367.[206]

This analysis may be contrasted with the *Bridal Expo* case, where the court examined whether the $5,000 loss requirement was met.[207]

> [I]n order to establish a civil violation of the CFAA, a plaintiff must also allege facts sufficient to establish one of the factors set forth under former § (a)(5)(b). 18 U.S.C. § 1030(g). The only factor applicable to Plaintiff's claims is "loss to 1 or more persons during any 1-year period . . . aggregating at least $5,000 in value." 18 U.S.C. § 1030(a)(5)(B)(i) (2008). The term "loss" means "any reasonable cost to any victim, including the cost of responding to an offense, conducting a damage assessment, and restoring the data, program, system, or information to its condition prior to the offense, and any revenue lost, cost incurred, or other consequential damages incurred because

206. *Id.* at *7-8.

207. *Bridal Expo, Inc. v. Van Florestein*, No. 4:08-cv-03777, 2009 U.S. Dist. LEXIS 7388, at *26-27 (S.D. Tex. 2009).

> of interruption of service." 18 U.S.C.A. § 1030(e)(11).[208]

Acknowledging the circuit split over the meaning of "without authorization" and "exceeds the authorized access," including other courts approving the use of the CFAA to cover instances of employees obtaining information in violation of their confidentiality agreements,[209] the court ultimately adopted the *Lockheed Martin* analysis.[210]

Two companion statutes to the CFAA are the Electronic Communications Privacy Act of 1986 (ECPA), 18 U.S.C. §§ 2510–2522, and the Stored Communications Act, (SCA) 18 U.S.C. §§ 2701-12. Although these statutes are largely criminal, they can be used in some civil instances. Recent cases indicate how the ECPA and SCA might be applied in the context of employment, such as *Garcia v. City of Laredo*, in which the court examined whether a party would be liable under the SCA for unauthorized review of information on a cell phone.[211] There, the city police department terminated an employee after discovering that she had violated departmental rules, a finding based on images and text messages they found on her cell phone.[212] Specifically, the police department downloaded a video and photographs from her cell phone before calling her to a meeting at which she was fired.[213] She then sued the City of Laredo, claiming a violation of the SCA.[214]

---

208. *Id.* at *25-26.

209. *See, e.g., International Airport Ctrs., LLC v. Citrin*, 440 F.3d 418, 420-21 (7th Cir. 2006); *ViChip Corp. v. Lee*, 438 F. Supp. 2d 1087, 1100 (N.D. Cal. 2006).

210. *Bridal Expo, Inc. v. Van Florestein*, No. 4:08-cv-03777, 2009 U.S. Dist. LEXIS 7388, at *32-33 (S.D. Tex. 2009) (adopting *Lockheed Martin Corp. v. L-3 Commc'ns Corp.*, No. 6:05-cv-1580-ORL-31KRS, 2006 U.S. Dist. LEXIS 53108 (M.D. Fla. Aug. 1, 2006))

211. *Garcia v. City of Laredo*, 702 F.3d 788, 790 (5th Cir. 2012).

212. *Id.*

213. *Id.*

214. *Id.*

After examining the statute, the court noted that the City of Laredo would be liable if it had "gained unauthorized access to a facility through which electronic communication services are provided (or the access must have exceeded the scope of authority given) and must thereby have access to electronic communications while in storage."[215] Garcia argued that her personal cell phone was a facility in which electronic communications were kept in electronic storage, particularly her text messages and pictures.[216] The court reviewed several other decisions and found generally that "a home computer of an end user is not protected by the SCA,"[217] and a cell phone does not "*provide* an electronic communication service just because the device *enables* use of electronic communication services, and there is no evidence here that the defendants ever obtained any information from the cellular company or network."[218] Consequently, access to an employee's Facebook account or cell phone records without permission does violate the SCA, but information left on a cell phone or iPad may not be unlawful.

In *Insurance Safety Consultants, LLC v. Nugent*,[219]an employee set up an email account for her manager and herself. When she joined a competitor she forwarded emails she had retained on those accounts to her new manager at her new employer. The old employer sued under the SCA and ECPA. Both claims were rejected. Following *Garcia*, the court found that the employee had transferred the emails from an end-user email account. Since she did not take information "stored" by an internet service provider, the SCA did not apply. In reaching this conclusion, the court noted that the SCA only applied to the improper "access" to stored electronic communications. Unlike the ECPA, the SCA

215. *Id.* at 791.

216. *Id.*

217. *Id.* at 792-93.

218. *Id.* at 793.

219. 2019 WL 7377031 (N.D, Tex. Dec. 31, 2019).

does not apply to the improper "use" or "disclosure" of stored information.[220]

Turning to the ECPA, the court again rejected the plaintiff's claim. While the ECPA applies to the improper use or disclosure, as well as improper access, of electronic information, the defendant had to have "intercepted" the information while it was in transit, not acquired it from an end-user email account.[221] Likening it to a football pass interception, the court held the ECPA was limited to an interception "in flight."[222]

Employers must be careful when accessing electronic information. In *Van Alstyne*, the Fourth Circuit reviewed an appeal by an employer found guilty of violating the SCA by accessing a former employee's private email account during an investigation of an employment lawsuit between the parties.[223] Van Alstyne claimed that she was terminated after being sexually propositioned by one of the owners.[224] As part of the case preparation, the owner accessed Van Alstyne's AOL account and took emails from that personal account.[225] The employee was not able to recover statutory damages because of lack of proof of actual damages, but the court did allow recovery of punitive damages and attorney's fees.[226]

The SCA provides a private cause of action for "any . . . other person aggrieved" by an SCA violation;[227] thus a private plaintiff can recover the actual damages it suffers and any profits made by the violator as a result of the violation, "but in no case shall a

---

220. *Id.* at 3.

221. *Id.* at 4.

222. *Id.*

223. *Van Alstyne v. Elec. Scriptorium, Ltd.*, 560 F.3d 199, 201-02 (4th Cir. 2009).

224. *Id* at 202.

225. *Id.*

226. *Id* at 206, 208-10.

227. 18 U.S.C. § 2707(a).

person entitled to recover receive less than the sum of $1,000."[228] A successful plaintiff also is entitled to recovery costs, including reasonable attorney's fees.[229] Finally, punitive damages may be awarded for willful or intentional violations.[230]At trial, *Van Alstyne* withdrew her claim for actual damages.[231] The defendants argued that an award of actual damages was a prerequisite to statutory damages.[232] Van Alstyne received a total of $175,000 in statutory damages ($1,000 for each violation of the SCA) and $100,000 in punitive damages, as well as $136,000 in attorney's fees and costs.[233] The Fourth Circuit found that actual damages were a prerequisite to statutory damages but not to an award of punitive damages and attorney's fees.[234]

The ECPA and the SCA may also affect disloyal departing employees. For example, in *United States v. Szymuszkiewicz*, a former employee revenue officer for the Internal Revenue Service was convicted for violating the ECPA.[235] In the appellate opinion, Judge Easterbrook described the offensive conduct as:

> monitor[ing] email messages sent to his supervisor, Nella Infusino. She found out by accident when being trained to use Microsoft Outlook, her email client. She discovered a "rule" that directed Outlook to forward to Szymuszkiewicz all messages she received. Szymuszkiewicz was convicted under the Wiretap Act for intentionally intercepting an electronic communication . . . agents found emails to Infusino stored in a personal

228. 18 U.S.C. § 2707(c).

229. 18 U.S.C. § 2707(c).

230. 18 U.S.C. § 2707(c).

231. *Van Alstyne v. Elec. Scriptorium, Ltd.*, 560 F.3d 199, 203 (4th Cir. 2009).

232. *Id.*

233. *Id.*

234. *Id.* at 206, 208-10.

235. *United States v. Szymuszkiewicz*, 622 F.3d 701, 703 (7th Cir. 2010).

> folder of Szymuszkiewicz's Outlook client—in other words, Szymuszkiewicz not only received the emails but also moved them from his inbox to a separate folder for retention—which is not what would have happened had all of Szymuszkiewicz's access been legitimate . . . . The jury could have chosen to believe Szymuszkiewicz's contention that he received Infusino's emails legitimately, or by mistake, but the evidence supported the more sinister inference that he obtained them intentionally and without her knowledge.[236]

5-6 ECONOMIC ESPIONAGE ACT OF 1996

The Economic Espionage Act of 1996 (EEA) was signed into law by President Clinton on October 11, 1996, and it created a broad criminal remedy for trade secret misappropriation, appearing to supplement the CFAA.[237]

The EEA provides a very broad definition of a trade secret:

> (1) the term "trade secret" means all forms and types of financial, business, scientific, technical, economic, or engineering information, including patterns, plans, compilations, program devices, formulas, designs, prototypes, methods, techniques, processes, procedures, programs, or codes, whether tangible or intangible, and whether or how stored, compiled, or memorialized physically, electronically, graphically, photographically, or in writing if—

---

236. *United States v. Szymuszkiewicz*, 622 F.3d 701, 703 (7th Cir. 2010) (internal citations omitted).

237. Pub. L. No. 104-294, 110 Stat. 3488, *codified at* 18 U.S.C. §§ 1831-1839 (1997). The Act creates a new Chapter 90 entitled "Protection of Trade Secrets" in Title 18, United States Code, immediately following Chapter 89 covering interstate transportation of unauthorized dentures.

(A) the owner thereof has taken reasonable measures to keep such information secret; and

(B) the information derives independent economic value, actual or potential, from not being generally known to, and not being readily ascertainable through proper means by, the public; and

(2) the term "owner," with respect to a trade secret, means the person or entity in whom or in which rightful legal or equitable title to, or license in, the trade secret is reposed.[238]

The Third Circuit opined that the EEA "protects a wider variety of technological and intangible information than current civil laws."[239] As with the TUTSA, under the EEA, an owner of a trade secret must take reasonable steps maintain secrecy.[240]

The EEA provides for two separate offenses for the theft of trade secrets: (1) the crime of "economic espionage" under § 1831; and (2) the crime of "theft of trade secrets" under § 1832. For both offenses, the government must prove beyond a reasonable doubt that: (1) the defendant stole or, without authorization by the trade secret owner, obtained, destroyed or conveyed information; (2) the defendant knew that information was proprietary; and (3) the defendant believed the misappropriated information was in fact a trade secret.[241]

Although the notion of economic espionage is not likely to involve

---

238. 18 U.S.C. § 1839(3)-(4).

239. *United States v. Hsu*, 155 F.3d 189, 196 (3d Cir. 1998).

240. 18 U.S.C. § 1839(3)(A).

241. *United States v. Hsu*, 155 F.3d 189, 203 (3d Cir. 1998) ("The government can satisfy its burden under § 1832(a)(4) by proving beyond a reasonable doubt that the defendant sought to acquire information which he or she believed to be a trade secret, regardless of whether the information actually qualified as such.").

departing employees, "theft of trade secrets" under § 1832 may apply. Attempts and conspiracies to steal trade secrets also are covered by the Act, as well as the knowing receipt, purchase or possession of a stolen trade secret.[242] However, there is no private right of action under the EEA.[243]

5-7 DUTY OF LOYALTY

Texas law generally does not recognize a fiduciary duty or duty of good faith in fair dealing owed by an employer to an employee.[244] Texas also does not impose a formal fiduciary duty on employees to their employers.[245] However, Texas courts have long acknowledged that employees may have a duty of loyalty to their employers. Indeed, the Texas Supreme Court recognized that "informal" relationships may give rise to special duties, sometimes characterized as fiduciary duties where there is a high degree of trust and confidence,[246] such that the duty of loyalty imposed on employees arises from the concepts of both fiduciary duty and agency.[247] Thus, an employee has a duty to act primarily for the benefit of his or her employer in all matters concerning employment, including a duty not to compete with the employer for self-interested purposes in any matter relating to the scope and course of employment and a duty to deal forthrightly and

---

242. *Id.* The Computer Crime and Intellectual Property Section (CCIPS) of the Department of Justice website, http://www.usdoj.gov/criminal/cybercrime/eeapub.htm, maintains an up-to-date listing of prosecutions under the Act.

243. *Vest Safety Medical Services, LLC v. Arbor Environmental, LLC*, 2020 WL 4003642, slip op. at *3 (S.D. Tex. July 15, 2020).

244. *Midland v. O'Bryant*, 18 S.W.3d 209, 216 (Tex. 2000).

245. *Merritt Hawkins & Assoc. LLC v. Gresham*, 79 F. Supp. 3d 625, 637 (N.D. Tex. Jan. 13, 2015).

246. *Johnson v. Brewer & Pritchard* PC, 73 S.W.3d 193, 203 (Tex. 2002); *Crim Truck & Tractor Co. v. Navistar Int'l Transp. Corp.*, 823 S.W.2d 591, 594 (Tex. 1992); *Merritt Hawkins & Assoc. LLC v. Gresham*, 79 F. Supp. 3d 625, 637 (N.D. Tex. Jan. 13, 2015).

247. *See Johnson v. McDonald*, 73 S.W.2d 128, 203 (Tex. App.—El Paso 1934, no writ) (An agent's duties to a principal include "the duty to account for profits arising out of the employment, the duty not to act as or on account of, an adverse party without the principal's consent, the duty not to compete with the principal on his or her own account or for another in matters relating to the subject matter of the agency, and the duty to deal fairly with the principal in all transactions between them.").

fairly with the employer in all matters between them.[248] This duty of fairness also entails a duty to be open and honest about any information that affects the employer's business.[249] This duty does not preclude an employee from making some initial preparations to go into competition with the employee's current employer. The employee, however, cannot (1) appropriate trade secrets, (2) solicit the employer's customers while still employed, (3) solicit employees to leave while still employed, or (4) take confidential information (whether or not a trade secret), such as customer lists.[250]

Whether a fiduciary relationship exists is a question of law,[251] but whether a fiduciary duty exists as a result of a confidential relationship is a question of fact.[252] Typically, the nature and extent of the fiduciary duty depends on the circumstances of each case and is analyzed most often in the context of an agent-principal relationship.[253]

Despite these constraints, the duty of loyalty does not preclude a fiduciary from preparing to compete in a future business.[254] An employee may *plan* to compete with the employer without a duty to disclose the plan and may secretly join with other employees in the competing business.[255] Courts are careful in defining the

---

248. *Critical Path Res., Inc. v. Huntsman Int'l, LLC*, 2020 Tex. App. LEXIS 2310, slip op. at **14-15 (Tex. App. – Beaumont March 19, 2020, no pet. h.); *McGowan & Co., Inc. v. Bogan*, 93 F. Supp. 3d 624, 652-53 (S.D. Tex. 2015); *Daniel v. Falcon Interest Realty Corp.*, 190 S.W.3d 177, 185 (Tex. App.—Houston [1st Dist.] 2005, no pet.).

249. *Daniel v. Falcon Interest Realty Corp.*, 190 S.W.3d 177, 185 (Tex. App.—Houston [1st Dist.] 2005, no pet.).

250. *Nuerodiagnostic Consultants, LLC v. Nallia*, 2019 Tex. App. LEXIS 8156, slip op. at *27 (Tex. App. Austin, Sept. 6, 2019, no pet.); *McGowan & Co., Inc. v. Bogan*, 93 F. Supp. 3d 624, 653 (S.D. Tex. 2015).

251. *Kiger v. Balestri*, 376 S.W.3d 287, 290 (Tex. App.—Dallas 2012, pet. denied).

252. Crim Truck & Tractor Co. v. Navistar Int'l Transp. Corp., 823 S.W.2d 591, 594 (Tex. 1992).

253. *Navigant Consulting, Inc. v. Wilkinson*, 508 F.3d 277, 284 n.4 (5th Cir. 2007).

254. *Abetter Trucking Co. v. Arizpe*, 113 S.W.3d 503, 510 (Tex. App.—Houston [1st Dist.] 2003, no pet.).

255. *Id.* at 511.

scope of the fiduciary obligations of an employer and an employee because of the competing interests of the duty of loyalty and encouraging competition.[256] As a result, absent a written agreement to the contrary, an employee may resign and immediately compete with a former employer, even if such competition causes the employer great harm.[257]

The scope of the duty of loyalty may be defined by contract or by an employee's position. For example, corporate officers and directors owe a strict fiduciary obligation to their corporation.[258] It is a duty greater than that imposed on an ordinary employee, and it entails obedience, loyalty, and due care.[259] A corporate officer or director must act in good faith and "must not allow his or her personal interests to prevail over the interest of the corporation."[260] This duty of loyalty demands an "extreme measure of candor, unselfishness and good faith on the part of the officer or director."[261] Neither may such a fiduciary usurp corporate opportunities for personal gain.[262] To demonstrate, a president and operations manager resigned, formed a competing business, and recruited many of his former company's employees, and work crews.[263] The jury was permitted to infer breach and causation because:

1. the departing employees set up a competing company months before they resigned;
2. the departing employees began telling

256. *Id.*

257. *See Rugen v. Interactive Bus. Sys., Inc.*, 864 S.W.2d 548, 551 (Tex. App.—Dallas 1993, no writ).

258. *Loy v. Harder*, 128 S.W.3d 397, 407 (Tex. App.—Texarkana 2004, pet. denied).

259. *Id.*

260. *Id.*

261. *Id.*

262. *Id.*

263. *Meaux Surface Prot., Inc. v. Fogleman*, 607 F.3d 161, 169 (5th Cir. 2010).

others, including clients, of their plan to compete;

3. the departing employees recruited employees prior to leaving; and
4. the departing employees procured insurance and other contracts with several customers shortly after their resignations.[264]

In *Grant v. Laughlin Environmental, Inc.*, the employee project manager owed a fiduciary duty to the company, comprised of a duty not to compete with the company in matters related to his employment, a duty to deal openly, and a duty to fully disclose to his employer information that affected the employer's business.[265] The employee breached those duties by:

1. using the company's equipment to build a driveway for himself and others;
2. using the company's phone to make calls on behalf of a competitor while still employed;
3. taking a business opportunity for a competitive company; and
4. using the company credit card for personal purchases and concealing his actions.[266]

Similarly, a former salesman was found guilty of breach of fiduciary duty for taking kickbacks that violated both his contractual and fiduciary duties.[267] In comparison, a consulting firm sued a former salesman who resigned to work for a competing company, arguing that the employee breached his fiduciary duty

---

264. *Id.* at 170.

265. *Grant v. Laughlin Envtl., Inc.*, No. 01-07-00227-CV, 2009 Tex. App. LEXIS 2092, at *21-22 (Tex. App.—Houston [1st Dist.] 2009, pet. denied) The court relied on *Daniel v. Falcon Interest Realty Corp.*, 190 S.W.3d 177, 185 (Tex. App.—Houston [1st Dist.] 2005, no pet.).

266. *Id.* at *23.

267. *Always at Mkt., Inc. v. Giradi*, 365 Fed. Appx. 603, 605, 607 (5th Cir. 2010).

by delaying a deal.[268] The court found in favor of the employee because there was no evidence that he had delayed the closing of a deal.[269] Here, the court emphasized the distinction between *preparing* to compete before going into a new business and actually competing.[270]

Generally, an employer may recoup the damages that flow naturally from an employee's breach of fiduciary duty. The Texas Supreme Court addressed the issue of restitution for breach of fiduciary duty in a case involving a partner who fraudulently induced another party to buy out his interest in the business.[271] A month before the buyout, defendant Swinnea's wife and another employee created a competing company, which Swinnea failed to disclose during the buyout negotiations.[272] After the buyout, Swinnea's revenue production increased by 30-50 percent as he encouraged clients to use his wife's competing company.[273] The court found that the placement of his wife and other former employees in the competing company was "deceptive, sham, and constituted fraud," and the court awarded exemplary damages, forfeiture of the consideration paid to Swinnea to buy him out, and other forfeiture damages and lost profits.[274] The Texas Supreme Court reversed the Court of Appeals, which found the evidence legally insufficient to support the trial court's damages award.[275] Because Swinnea was a fiduciary, an equitable remedy could "cross the line from actual damages for breach of contract or fraud" to the equitable return of contractual consideration.[276] Just as forfeiture is an appropriate remedy for an agent's disloy-

268. *Alliantgroup, L.P. v. Feingold*, 803 F. Supp. 2d 610, 628 (S.D. Tex. 2011).

269. *Id.*

270. *Id.*

271. ERI Consulting Eng'rs, Inc. v. Swinnea, 318 S.W.3d 867, 870 (Tex. 2010).

272. *Id.* at 871.

273. *Id.*

274. *Id.*

275. *Id.* at 870, 882.

276. *Id.* at 873.

alty, it also is appropriate when a fiduciary takes advantages of an employment position "regardless of proof of actual damages."[277]

Some courts recognize a cause of action for aiding and abetting a breach of a fiduciary duty.[278] For example, the Fort Worth Court of Appeals found that a claim could be made against a sole stockholder of a newly organized competitor company for aiding former employees in breaching their fiduciary duties to their former company.[279] Expressly stated, "the equitable cloak of protection must, of necessity, be full and complete so that those who acted wrongfully and have breached their fiduciary relationship, as well as those who willfully and knowingly have aided them in doing so, will be effectively denied the benefits and profits flowing from the wrongdoing."[280]

5-8 CONVERSION

Conversion is the unauthorized, wrongful assumption and exercise of dominion and control over the personal property of another to the exclusion of, or inconsistent with, another person's rights.[281] Importantly, intent is not an element of conversion.[282] The elements of a claim for conversion are: (1) the plaintiff owned or had legal possession of the property or entitlement to possession; (2) the defendant unlawfully and without authorization

---

277. *Id.* at 874.

278. *Mabrey v. Sandstream, Inc.*, 124 S.W.3d 302, 316-317 (Tex. App.—Fort Worth 2003, no pet.); *Toles v. Toles*, 113 S.W.3d 899, 912 (Tex. App.—Dallas 2003, no pet.); *Elcor Chem. Corp. v. Agri-Sul, Inc.*, 494 S.W.2d 204, 208-09 (Tex. Civ. App.—Dallas 1973, writ ref'd, n.r.e.).

279. *Mabrey v. Sandstream, Inc.*, 124 S.W.3d 302, 316 (Tex. App.—Fort Worth 2003, no pet.).

280. *Id.* at 316-317. (quoting *Elcor Chem. Corp. v. Agri-Sul, Inc.*, 494 S.W.2d 204, 212 (Tex. Civ. App.— Dallas 1973, writ ref'd, n.r.e.)), *see also Critical Path Res., Inc. v. Huntsman Int'l, LLC*, 2020 Tex. App. LEXIS 2310, slip op. at **14-15 (Tex. App. – Beaumont March 19, 2020, no pet. h.) (affirming award against vendor found to have knowingly participated in employee's own fiduciary breach concerning that vendor's retention and overbilling).

281. *Waisath v. Lack's Stores, Inc.*, 474 S.W.2d 444, 446 (Tex. 1971).

282. *Cargal v. Cargal*, 750 S.W.2d 382, 384 (Tex. App.—Fort Worth 1988, no writ).

assumed and exercised dominion and control over the property to the exclusion of, or inconsistent with, the plaintiff's rights as an owner; (3) the plaintiff demanded return of the property; and (4) the defendant refused to return the property.[283]

When considering a claim for conversion, a prudent practitioner also will consider the Texas Theft Liability Act284 because of the similarity of the elements and the ability to obtain actual damages, attorney's fees, and a statutory penalty of $1,000.[285] Some courts, however, have held that the Texas UTSA preempts a conversion claim based on the alleged misappropriation of trade secrets.[286]

Conversion only applies to tangible personal property, not real property, and intangible property is not subject to conversion.[287] For example, unauthorized use of a trade name is not conversion;[288] neither is an internet web page address,[289] nor is misdirected email communication.[290] However, a customer list or other confidential information reduced to writing may be converted because of the distinction between the information and the actual list itself.[291] The determining factor seems to be whether

283. *J.P. Morgan Chase Bank, N.A. v. Tex. Contract Carpet, Inc.*, 302 S.W.3d 515, 536 (Tex. App.—Austin 2009, no pet.).

284. *See* discussion on Texas Theft Liability Act *in* § 5-4.

285. Tex. Civ. Prac. & Rem. Code Ann. § 134.005.

286. *See 360 Mortg. Grp., LLC v. HomeBridge Fin. Servs., Inc.*, No. A-14-CA-00847-SS, 2016 U.S. Dist. LEXIS 25652, slip op. at *7 (W.D. Tex. Mar. 2, 2016) (citing cases under UTSA).

287. *Rodriguez v. Dipp*, 546 S.W.2d 655, 658 (Tex. Civ. App.—El Paso 1977, writ ref. n.r.e.).

288. *Express One Int'l, Inc. v. Steinbeck*, 53 S.W.3d 895, 901 (Tex. App.—Dallas 2001, no pet. h.).

289. *CIC Corp, Inc. v. Aimtech Corp.*, 32 F. Supp. 2d 425, 430 n.9 (S.D. Tex. 1998).

290. *Robin Singh Educ. Servs. v. Test Masters Educ. Servs.*, 401 S.W.3d 95, 98 (Tex. App.— Houston [14th Dist.] 2011, no pet.).

291. *See, e.g., Beardmore v. Jacobsen*, 131 F. Supp. 3d 656, 667 (S.D. Tex. 2015); *Merritt Hawkins & Assoc. LLC v. Gresham*, 79 F. Supp. 3d 625, 636 (N.D. Tex. 2015); *Deaton v. United Mobile Networks, L.P.*, 926 S.W.2d 756, 763-765 (Tex. App.—Texarkana 1996, writ denied), aff'd in part, rev'd in part on other grounds, 939 S.W.2d 146 (Tex. 1997).

the confidential and proprietary information or trade secret has been reduced to tangible form.[292]

Under the Texas UTSA, however, a conversion claim based on the improper use or disclosure of trade secret information is preempted.[293] To survive preemption, the conversion claim must be based on value of the lost tangible item itself.[294]

Although a plaintiff must prove that he or she was the owner of the property, possessed the property, or had a right to possess the property, conversion does not require actual ownership.[295] Rather, conversion can be based on a denial of the right to possession.[296] A conversion claim mandates a showing of a wrongful exercise of dominion and control over the property to the exclusion of the person with superior rights over the property.[297] Of particular interest in departing employee cases is that someone can exercise lawful possession of property and then later assert rights inconsistent with the owner's control of the property.[298] For instance, when an employee lawfully obtains possession of an employer's property but later loses the right to such property, such as when employment is terminated, the former employee can be guilty of conversion. Remember, no wrongful intent is necessary.[299] However, the claim does require injury; therefore,

---

292. *Vest Safety Medical Services, LLC v. Arbor Environmental, LLC*, 2020 WL 4003642, slip op. at *5 (S.D. Tex. July 15, 2020); *DHI Grp., Inc. v. Kent*, 2017 U.S. Dist. LEXIS 42253, slip op. at *10-11 (S.D. Tex. Mar. 3, 2017).

293. *Computer Sciences Corp. v. Tata Consultancy Services Limited,* 220 WL 2487057, slip op. at ** 7-8 (N.D. Tex. Feb. 7, 2020).

294. *Id.*

295. *Lone Star Beer, Inc. v. First Nat'l Bank*, 468 S.W.2d 930, 933 (Tex. App.—El Paso 1971, writ ref'd n.r.e.).

296. *Kirkland v. Mission Pipe & Supply Co.*, 182 S.W.2d 854, 855 (Tex. App.—Austin 1944, writ ref'd w.o.m.).

297. *Waisath v. Lack's Stores, Inc.*, 474 S.W.2d 444, 447 (Tex. 1971).

298. *Sharpe v. Roman Catholic Diocese of Dallas*, 97 S.W.3d 791, 796-97 (Tex. App.—Dallas 2003, pet. denied) (cause of action accrued for limitations purposes when party in possession unequivocally exercised acts of dominion).

299. *Winkle Chevy-Olds-Pontiac v. Condon*, 830 S.W.2d 740, 746 (Tex. App.—Corpus Christi 1992, writ dismissed).

a claimant must establish that the defendant proximately caused his or her injury.[300] Third, where a person lawfully acquires property, a proper conversion claim requires a showing that the plaintiff demanded return of the property and that the defendant refused.[301] This is not required when the facts demonstrate an exercise of dominion and control inconsistent with the claimant's possessory interest.[302] In that regard, the demand serves as proof that conversion occurred, rather than as an element of the cause of action.[303] In defense to a conversion claim, a defendant may plead superior title and right to possession.[304] Therefore, if someone takes property over which that person has a superior possessory interest to the opposing party, then there is no conversion.[305] Express or implied consent is also a defense to a conversion claim.[306] Relatedly, a defendant can plead proportionate responsibility by proving that the plaintiff's own actions or omissions caused some or all of the plaintiff's injury.

Another defense is a qualified, good faith refusal. A defendant may prove that, at the time of refusal, he had a reasonable doubt that the plaintiff had a right to possession, and he made the refusal in good faith.[307] The refusal must not be absolute, and must be qualified by conditions that are reasonable, justifiable, and imposed in good faith and in recognition of the owner's rights.[308] The reason for qualified refusal must be articulated clearly to the

300. *United Mobile Networks, L.P. v. Deaton*, 939 S.W.2d 146, 148 (Tex. 1997).

301. *Hull v. Freedman*, 383 S.W.2d 236, 238 (Tex. Civ. App.—Fort Worth 1964, writ ref. n.r.e.).

302. *Loomis v. Sharp*, 519 S.W.2d 955, 958 (Tex. Civ. App.—Texarkana 1975, writ dismissed w.o.j.).

303. *Presley v. Cooper*, 284 S.W.2d 138, 141 (Tex. 1955).

304. *Enduro Oil Co. v. Parish & Ellison*, 834 S.W.2d 547, 549 (Tex. 1992).

305. *French v. Moore*, 169 S.W.3d 1, 13-14 (Tex. App.—Houston [1st Dist.] 2004, no pet.).

306. *Gronberg v. York*, 568 S.W.2d 139, 144-45 (Tex. Civ. App.—Tyler 1978, writ ref. n.r.e.).

307. *Khorshid, Inc. v. Christian*, 257 S.W.3d 748, 759 (Tex. App.—Dallas 2008, no pet.).

308. *Earthman's, Inc. v. Earthman*, 526 S.W.2d 192, 204 (Tex. Civ. App.—Houston [1st Dist.] 1975, no writ).

party seeking possession; no explanations may be given after the time of refusal.[309] Whether the refusal was qualified is a question for the jury.[310] Innocence is not a defense to conversion,[311] but it may be a defense to punitive damages.[312]

In general, damages for conversion are measured as the sum of money that would fairly compensate a plaintiff for all losses or injuries proximately caused by a defendant's conversion.[313] Normally, the measure of damages is the fair market value of the property at the time of conversion.[314] A plaintiff may recover other damages if they are proximately caused by the conversion. The loss of value is measured in three ways:

1. fair market value plus interest;
2. fair market value at its highest rate plus interest; and
3. intrinsic value.[315]

Further, punitive damages are recoverable with proof of actual malice.[316] Because equitable relief is authorized, a plaintiff can receive a temporary restraining order or temporary injunction.[317] However, attorney's fees are not recoverable in a conversion

309. *Stein v. Mauricio*, 580 S.W.2d 82, 83 (Tex. Civ. App.—San Antonio 1979, no writ).

310. *Smith v. Maximum Racing, Inc.*, 136 S.W.3d 337, 344 (Tex. App.—Austin 2004, no pet.).

311. *Henson v. Reddin*, 358 S.W.3d 428, 435 (Tex. App.—Fort Worth 2012, no pet.).

312. *Killian v. Trans Union Leasing Corp.*, 657 S.W.2d 189, 192 (Tex. App.—San Antonio 1983, writ ref'd n.r.e.).

313. *Groves v. Hanks*, 546 S.W.2d 638, 647 (Tex. Civ. App.—Corpus Christi 1976, writ ref. n.r.e.).

314. *First Nat'l Bank v. Gittelman*, 788 S.W.2d 165, 169 (Tex. App.—Houston [14th Dist.] 1990, writ denied).

315. *Williams v. Dodson*, 976 S.W.2d 861, 864-65 (Tex. App.—Austin 1998, no pet.).

316. *Green Int'l v. Solis*, 951 S.W.2d 384, 391 (Tex. 1997).

317. *See Taiwan Shrimp Farm Vill. Ass'n v. U.S.A. Shrimp Farm Dev., Inc.*, 915 S.W.2d 61, 65 (Tex. App.—Corpus Christi 1996, writ denied).

claim,[318] except when permitted by a specific statute or by a contract between the parties.[319]

5-9 TORTIOUS INTERFERENCE

Tortious interference claims fall into two categories: interference with an existing contract or interference with prospective business relations. The elements of each are slightly different and will be dealt with separately.

5-9:1 TORTIOUS INTERFERENCE WITH EXISTING CONTRACT

To assert a claim for tortious interference with a contract under Texas law, a plaintiff must prove:

(a) The existence of a contract subject to interference;

(b) Willful and intentional interference with the contract;

(c) The interference proximately caused damages; and

(d) Actual damages or loss incurred.[320]

The new employer should be wary of a tortious interference claim when hiring an employee who is or may be violating duties to his/her former employer.

To demonstrate, in *Downing v. Burns*' former employers told

318. *Broesche v. Jacobson*, 218 S.W.3d 267, 277 (Tex. App.—Houston [14th Dist.] 2007, pet. denied).

319. *Holland v. Wal-Mart Stores*, 1 S.W.3d 91, 95 (Tex. 1999).

320. *Global Supply Chain Sols, LLC v. Riverwood Sols., Inc.*, 2019 Tex. App. LEXIS 7261 slip op. at * 49 (Tex. App. – Dallas, Aug. 16, 2019, no pet.); *BHLBoresight, Inc. v. Geo-Steering Sols., Inc.*, No. 4:15-CV-00627, 2016 U.S. Dist. LEXIS 44729, slip op. at *9 (S.D. Tex. Mar. 29, 2016); *Faucette v. Chantos*, 322 S.W.3d 901, 913 (Tex. App.—Houston [14th Dist.] 2010, no pet.).

a new employer that they would sue anyone who employed their former employee who had stolen a policy and procedure manual.[321] As a result, the next two employers fired the employee to avoid the threatened litigation.[322] The employee clearly had evidence of harm in the termination and proved willful and intentional interference with an existing contract that proximately caused the damage or loss.[323]

In a second case, the Houston Court of Appeals discussed the difference between tortious interference with contract and tortious interference with prospective business relations.[324] In this case, an employer sued two former employees for breach of contract and tortious interference with a contract.[325] The employees initially considered buying the company, but the plan fell through as the relationship between the owner and employees became strained.[326] The employees later resigned, and one of the company's long-term client-manufacturers gave notice that it was terminating its sales agreement with the employer.[327] Three days later, another large manufacturer gave its notice of the same.[328] Next, those manufacturers entered into contracts with the new company developed by the former employees, even though the original employer had worked with those manufacturers for nearly 20 years.[329]

The jury found tortious interference.[330] The employer argued that

---

321. *Downing v. Burns*, 348 S.W.3d 415, 418 (Tex. App.—Houston [14th Dist.] 2011, no pet.).

322. *Id.*

323. *Id.* at 418-19.

324. *Faucette v. Chantos*, 322 S.W.3d 901, 913-14 (Tex. App.—Houston [14th Dist.] 2010, no pet.).

325. *Id.* at 904.

326. *Id.* at 906.

327. *Id.* at 906-07.

328. *Id.* at 907.

329. *Id.*

330. *Id.* at 904, 913.

he met the elements of a claim for tortious interference with a contract because the employees caused the two manufacturers to terminate their 20-year contracts with the original employer.[331] In response, the employees argued that the claim related to tortious interference with prospective contracts and business relationships because the manufacturers had given 30-day notices of cancellation, such that the claim was really about prospective business.[332] The Faucette court focused on the Texas Supreme Court's *Wal-Mart Stores* decision, finding that the plaintiff had to prove that the defendant's conduct was independently tortious and wrongful.[333] Basically, the plaintiff did not prove the existence of a valid contract and, therefore, did not meet the elements of tortious interference with prospective relationships.

One federal court emphasized the difference between tortious interference with contract and tortious interference with prospective business relations. The latter requires proof of an independently wrongful act, while the former does not.[334]

The *Faucette* case stresses the importance of the first element of tortious interference with contract, namely the existence of a valid contract. An employee handbook is not a contract,[335] but a voidable contract may be the subject of interference, even though it is unenforceable between the two parties.[336] Additionally, a terminable, at-will employment contract may support a tortious interference claim.[337] Second, a plaintiff must prove that the

---

331. *Id.* at 913.

332. *Id.*

333. *Id.*

334. *BHLBoresight, Inc. v. Geo-Steering Sols., Inc.*, No. 4:15-CV-00627, 2016 U.S. Dist. LEXIS 44729, slip op. at *9 (S.D. Tex. Mar. 29, 2016).

335. *Cote v. Rivera*, 894 S.W.2d 536, 542 (Tex. App.—Austin 1995, no writ) (no claim for tortious interference because employee handbook did not constitute contract).

336. Juliette Fowler Homes, Inc. v. Welch Assocs.,Inc., 793 S.W.2d 660, 664 (Tex. 1990).

337. *Hood v. Edward D. Jones & Co., L.P.*, 277 S.W.3d 498, 502 (Tex. App.—El Paso 2009, pet. denied); see generally *Health Call v. Atrium Home & Health Care Servs.*, 706 N.W.2d 843 (Mich. 2005).

defendant willfully and intentionally interfered[338] with a contract to which it is *not* a party.[339] For a corporate agent to be liable for interference with a corporation's contract, the agent must have actually interfered,[340] willfully and intentionally, to serve personal interests.[341] Further, a defendant must have actual knowledge of the contract or knowledge of facts and circumstances that would lead a reasonable person to believe that there was a contract in which the plaintiff had an interest.[342] Finally, the interference must cause injury that proximately results in damages or loss.[343]

Departing employee cases are particularly susceptible to tortious interference claims. Seldom will an employer hire an employee without knowledge at the time of hire, or shortly thereafter, of the existence of restrictive covenants, non-disclosure agreements, or no-hire agreements concerning that employee. Indeed, standard practice encourages the former employer to send a letter notifying the new employer of such agreements. Once the new employer is put on notice and then continues to suffer the breach or continuing breach of the restrictive covenants, intent is much easier to prove. Rarely do privilege and justification apply as defenses.[344] A better defense is that the agreement is unenforceable or partially unenforceable.

---

338. *Browning-Ferris, Inc. v. Reyna*, 865 S.W.2d 925, 926-27 (Tex. 1993).

339. *In re Vesta Ins. Grp., Inc.*, 192 S.W.3d 759, 761 (Tex. 2006) (to be liable, a defendant must be a stranger to the contract).

340. *Southwestern Bell Tel. Co. v. John Carlo Tex., Inc.*, 843 S.W.2d 470, 472 (Tex. 1992).

341. *Powell Indus., Inc. v. Allen*, 985 S.W.2d 455, 457 (Tex. 1998).

342. *Exxon Corp. v. Allsup*, 808 S.W.2d 648, 656 (Tex. App.—Corpus Christi 1991, writ denied).

343. *Davis v. HydPro, Inc.*, 839 S.W.2d 137, 139-40 (Tex. App.—Eastland 1992, writ denied); *KTRK TV, Inc. v. Fowkes*, 981 S.W.2d 779, 790 (Tex. App.—Houston [1st Dist.] 1998, pet. denied) (plaintiff who was still employed with same salary and benefits did not suffer injury for tortious interference with employment contract).

344. *Butnaru v. Ford Motor Co.*, 84 S.W.3d 198, 207 (Tex. 2002); Prudential Ins. Co. of Am. v. Fin. Review Servs., 29 S.W.3d 74, 77-78 (Tex. 2000).

5-9:2 TORTIOUS INTERFERENCE WITH PROSPECTIVE RELATIONS

To assert a claim for tortious interference with prospective business relations, a plaintiff must prove: (1) A reasonable probability that the parties would have entered into a contractual relationship; (2) the defendant committed an "independently tortious or unlawful act;" (3) the defendant committed the act with a conscious desire to prevent the relationship from occurring; and (4) the plaintiff suffered actual harm or damage as a result of the defendant's interference—that is that the defendant's actions prevented the relationship from occurring.[345]

To establish a reasonable probability of contract, a plaintiff only needs to prove that entering the contract would be "reasonably probable, considering all the facts and circumstances attended to the transaction."[346] Emphasizing an earlier point, a defendant's conduct must be "independent[ly] tortious or unlawful," meaning that the defendant violated some other recognized tort or duty.[347] Most often the independent torts are breach of a confidentiality agreement, misappropriation of trade secrets, or breach of the duty of loyalty.348 In meeting the causation element, the plaintiff is not required to establish "but for causation" but only that the act or omission was a substantial factor in causing the injury.349

An insightful example of tortious interference involving a departing employee is *Alliantgroup*, where the court granted summary

345. *Wal-Mart Stores, Inc. v. Sturges*, 52 S.W.3d 711, 726 (Tex. 2001); *M-I LLC v. Stelly*, 733 F. Supp. 2d 759, 775-76 (S.D. Tex. 2010); *Alliantgroup, L.P. v. Feingold*, 803 F. Supp. 2d 610, 628 (S.D. Tex. 2011) (plaintiff need not show that the contract would have been created but for interference); *DHI Grp., Inc. v. Kent*, No. H-16-1670, 2017 U.S. Dist. LEXIS 42253, slip op. at *13 (S.D. Tex. Mar. 3, 2017).

346. *Advanced Nano Coatings, Inc. v. Hanafin*, 478 Fed. Appx. 838, 845 (5th Cir. May 31, 2012) (a plaintiff need not show but for causation from the interference).

347. *Id.*

348. *Faucette v. Chantos*, 322 S.W.3d 901, 916, n.8 (Tex. App.—Houston [14th Dist.] 2010, no pet.).

349. *Advanced Nano Coatings, Inc. v. Hanafin*, 478 Fed. Appx. 838, 845 (5th Cir. May 31, 2012).

judgment in favor of the former employee on a tortious interference with contract claim.[350] The employee clearly had confidential information and worked on transactions with several clients shortly before his resignation.[351] There was no evidence, however, that the employee's actions prevented the employer from entering into business relationships with those clients.[352]

Moreover, there was no evidence that the employee used the employer's business information, solicited former clients, or took the employer's business.[353] Similarly, in *M-I LLC* the court granted a motion to suppress because the plaintiff failed to allege facts showing a reasonable probability that the plaintiff would have entered into a contract with third parties.[354] The complaint also failed to demonstrate independent tortious conduct, the identity of any prospective business relationships, or actual damages.[355]

Finally, similar to a conversion claim, a tortious interference claim cannot be based on the misappropriation of trade secrets, even in part. Damages resulting from such misappropriation must be obtained under the Texas UTSA.[356]

5-10 CONCLUSION

Other causes of action against departing employees range from breach of contract claims to trade secret misappropriation to conversion. Breach of contract claims often involve covenants not to compete, covenants for nonsolicitation of employees or customers, and nondisclosure agreements. To bring a claim for breach, the person bringing suit must be the proper plaintiff, which she

350. *Alliantgroup, L.P. v. Feingold*, 803 F. Supp. 2d 610, 614 (S.D. Tex. 2011).

351. *Id.* at 616.

352. *Id.* at 628-29.

353. *Id.* at 629.

354. *M-I LLC v. Stelly*, 733 F. Supp. 2d 759, 774-76 (S.D. Tex. 2010).

355. *Id.*

356. *Computer Sciences Corp. v. Tata Consultancy Services Limited*, 220 WL 2487057, slip op. at * 9 (N.D. Tex. Feb. 7, 2020)

can demonstrate by being a party to a valid and enforceable contract. Additionally, the plaintiff must have performed her obligations under the contract, or have been excused from performance, and the defendant must have failed to perform his or her obligations, resulting in plaintiff's injury.

Regarding trade secret misappropriation, the Texas Uniform Trade Secrets Act, passed in May 2013, adopts the model Uniform Trade Secrets Act and covers a broader category of trade secrets than previously recognized under Texas law. Significantly, the Texas UTSA provides injunctive relief for actual and threatened misappropriation, protective orders, and attorney's fees. New employers of former employees guilty of misappropriation also may be liable when the new employer seeks to profit from such misappropriation. Remember, however, that an employee's general skills, knowledge, and experience are not trade secrets.

A third cause of action is inevitable disclosure, such as when an employee's skill is so entwined with the former employer's business that work for future employers would necessarily disclose aspects or details of the former employer's business. A fourth claim against departing employees arises under the Texas Theft Liability Act enacted in 1989 to provide a civil remedy for theft, including trade secret misappropriation. Notably, the TTLA requires intent, such that the innocent taking of property will not result in liability. As with the Texas UTSA, the TTLA provides attorney's fees to the prevailing *party*, be it the plaintiff or defendant.

The Computer Fraud and Abuse Act also sets forth a private right of action against departing employees with resulting monetary and injunctive relief. Like the TTLA, the CFAA requires intent. A plaintiff also must prove the defendant did not have access to the computer or its stored information and that the CFAA violation caused $5,000 or more in damages or loss. Relatedly, the Economic Espionage Act, which entered into law in 1996 and supplements the CFAA, created a criminal remedy for trade secret misappropriation but no private right of action.

As to the duty of loyalty, employees owe such a duty to their employers but not vice versa. The duty demands that the employee act to serve the interests of the employer. The scope of the duty is defined by contract terms or the employee's position (e.g., an executive or director has a higher duty than does an ordinary, low-level employee). Similarly, courts impose liability for those who aid and abet a breach of a fiduciary duty, such as the duty of loyalty.

The seventh cause of action discussed above is a claim for conversion, which is the wrongful assumption and exercise of dominion and control over another's property in a manner inconsistent with the property owner's rights. Liability may lie even when a party lawfully obtains the property but later acts inconsistently with the original owner's rights (*e.g.*, when an employee loses authorization upon termination, making use of property under prior authorization an actionable violation). Importantly, no intent is required to bring a conversion claim, but proof of malice will support an award of punitive damages.

Finally, a former employer may assert a claim for tortious interference with an existing contract or with prospective business relations. These distinct causes of action each have a scienter requirement. While an element of tortious interference with an existing contract is the actual existence of a contract, tortious interference with prospective business relations only requires a reasonable probability that the parties would have entered into a contract. In addition, each includes an element of resulting damages or loss.

Aside from covenants not to compete as discussed previously in chapter three, employers can assert other causes of action against departing employees who negatively impact or injure that employer's business upon departure and thereafter. Such harm may range from trade secret misappropriation to tortious interference. Remember to adhere to each cause of action's specific, nuanced elements.

Chapter 6

Negotiation, Mediation and Settlement[1]

Edited by John DeGroote

Context is important in any case, but cases involving departing employees aren't just any case. These disputes are intense, the settlement window is small and the stakes are high—making them harder than most cases to resolve. To successfully settle them, effective negotiators understand what the barriers to settling these cases are and creative ways to get around them.

6-1 WHAT MAKES SETTLING THESE CASES DIFFERENT?

6-1:1 THE STAKES OF THESE CASES MAKES THEM HARDER TO SETTLE.

In today's environment, any case can be important and few are irrelevant. Your client's bad emails are only a few clicks from Internet stardom, and the 24-hour news cycle can shift the public's focus to most any case with little effort. These new downsides only add to the ever-present risks of uncapped costs, endless ediscovery demands, unpredictable litigation outcomes, and more.

1. The author thanks Blake M. Guy for his helpful contributions to this chapter.

While any lawsuit can be dangerous, litigation between companies and their departing employees generates its own level of focus, expense, and risk. This is true for several reasons. First and perhaps most important, departing employee disputes involve more than arguments over past conduct: the future of the company, and an individual's livelihood, are both at stake. The employee's ability to work in her chosen field, in her area of expertise, with coworkers and clients she knows are at risk. On the other side of the dispute, the company's trade secrets, its future revenues, and its market share often hang in the balance, and its clients and competitors are just a subpoena away. The stakes couldn't be higher.

With added importance comes added scrutiny from several important audiences. Threats to revenue and future market share mean this isn't just a "legal problem." This draws the attention of the CEO and, often, the Board. Copycat cases, pattern settlements, and the potential for a negative ruling on the company's employment agreements add to the tension.

6-1:2 EMOTION OFTEN DRIVES DISPUTES INVOLVING DEPARTING EMPLOYEES.

While the financial stakes of these cases might be high, emotion can make them more expensive to litigate and harder to settle. Few disputes carry as much emotion as one with a departing employee: a once trusted member of the team is gone and so is the trust the company had in her. Longtime friends and colleagues are now litigation opponents and business competitors. All involved risk a loss of reputation in the shrinking world that is their industry. Individual alliances and long-term personal interests become unclear, and a sense of betrayal colors it all.

Most cases involving departing employees are predicated on a genuine belief that the other side did something wrong, which can fuel a sense of anger and fear—and a need for revenge—that makes these cases more intractable. And things can get worse:

emotion can drive regretful choices and poorly-worded communications even after the case is filed, all of which are subject to the discovery microscope.

6-1:3 THE SPEED OF THESE CASES MAKES THEM HARDER TO SETTLE.

While heightened emotions and increased focus make cases with departing employees difficult to settle, the speed at which they are litigated makes the negotiator's job even more difficult.

Traditional litigation enjoys a timeline that gives parties and counsel an opportunity to consider what is alleged, to plan their response, and to react in a measured way. This can provide the "acceptance time" that Chester Karrass tells us we often need in negotiation.[2] Unfortunately, when employees depart, the litigation that follows is both compressed and intense, leaving few if any windows for negotiation.

The timeline for cases involving departing employees is driven by the schedule for the temporary injunction hearing, which has to take place within 28 days of the entry of a temporary restraining order.[3] The temporary injunction hearing is often the only time both sides are heard in these matters, since the results of any final hearing usually track the results of the temporary injunction hearing.

---

2. For an exploration of acceptance time in settlement, see John DeGroote, Why We Can't Just "Cut to the Chase": Acceptance Time in Negotiation, Settlement Perspectives, September 16, 2008 http://www.settlementperspectives.com/2008/09/why-we-cant-just-cut-to-the-chase-acceptance-time-in-negotiation/. Karrass articulated the need for acceptance time as follows:

People need time to accept anything new or different. Both parties walk into a negotiating session with somewhat unrealistic goals. They start with all kinds of misconceptions and assumptions. Being human they hope against hope that their goals will, for a change, be easily met. The process of negotiating is usually a rude awakening. . . .

Can we expect the buyer or seller to adjust to these new and undesired realities immediately? Of course not. Resistance to change is universal. It takes time to get used to ideas that are foreign or unpleasant.

Chester L. Karrass, Give and Take 1 (1974).

3. Tex. R. Civ. P. 680.

Within those 28 days, the parties and their lawyers engage in expedited discovery, which by necessity involves immediate, executive-level depositions and ediscovery, and may include discovery on clients, competitors, and more. As the temporary injunction hearing nears, the personal toll on all involved continues to escalate. Customers and families are impacted, and even the lawyers aren't immune—and the "trial" hasn't yet begun.

With fact discovery, expert discovery and trial preparation occurring within a month and customers, employees and financial stability at risk, settlement opportunities can be lost in the melee.

6-2 NEGOTIATION STRATEGIES FOR SETTLING CASES INVOLVING DEPARTING EMPLOYEES.

Since most cases involving departing employees involve a genuine belief that the other side did something wrong, it's tough to resolve the dispute until both sides know more about what actually happened. The challenge in settling these cases is to move the parties quickly through the facts—at least the important facts—so that their focus can move from their opening positions to their underlying interests and, ultimately, to a path to settlement that serves those interests.

Getting there in time is the challenge.

6-2:1 THE PARTIES NEED TO KNOW THE FACTS — OR AT LEAST MORE OF THEM.

If all the facts were known at the outset, settlement of these cases would be a lot easier. But given the "hurry up" nature of cases involving departing employees, the parties will never know all the facts. They need to decide quickly whether locking down that next fact is worth the additional attorneys' fees—and settlement delay—it will take to get there.

Since each side may impute the most nefarious of motives and the most egregious of conduct to the other, some exchange of information, whether by formal discovery or otherwise, has to be done. Once the company realizes that its trade secrets are in fact still secret, or once the departing employee confirms that the company hasn't disparaged her to her clients, the parties' focus can move from survival to resolution.

The negotiator's challenge is to facilitate a process in which sufficient information can be exchanged—credibly, timely, and efficiently—before the parties' positions have hardened.

6-2:2 INTERESTS, NOT POSITIONS, SETTLE CASES.

At the outset of any case, the parties focus on their perception of "right" and "wrong" and what actually happened: Did Ms. Smith create any intellectual property on her company laptop? Has she violated her employment agreement by approaching customers near the company's old sales office in Texarkana?

As the case proceeds, the questions should change from positions to interests. Skilled negotiators focus less on "What, specifically, happened?" and focus more on "Setting aside the dispute for a moment, what do you really want here?" or "What are you really worried about, and how can we protect it?"

MIT highlighted the difference between positions and interests years ago, when it retold the story of two chefs who divided an orange in half after disagreeing on who most deserved the whole. After dividing the orange, one chef squeezed his half to put the juice into a sauce he was making, but the sauce still needed a bit more. The other chef grated the peel from his half for a cake batter he was preparing, but it wasn't quite enough. Had the two simply discussed why they wanted what they had asked for—the *interests* driving their *positions*—they could have divided the orange in a way that would have truly satisfied everyone involved.[4]

---

4. Mary Rowe, Nils Fonstad, and Robert McKersie, *Interests vs. Positions*, Negotiation

The MIT example isn't just academic. The company may care less about what Ms. Smith did with her laptop last year than what she might do with a new customer—one not referenced in her legacy employment agreement—next week. Ms. Smith, on the other hand, may have no desire to approach that new customer but may want to sell products near her home in Texarkana, even though the company shuttered its office there years ago. A good negotiator will push to find a way to share the orange—or the territory around Texarkana—that works for both sides.

6-2:3 EFFECTIVE NEGOTIATORS KNOW AND ADDRESS SETTLEMENT OBSTACLES EARLY ON.

Getting the parties to look past their opening positions to focus on their underlying interests sounds simpler than it is. Time pressures, executive focus, and high stakes aren't the only obstacles for the negotiator. Quickly resolving high-stakes, emotionally-driven cases is never easy, and there are a few more obstacles to getting them done.

Whether she uses them to her advantage or works to avoid their impact, a skilled negotiator needs to be aware of a few more issues before any deal can get done:[5]

1. **Finding the Decision Makers and Decision Influencers.** Cases with departing employees, like any case, involve more than a former employee and her old company. Spouses, lawyers, customers, and others can impact how and if the case settles. To be effective, a good negotiator needs to

Basics (1996), http://web.mit.edu/negotiation/www/NBivsp.html.

5. This list is based in part on one first published by Michael R. Greco in *Mediating Non-Compete Disputes in the Medical Device Industry*, Non Compete and trade Secrets (March 17, 2013), http://www.noncompetenews.com/post/2013/03/17/Mediating-Non-Compete-Disputes-in-the-Medical-Device-Industry.aspx.

figure out who these influencers are, and she needs to do it quickly.

2. **The Need for a Story.** Everyone connected with the case—the decision makers and decision influencers—needs a story. Rarely do people capitulate, and they almost never fold early in the case. A good negotiator will help the other side craft a narrative that satisfies all constituencies. If the employee can save face, she's more likely to settle.[6]
3. **Imbalance of Power.** Setting aside the occasional lawsuit between competitors, most of these cases involve an imbalance of power. The typical case is when an established company sues a former employee and her startup employer. An effective negotiator will perceive and address this imbalance during the negotiations, whether by exploiting it or minimizing it.
4. **Reactive Devaluation.** "The very offer of a particular proposal or concession—especially if the offer comes from *an adversary*—may diminish its apparent value or attractiveness in the eyes of the recipient."[7] This cognitive bias, reactive devaluation, may make proposals directly conveyed from one adversary to another less palatable. A good negotiator will use a mediator, joint brainstorming sessions, or other means to circumvent this obstacle.

6. See John DeGroote, *What Will She Tell Her Husband?* Settlement Perspectives (March 1, 2010), http://www.settlementperspectives.com/2010/03/what-will-she-tell-her-husband/.

7. Lee Ross, *Reactive Devaluation in Negotiation and Conflict Resolution, in* Barriers to Conflict Resolution 26, 28 (Kenneth Arrow, et al. eds. 1995).

5. **Sunk Costs.** Is the other side an individual who can't afford this litigation? Realistically, can the company afford it if it goes the distance? Both sides likely view attorneys' fees and discovery expenses as "sunk costs" that can't be recovered if the case settles,[8] and each party's desire to be repaid these sums in settlement can taint the negotiation process. While this issue can be minimized if the case is settled early, the good negotiator will factor each side's ability to pay and risk tolerance into her settlement strategy as the temporary injunction hearing approaches.

6-2:4 CREATIVE SOLUTIONS — THAT ADDRESS THE PARTIES' REAL INTERESTS — CAN GET CASES SETTLED.

Cases involving departing employees almost always involve companies and circumstances that have changed since the operative agreements were written. Product lines, customer lists, sales territories, and more have changed since the noncompete agreement, the nonsolicitation agreement or the confidentiality agreement were executed. The good news is that, you now have a chance to negotiate and write a solution that addresses your current circumstances.

How does an effective negotiator arrive at a deal that addresses the parties' interests, rather than their positions? A good negotiator will employ approaches that get the parties to focus away from their current positions and how they got here, and instead turn to their underlying interests and where they're going.

8. The threat of statutory fee shifting under Tex. Civ. Prac. & Rem. Code Section 38.001, et. seq. may increase this threat, but the possibility that attorneys' fees may be awarded if the case does not settle may impact the parties' negotiating positions.

No single book chapter can begin to catalog all the ways these cases can be settled, but a few are listed below. [9]

6-2:4.1 ACTUALLY TALK — AND LISTEN.

Texas Rule of Evidence 408 protects settlement-related communication, and it's there for a reason. In some cases, the simplest approach may work, and it's very rarely ever attempted: a face-to-face meeting between the former employee and someone from her old company, where a true exchange of ideas can take place. The particulars of the meeting can be tailored to the circumstances, but all should focus both on reducing perceived threats to either side and on promoting an open discussion of interests and alternatives. The meeting should take place before the "sunk costs" discussed above mount and may involve a nonthreatening company representative, a neutral site, a whiteboard (to promote joint input rather than formal, individual notes), and/or an open acknowledgement that it's a protected settlement communication. At this meeting, the parties can look beyond their own positions to what all parties at the table truly need and want—because it's often in everyone's interests to satisfy everyone's interests.

6-2:4.2 BREAK THE DISPUTE INTO SMALL ISSUES AND LOOK FOR MOMENTUM.

Smaller negotiating successes can build settlement momentum, and one mediator suggests that the parties "[b]reak the dispute into small issues and see if momentum to settle can build."[10] Smaller pieces can include (i) the noncompete agreement; (ii) the

9. For additional resources on creative settlement techniques, see John DeGroote, *Advanced Settlement Techniques & the Use of Mediation & Arbitration to Resolve Disputes* (October 2004) (unpublished paper), *available at* http://www.settlementperspectives.com/wp-content/uploads/2004-Impasse-Paper.pdf); John W. Cooley, Creative Problem Solver's Handbook for Negotiators and Mediators 197 (vol. 1 2005); and John W. Cooley, Creative Problem Solver's Handbook for Negotiators and Mediators 116 (vol. 2 2005).

10. Russel Murray, *Mediating the Non-Compete and Non-Disclosure Dispute*, Russel's Biz Blog (May 22, 2013), http://www.ormlaw.com/uncategorized/mediating-the-non-compete-and-non-disclosure-dispute/.

nondisclosure agreement; (iii) the identity of the former employee's intended employer; and (iv) the new territory for the former employee:

> Why smaller pieces? Because little problems are easier to resolve than big ones, especially if they can be unlinked. NDAs are usually easy—the former employee just agrees not to disclose and returns all documentation, which is about all a court would usually order anyway. Then, on the noncompete, it gets whittled away piece by piece—different geographic area, different responsibilities, different product, different customers, whatever—as the company comes to recognize that the departing employee isn't really a threat, anyway.[11]

6-2:4.3 CONSIDER SOLUTIONS THAT ADDRESS THE PUBLIC FACE OF THE DISPUTE.

As discussed above, reputational threat, industry focus, and pride have an outsized impact on cases involving departing employees. One area ripe for compromise is the public face of the dispute:

- How will the industry see this dispute?
- Does the company need to manage how its remaining employees, customers, and competitors perceive what happened?
- What will the departing employee's colleagues at the new company think?
- What will an Internet search for that employee's name turn up?

Since the past is past and the future will be written by a judge and jury if the parties can't come to agreement, now is the best chance

11. *Id.*

the parties have to put their own spin on the dispute. The parties and the lawyers who serve them can address this as a standalone issue or as part of an overall package. Whether it's a press release, a reference letter, a joint statement of facts, or something else, there are ways to craft a workable narrative for this dispute—if the parties want to.

6-2:4.4 TAILOR YOUR PROCESS TO YOUR PROBLEM.

Not everything on the parties' checklist can be agreed to. At times the negotiators need to design a process that addresses remaining open items in a way that simply gets the deal done. While each case is different, one example in the customer list context is a mock fantasy football draft employed to pick customers from a customer list:

> By this process, one trial lawyer resolved a dispute over a customer list between two former partners by listing all the customers and implementing a "draft" by each side—the parties alternated selecting customers from a list of all the customers until there were none left to pick from. At the end of the process the parties did a little more trading, decided they could live with what they had, and moved on.[12]

The specific process outlined above won't be appropriate in every case, but it does emphasize how creative thinking can tweak the process to get the parties to what they need, and the momentum for settlement may not stop there. Creativity can be applied to "designing the problem and designing the process to solve the problem and designing the solution(s)."[13]

---

12. John DeGroote, *Advanced Settlement Techniques & the Use of Mediation & Arbitration to Resolve Disputes* (October 2004) (unpublished paper), *available at* http://www.settlementperspectives.com/wp-content/uploads/2004-Impasse-Paper.pdf) (technique submitted by Michael P. Cash).

13. Email from John W. Cooley, to author (January 3, 2009) (on file with author) (selected capitalizations omitted).

> The use of creativity applies to designing (defining) the **PROBLEM** AND designing the **PROCESS** to solve the problem and designing the **SOLUTION(S)**. . . . Many other creative process designs may flow from the process design you initially consider undertaking. That's why, in my opinion, more time should be spent up front by counsel and parties to design the process. This is partially true because the process you select may minimize (or better yet, maximize) the number of potential solutions available.[14]

6-2:4.5 TRY NONBINDING ARBITRATION TO ACHIEVE ANOTHER PERSPECTIVE.

The parties' belief in their own positions is often very strong, and their lawyers, paid to advocate *for* their clients, often find it difficult to argue *against* their clients to suggest a settlement as the case progresses. Although some parties demand their "day in court," rarely do they require a full-scale court experience. What they often crave is outside input and vindication from a neutral third party. Nonbinding arbitration can be a quick and efficient means to achieve that input:

> [N]on-binding arbitration resembles conventional arbitration in that some discovery and briefing usually take place, and there are often formal hearings where evidence is presented and witnesses are examined and cross- examined. A non-binding arbitration award differs from a traditional arbitration award only in that it is not binding.[15]

---

14. *Id.*

15. Steven C. Bennett, *Non-Binding Arbitration: An Introduction*, Disp. Res. J. 1 (May-July 2006); see also John DeGroote, *Non-Binding Arbitration: Get Your Day in Court Without One Day in Court,* Settlement Perspectives (October 7, 2008), *available at* http://www.settlementperspectives.com/2008/10/non-binding-arbitration-get-your-day-

In cases where the temporary injunction hearing looms, an involved parallel process for a nonbinding arbitration won't help—but a truncated presentation of agreed facts, paired with a few documents and the noncompete agreement or other contract in dispute—may be enough to support a written, nonbinding opinion from a respected authority. This opinion can give the parties the neutral perspective they're looking for, which can be the next step toward settlement.

6-2:5 DECISION TREES CAN FOSTER COMMUNICATION AND UNDERSTANDING.[16]

Often used in the business world, decision trees are "tree-shaped models of [a] decision to be made and the uncertainties it encompasses."[17] A decision tree "shows the various possible outcomes in a lawsuit and helps the parties evaluate the costs, risks and benefits of each outcome."[18] Decision trees, which help parties organize outcomes and the probabilities associated with each, are valuable in part because "even very smart and very intuitive people are not good at juggling multiple uncertainties."[19]

Stated simply, the decision tree is a tool used to value the multiple financial outcomes possible in any litigation—whether summary judgment is granted, the plaintiff "wins" a small amount, or something else happens. Just as important, decision trees arrive at these values by translating the subjective judgment of trial counsel into objective terms, since a trial lawyer's interpretation of "a good chance of winning" or a "probable loss" might be

---

in-court-without-one-day-in-court/

16. This section is based in part on John DeGroote, *Decision Tree Analysis In Litigation: The Basics,* Settlement Perspectives (January 4, 2009), *available at* http://www.settlementperspectives.com/2009/01/decision-tree-analysis-in-litigation-the-basics/.

17. Dwight Golann, Mediating Legal Disputes (1995).

18. Daniel Klein, *What is a Decision Tree?* Daniel Klein Mediation, *available at* http://decisiontree.kleinmediation.com.

19. Marc B. Victor, Decision Tree Analysis: A Means of Reducing Litigation Uncertainty and Facilitating Good Settlements, 31 Ga. St. U. L. Rev. (2015) 715, 720.

very, very different from yours. A decision tree can eliminate this latent disconnect.

Decision trees are created by:

1. Listing the various possible events which might occur in the course of litigation (or beyond);
2. Considering the costs or gains associated with each possibility;
3. Discounting each possibility by its probability-estimated likelihood that it will occur; and
4. Evaluating the overall picture by multiplying each possibility by its probability.[20]

These four steps therefore require lawyers and their clients to understand (i) what events are anticipated; (ii) how much each event will cost; and (iii) what the possible outcomes are and how likely each is to occur. Whether each side to a dispute keeps their decision tree private—but acts on the understanding of the case they have developed—or works collaboratively with the other side to see where they can agree and where they can't, a decision tree can be an invaluable tool in the settlement process.

6-2:6 SPECIAL SETTLEMENT COUNSEL SETTLE CASES.

As the noncompete dispute moves toward the temporary injunction hearing and expedited discovery and trial preparation near their peaks, is trial counsel in a good position to extend the olive branch? William F. Coyne Jr. once said "[w]e do not ask our generals to be diplomats, nor our diplomats to be generals,"[21] and

20. Kathleen M. Scanlon, Mediator's Deskbook (1999).

21. William F. Coyne Jr., *Using Settlement Counsel for Early Dispute Resolution*, 15 Negotiation J. 1, 11 (1999).

his perspective may have particular relevance in cases involving departing employees.

A host of sources have explored the idea that a separate lawyer from a separate firm whose sole job it is to focus on settlement—while remaining above the litigation fray—may make sense in significant cases.[22] Separate settlement counsel can leverage their training and their emotional distance to get beyond legal positions to actual interests, since "the types of questions that are asked when focusing on settlement are different from the types of questions that a litigator needs to ask to prepare a complaint and commence a suit."[23] Settlement counsel thus focus on interests, while legal positions advance in parallel.

Given the stakes, the speed, the emotional nature, and the expense of cases involving departing employees, settlement counsel may make particular sense in these cases.

6-3 MEDIATION STRATEGIES FOR SETTLING DEPARTING EMPLOYEE CASES

With genuine effort by both sides, proactive negotiation can lead to settlement of many cases involving departing employees. For some cases, mediation is the first opportunity the parties take to try to resolve the dispute, and in others mediation comes from impasse. A good negotiator can use the techniques listed in this chapter, and more, in mediation, and a good mediator will need every tool at her disposal:

> A significant number of cases involve a true, good faith disagreement, and gap, based upon a recipe of intersecting factors such as different

22. For a partial list of settlement counsel resources, *see* John DeGroote, *Settlement Counsel: 10 Free Internet Resources*, Settlement Perspectives (April 4, 2013), *available at* http://www.settlementperspectives.com/2013/04/settlement-counsel-10-free-internet-resources/.

23. John DeGroote, *Why Settlement Counsel? A Lesson from the Scorpion and the Frog*, Settlement Perspectives (May 29, 2012), *available at* http://www.settlementperspectives.com/2012/05/why-settlement-counsel-a-lesson-from-the-scorpion-and-the-frog/.

> perceptions as to the facts, credibility, law, skill of counsel, venue, risk tolerance, party values/principles, precedents, historical and personal narratives, strategic goals and priorities. Breaking impasse involves an actual transformation of the choices, and or perspectives, of at least one of the stakeholders of the dispute.[24]

Mediators are well equipped to identify and eliminate obstacles to settlement as they arise. By managing the discussions, asking the right questions, and truly listening to the parties, mediators can identify the real interests at play and often find the path to a settlement that satisfies those interests.

6-3:1 WHY MEDIATE AT ALL? CAN'T THE PARTIES JUST WORK IT OUT?[25]

Mediation has been a primary mechanism for settling cases involving departing employees for over 20 years, and there are reasons why it works. As the parties consider mediation—typically between the TRO hearing and the temporary injunction hearing—they should consider why it works so often:

1. **Mediation Fosters Simultaneous Focus on Settlement.** Mediation, which by definition involves clients, requires some degree of preparation and advance thought about positions, interests, reasonable settlement ranges, and more. Effective negotiators will leverage this simultaneous focus on the problem at hand and potential solutions.

24. John W. Cooley, Creative Problem Solver's Handbook for Negotiators and Mediators, Volume One 197 (2005).

25. This section is based on John DeGroote, *Why Mediate At All? Can't We Just Work It Out?*, Settlement Perspectives (November 21, 2008), *available at* http://www.settlementperspectives.com/2008/11/why-mediate-at-all-cant-we-just-work-it-out/.

2. **The Decision Makers Are Present.** Hand in hand with simultaneous focus is the fact that the decision makers are present or at least available. Mediation generates an audience—with authority—to understand and evaluate each party's arguments, its revealed interests, and the mediator's proposed path forward.
3. **Mediators Are Paid to Settle Your Case.** Mediators are paid to settle cases, and this economic incentive means you'll have at least one person in the room working hard to settle the case.
4. **Mediators Are Neutral.** Usually the only one in the room who has no stake in the outcome is the mediator, and effective negotiators use this to their advantage by seeking the mediator's input on negotiation strategies, bargaining positions, and, in some cases, underlying positions.
5. **The Physical Setup Can Foster Protected Discussions.** In most cases, mediation allows parties to be in the same location but in different rooms for difficult parts of the negotiations. This allows participants to pause before reacting, and it encourages each party to compose their thoughts before communicating their positions to the other side. Whoever said "give good news in public, give bad news in private" knew something about mediation.

These factors, and confidentiality as discussed below, are available for all parties to leverage in mediation.

6-3:2 WHEN DO YOU MEDIATE?

There is no hard and fast rule on the best time to mediate. While most cases involving departing employees that go to mediation do so between the TRO and the temporary injunction hearings, presuit mediation is becoming more common, as is appellate mediation. If mediation doesn't occur before the case is filed, effective negotiators will look for inflection points in the case as windows for mediation, such as the day before a key customer's deposition, the day before an important hearing, or the week before an important executive's deposition.

As shown later in this chapter, the parties can achieve a better understanding of the other side's position, a more streamlined case, and a more thorough mediation even if it isn't successful the first time, so there are few arguments against mediating the case early. There is no rule against mediating it again when the parties have a little more knowledge and a little less money.

6-3:3 USE MEDIATION AS A PLATFORM FOR CANDID DISCUSSIONS AND EMOTIONAL RELEASE.

As mentioned above, cases involving departing employees "are driven in large part by emotion. Parties feel betrayed by their opponents' misconduct, which is frequently fresh in their minds."[26] Very often the dispute between a company and its departing employee involves indirect communication by email, by conference call, or by other remote means.

Mediation gives both sides a unique opportunity to actually sit in the same room and discuss how they got there and, later, where they're going. "Providing [the parties] with an opportunity to speak their mind (in a respectful way) can be cathartic

26. Michael R. Greco, *5 Keys to Mediating Non-Compete and Trade Secret Disputes,* Non-Compete and Trade Secrets (February 12, 2012), *available at* http://www.noncompetenews.com/post/2012/02/21/5-Keys-to-Mediating-Non-Compete-and-Trade-Secret-Disputes.aspx.

and productive."[27] The simple fact of working on the problem together can make a real difference.

6-3:4 USE MEDIATION CONFIDENTIALITY TO YOUR ADVANTAGE.

Under Tex. Civ. Prac. & Rem. Code 154.073 and with only limited exceptions, a statement made in mediation is "confidential, is not subject to disclosure, and may not be used as evidence against the participant in any judicial or administrative proceeding." What the parties and their counsel say in mediation governed by this statute is generally nondiscoverable and inadmissible.[28]

The experienced negotiator will use this shield to get the parties closer to settlement, as it can cover a number of things a party may wish to convey confidentially to the other side, including:

1. An apology;
2. A summary of the facts in the case from one party's perspective;
3. The results of an investigation;
4. An exchange of documents that might be embarrassing to the parties or their counsel, including:
    a. Motions that may be filed, such as spoliation motions;
    b. Arguments about privilege waiver; and
    c. Documents not yet produced that are embarrassing to the parties (although these may be discoverable if they existed outside the mediation context); and

27. *Id.*

28. *See* Tex. Civ. Prac. & Rem. Code 154.073. Note that many practitioners also rely on Tex. R. Evid. 408, which provides protections for settlement-related communications.

5. A discussion of the parties' underlying interests.

Although mediation confidentiality is often appreciated, it is rarely leveraged. Why file that fraud counterclaim—which can never be retracted—when it might be more valuable unfiled? Could it help the parties get beyond today's dispute if one client would look the other in the eye and (confidentially) apologize for the things she knows she did wrong?

6-3:4 USE MEDIATION TO SETTLE HALFWAY.

If a mediation isn't successful—or stated more accurately, if a case doesn't settle in mediation—the parties and their lawyers have the opportunity to "settle halfway":

> In disputes where [the parties] aren't ready—or able—to settle the entire case, [the parties can] look for ways to eliminate parts of it to streamline the matter, limit expenses, and refocus the parties on resolving what's left.[29]

Stated differently, if settlement can't be reached, the parties can (i) agree on what's really in dispute and focus on that issue; (ii) develop a tailored discovery plan to get to the facts actually in dispute; and (iii) agree on claims that can be dropped, defenses that can be abandoned, stipulations that can be entered, and other measures designed to narrow the dispute so it can proceed more efficiently or, possibly, be settled once the parties know more about what's truly in dispute.

By settling halfway, no one is asking any party to capitulate or to abandon truly valuable claims. If each side will carefully consider what motivates the other party and their lawyers, a great deal can still be negotiated. Examples include:

---

29. John DeGroote, *You Can Win By Settling Halfway: Settlement Structures Part I*, Settlement Perspectives (October 10, 2008), *available at* http://www.settlementperspectives.com/2008/10/you-can-win-by-settling-halfway-settlement-structures-part-i/.

1. Will the plaintiff agree to a bench trial if the defendant agrees not to challenge her expert?
2. Is that laches defense really important or can it be abandoned in exchange for a waiver of the third customer representative's deposition?
3. Would the plaintiff waive its claim for punitives in exchange for an agreement to arbitrate?

6-4 CONCLUSION

As outlined above, cases involving departing employees are by their very nature important, emotional, fast-paced, and expensive. The parties can, and often should, find ways to resolve these disputes earlier, whether through a cooperative information exchange, the strategic use of mediation, or some other process designed to address the parties' actual interests rather than their legal positions.

Effective negotiators will realize that the challenges that distinguish litigation with departing employees, when recognized and accounted for, simply give the parties and their lawyers more reasons—and more ways—to get them resolved earlier.

Chapter 7
Discovery

Edited by Greg McAllister and Dave Wishnew

7-1 FACT DISCOVERY IN INJUNCTION CASES

7-1:1 OVERVIEW

Lawyers obtain the essential evidence needed to prove their cases through discovery. The author will presume (for purposes of this subsection) that the reader has sufficient knowledge regarding general discovery and, therefore, will use this subsection to focus on fact discovery in injunction cases. Discovery in preparation for a temporary injunction hearing is often limited by the scope of discovery that the court is willing to grant on an expedited basis and/or the fact that a temporary injunction hearing will only determine some (not all) of the issues in any particular case.

7-1:2 DISCOVERY PLANNING

Quite often, both the client and the lawyer are in a hurry while preparing a petition for a temporary restraining order and/or temporary injunction. Furthermore, because so much energy is expended on preparing a technically correct petition, discovery planning is frequently shortchanged. At some point, however, the lawyer *must* turn his or her attention to discovery planning because discovery planning can often determine whether or not the petitioner can prove his or her case. In the simplest terms, discovery planning should start with the following assessment:

1. Determine what you can prove;
2. Determine what you *think* you can prove (but will need to confirm with more discovery);
3. Determine what *might* be true (but can only be confirmed with more discovery); and
4. Determine what facts and legal principals are essential for you to prove at the temporary injunction stage.

When conducting discovery, practitioners often fail to differentiate between a case for equitable relief and a case for damages. For example, while you need to prove harm at the temporary injunction stage, you do not need to prove all of your damages.

Once you have gone through the recommended exercise above, you will be able to develop a checklist of what you need to prove as well as what discovery you need and—as a result—you can remain focused on how you must develop your evidence to prove each element of your claim for equitable relief and how you must respond to any defenses the other party asserts in response to your claim.

7-1:3 SCOPE OF EXPEDITED DISCOVERY

As previously mentioned, prudent counsel will want to move for expedited discovery with their petition for a temporary restraining order or temporary injunction. Remember, temporary restraining orders expire in 14 days (barring a possible 14-day extension).[1] Of course, the parties can extend a temporary restraining order

1. *See* Tex. R. Civ. P. 680.

by agreement. During that time, you need to obtain documents from the other side, produce documents for the other side, potentially serve (and respond to) written discovery, take and defend depositions, and marshal your evidence for the hearing. Clearly, there is a lot to do. Therefore, you should request discovery early on and narrow your approach to discovery, focusing on the issues that are a matter of proof at the temporary injunction hearing, so you do not spread yourself too thin on less imperative issues.

Most judges will grant expedited discovery in a temporary restraining order and/or temporary injunction case. However, most will also want to make certain that the expedited discovery is narrowly focused and balanced—meaning that both sides can conduct the necessary expedited discovery. If you present the judge with a motion and order demonstrating these characteristics, you will be more likely to obtain a grant for expedited discovery. Many lawyers fail to think through their discovery needs prior to filing, which can delay or even prevent discovery in a temporary injunction case. Discovery in injunction matters is extremely important and should be considered thoughtfully prior to going down to the courthouse.

7-1:4 DEPOSITIONS

In many cases, you will be allowed to take expedited depositions. However, in these instances, the number of depositions (and length) is usually limited. You should be prepared to tell the court exactly which depositions you want, how long you want them to be, and why it should grant your requests. The easiest way to prepare for this is to work backward from your proof outline. Do your best to determine which witnesses are most likely to know the facts associated with your necessary proof. If the defendant is an entity, deposing a representative of the entity is almost always the best choice[2] because the entity will be forced to prepare a witness to testify on the list of subject matters you

2. *See* Tex. R. Civ. P. 199.2(b)(1).

will have provided ahead of time. Consequently, "I don't know" or "I don't recall" will not typically be acceptable answers in this type of deposition. If possible, a videotaped deposition is almost always preferable. Lawyers and judges are nearly uniform in their belief that videotaped depositions hold a judge's (and, later, the jury's) attention much more effectively than a transcript. Finally, with the prevalence of remote depositions through video conferencing software (i.e. Zoom), lawyers should weigh the benefits and costs of in-person depositions in preparing for a temporary injunction hearing and consider a hybrid of in-person and remote depositions depending on the length of deposition expected and the importance of information expected from each witness.

7-1:5 WRITTEN DISCOVERY

An order for expedited discovery will likely allow requests for production. These requests should be simple, direct, and focused. Once again, you should determine what you will need to have in order to properly prepare for the injunction hearing. Again, the best place to start is your proof outline. Occasionally, interrogatories are necessary, but this practitioner's experience is that interrogatories (and also requests for admissions) yield very little valuable information.

7-1:6 DISCOVERY FROM THIRD PARTIES

Discovery from third parties can be problematic in expedited discovery. Typically, judges disfavor requiring nonparties to respond to document requests on an expedited basis. And, while you can serve a subpoena, an uncooperative third party can make obtaining the meaningful documents in time for your hearing difficult. Moreover, departing employee cases often involve battles over customers, prospective customers, former employees, or suppliers. A prudent practitioner should think carefully about whether or not the inconvenience (and likely irritation) that could easily result from serving a subpoena on and/or deposing a third party is worth the business risk.

7-1:7 PROTECTIVE ORDERS

Since departing employee cases tend—by their very nature—to contain confidential information, the parties involved must regularly enter into a protective order, which can preserve confidentiality. Usually, there are two classes of people that are allowed to see the documents subjected to a protective order. The first group includes the parties, witnesses, and experts. The second can be summarized with the phrase, "attorney's eyes only." The use of the "attorney's eyes only" designation is often a matter of great controversy among lawyers because dealing with these documents can result in clumsy litigation, especially when the lawyer cannot show her own client certain documents while preparing for litigation.

7-2 ELECTRONIC INFORMATION[3]

Understanding the universe of electronically stored information (ESI) relevant to your case is critical and should begin (if possible) before the lawsuit is filed. ESI in departing employee cases often differs from ESI in civil commercial litigation because the former employer usually controls the majority of the electronic evidence. In all likelihood, the employer and employee shared the same network and servers. Therefore, an analysis of the employee's activities in the days and weeks prior to and/or immediately following his or her termination will yield an electronic trail of evidence the employer can use to bolster the claim for immediate injunctive relief. This examination of the available electronic information may show that the employee was breaching (or intended to breach) his restrictive covenants. Often, an employee downloads or emails the employer's confidential and proprietary

3. The author thanks Dave Wishnew, a partner at Crawford, Wishnew & Lang, PLLC, and his associate T.J. Jones for contributing this section of the chapter.

information to his personal accounts and then attempts to cover up the duplicitous activity. Similarly, departing employees often copy confidential information to cloud storage platforms like a personal Dropbox account. Fortunately for the employer, the employee's actions will often leave an electronic imprint, which an employer can use as convincing evidence of irreparable harm and a probable right to relief.

By no means will this section attempt to cover the entire, expansive world of ESI. Rather, it is designed to give the practitioner some helpful background information and strategic considerations that will allow her to efficiently analyze and utilize ESI in departing employee cases.

7-2:1 ESI UNDER THE TEXAS AND FEDERAL RULES

Texas Rule of Civil Procedure 196.4 governs the discovery of ESI:

> To obtain discovery of data or information that exists in electronic or magnetic form, the requesting party must specifically request production of electronic or magnetic data and specify the form in which the requesting party wants it produced. The responding party must produce the electronic or magnetic data that is responsive to the request and is reasonably available to the responding party in its ordinary course of business. If the responding party cannot—through reasonable efforts—retrieve the data or information requested or produce it in the form requested, the responding party must state an objection complying with these rules. If the court orders the responding party to comply with the request, the court must also order that the requesting party pay the

> reasonable expenses of any extraordinary steps required to retrieve and produce the information.[4]

The Texas Supreme Court in *In re Weekley Homes, L.P.*,[5] cited to the Conference of Chief Justices, *Guidelines for State Trial Courts Regarding Discovery of Electronically-Stored Information*, to define ESI as:

> Any information created, stored, or best utilized with computer technology of any sort, including business applications, such as word processing, databases, and spreadsheets; Internet applications, such as e-mail and the World Wide Web; devices attached or peripheral to computers, such as printers, fax machines, pagers; web-enabled portable devices and cell phones and media used to store computer data, such as disks, tapes, removable drives, CDs, and the like.[6]

Federal Rule 26 addresses the discovery of ESI in federal cases:

> *Specific Limitations on Electronically Stored Information.* A party need not provide discovery of electronically stored information from sources that the party identifies as not reasonably accessible because of undue burden or cost. On motion to compel discovery or for a protective order, the party from whom discovery is sought must show that the information is not reasonably accessible because of undue burden or cost. If that showing is made, the court may nonetheless order discovery from such sources if the requesting party shows good cause, considering the limitations of

4. Tex. R. Civ. P. 196.4

5. *In re Weekley Homes, L.P.*, 295 S.W.3d 309, 314 (Tex. 2009) (orig. proceeding).

6. *See* Conference of Chief Justices, *Guidelines for State Courts Regarding Discovery of Electronically-Stored Information* (Aug. 2006).

> Rule 26(b)(2)(C). The court may specify conditions for the discovery.[7]

Texas Rule 196.4 is not a mirror image of the two-tier approach provided by Rule 26. Although Rule 196.4 does not specifically require a showing of "good cause," the Texas Supreme Court in *In re Weekley Homes, L.P.* dictated a similar analysis by incorporating Rule 192.4(b).

The factors provided by Rule 192.4 are

1. the needs of the case;
2. the amount in controversy;
3. the parties' resources;
4. the importance of issues at stake; and
5. the importance of the proposed discovery in resolving these issues.[8]

Notably, the Texas Rules differ from the Federal Rules by requiring the requesting party to bear the costs of any ESI that is discoverable but not reasonably accessible.

It is highly recommended that the practitioner familiarize himself with the most recent and relevant state and federal cases that discuss ESI. Texas courts often cite *Weekley Homes* regarding discovery issues related to ESI, and the Texas Supreme Court has since gone on to opine on more detailed ESI issues not addressed in that decision.[9] On the federal side, the *Zubulake* holdings from the Southern District of New York are largely followed in courts around the country, including Texas courts.[10] Likewise, the Sedona Conference has published several instructive and

---

7. Fed. R. Civ. P. 26(b)(2)(B).

8. Tex. R. Civ. P. 192.4(b); *In re Weekley Homes, L.P.*, 295 S.W.3d 309, 317 (Tex. 2009) (orig. proceeding).

9. *In re Harris*, 315 S.W.3d 685, 694 (Tex. App.—Houston [1st. Dist.] 2010, orig. proceeding); *In re State Farm Lloyds*, 520 S.W.3d 595, 606 (Tex. 2017)

10. *See MRT, Inc. v. Vounckx*, 299 S.W.3d 500, 511 (Tex. App.—Dallas 2009, no pet.)

authoritative texts regarding ESI that are often cited by state and federal judges.[11]

7-2:2 DISCOVERABILITY

In keeping with their federal brethren, Texas judges have an expansive definition regarding the types of discoverable ESI. While the discoverability of emails seems obvious in this day and age, the fact that some deleted files and metadata are discoverable is not as intuitive. However, an examination of these deleted files and metadata can often direct the practitioner to a wealth of evidence of an employee's clandestine activities. Like most people, employees often write in an email what they would never say in person.

When conducting expedited discovery, it is particularly important to have focused requests that describe the type of information the party is seeking to discover with as much accuracy as possible.[12] Although the Texas Supreme Court has stated that it is not necessary to know the method or means of retrieving ESI at the time the requests for information are made, it is good practice for the practitioner to specify the type and format of information to be produced.

If a party has specifically requested ESI, the responding party must produce the ESI that is reasonably available to the responding party in its ordinary course of business. Additionally, at a hearing on reasonable accessibility, the responding party has the burden to show that the requested ESI is not reasonably available due to cost and/or undue burden. If the responding party satisfies its burden, the requesting party must then demonstrate to the court that a cost-benefit analysis favors discovery of the requested ESI. In other words, the responding party will need to

11. *See* The Sedona Conference, *Publications*, https://thesedonaconference.org/publications (last updated 2021).

12. Forms 1-018 and 1-019 provide some common discovery requests that are used to discover relevant ESI.

demonstrate that the five factors of Rule 192.4 favor limiting the ESI production, while the requesting party should controvert the responding party to establish the importance of the ESI to the case.

When one party seeks access to the other party's personal storage devices, additional considerations must be made. For example, courts are typically wary of granting unfettered access to an employee's personal computer. Under *In re Weekley Homes, L.P.*, the party seeking production of personal storage devices must also demonstrate that (a) the responding party has defaulted in its obligations to search its records and produce the requested data; and (b) the responding party's production has been inadequate and a search of their storage devices could recover deleted relevant data, to the extent applicable.[13] Even if the court grants access to the personal devices, it will most likely require that a third-party computer expert conducts the ESI analysis. To that end, the parties will likely need to work together (and often with independent experts) to develop a protocol to analyze ESI on devices belonging to former employees. The protocol will outline the steps required to identify and collect relevant ESI, while preserving privilege and personal information.[14]

7-2:3 EARLY DIAGNOSIS

It is essential to quickly understand the breadth of information you are dealing with, the types of files, and the locations of ESI within the employer's network. Clients often forget how much information they have in their possession and where the relevant information might be located. Therefore, you should ask the client many probing questions regarding ESI. Do not be afraid to err on the side of redundancy. It can take five questions about an important thumb drive before the client informs you it is sitting in a desk drawer.

---

13. *In re Weekley Homes, L.P.*, 295 S.W.3d 309, 317 (Tex. 2009) (orig. proceeding).

14. A sample of a proposed protocol is attached as Form 1-025.

Craig Ball, a well-known lawyer and author of ESI-related topics, advocates for lawyers to habitually apply the "five Ws" to preserve and capture ESI.[15] Adapting Ball's analysis to a departing employee case, the practitioner should learn and document:

1) What information has the employee taken;
2) When did the employee take the information;
3) Where is the information now and where did the information originate;
4) Who is the employee sharing the information with; and
5) How is the employee using the information to the employer's detriment.

Barry Bray, Founder and President of Delphi Legal Technologies and an ESI expert with over twenty years of experience, also recommends early diagnosis of ESI issues[16]:

> Data collection is the hardest part of a case. Compile a list of all data sources day one from your client. Cost of ESI is a major factor in litigation today, if you have a good idea of the total amount of data you are facing your client can go into the case understanding what the cost will be and your firm will understand the resources need to review the data collection. Attorneys and law firm should try to be proactive and teach clients to plan for the day an employee will leave the company from the first day of hire. Information is as valuable as property, and in some cases more valuable. Employers should always know who

15. Craig Ball, *E-Discovery: Right from the Start; Smart First Steps in Electronic Discovery*, at 1 (2008), http://www.craigball.com/Ball_Right%20from%20the%20Start_20081106.pdf.

16. Bray, B. (July 24, 2013). Telephonic Interview.

> has access to data and how they access that data. On the other side, if you are an employee make sure and hand off any information you have to your employer on your last day and go over a check list to make sure any information or data is returned destroyed or deleted and that they sign off on its return.

Mr. Bray also believes that "not knowing" the answers to the following questions can be the lawyer's biggest downfall:

1. Where is the data stored?
2. How much data needs review?
3. How much time will it take to review the data?
4. How will counsel review the data once collected?
5. How much will it cost to format the data for review?

In order to run your case effectively, you must fully understand your data universe. Designating a lawyer or paralegal within the firm as "keeper" of the master guide to the ESI is a helpful strategy for effective case management. You should also create and maintain the list of ESI's "custodians," which are typically the key players (in possession of ESI) involved in the dispute. Additionally, interviewing co-workers can provide information about the types of ESI the former employee could access and may also provide insight into the former employee's motives for taking the information. If the employer has an in-house IT professional, counsel should engage her or him immediately in order to better understand the location and size of servers, drivers, computers/ laptops, the email system, and any smartphones devices. Lastly, be mindful of any third parties that may have received relevant ESI and include them on the list of potential custodians.

7-2:4 LEGAL HOLD AND STEPS TO ENSURE INFORMATION IS NOT DESTROYED

In departing employee cases, the duty to preserve evidence begins as soon as the employer becomes aware that a former employee is, or may be, violating contractual or common law obligations. It is fairly common for an employer to immediately reassign or recycle the departing employee's company computer and phone, or remove an employee from the company's cloud services, and an unaware IT professional may clear the devices and assign them to a new user, or delete an employee's cloud-based data, which can result in the inadvertent deletion of ESI. Too often, IT personnel do not know of the existence of a legal hold until important ESI has already been removed from the former employee's devices or the company's cloud storage services. Because ESI is routinely deleted or altered in the ordinary course of business, a forward-thinking lawyer should have the employer immediately institute a legal hold to avoid future problems, such as allegations of spoliation. Therefore, it is imperative to notify all custodians of information, IT personnel, relevant management, and new or reassigned employees who may acquire devices containing data that is subject to a legal hold. Legal holds are not uniform in nature but, instead, are unique to each departing employee case.

The first step is to identify the ESI that is potentially relevant to a claim or defense and send a preservation notice (*i.e.*, a legal hold letter) to all custodians and appropriate personnel in the human resources and IT departments.[17] The practitioner's next priority should be to meet with the client and potential custodians to discuss what ESI may be relevant to the case and which devices and storage accounts may contain the relevant ESI (including specific file types). You must be thorough when questioning custodians, as they may not initially recall certain documents or files that may contain pertinent ESI or the identification of employees that may have received relevant information.

---

17. *See* Forms 1-013 through 1-015.

If the hold for information is related to a specific date range, you should make sure this information is properly communicated to all custodians and IT personnel. Additionally, a legal hold may extend to information stored on an employee's personal email, home computer, or other storage devices and services. Requiring a response from those who have received notice is good practice, and a prudent practitioner will carefully track each response in order to maintain a strong grasp on the often transient universe of ESI in the case. All custodians of ESI should understand what is required of them and how to best comply with the legal hold. Periodic meetings and follow-up phone calls with the custodians are other good strategies to ensure that everyone is on the same page. IT departments should also confirm that all programs with automatic archiving and/or deletion functions are turned off for all custodians and that vendors the company uses to store data have been made aware of their changed preservation needs.

During this time, the practitioner should thoroughly document all preservation actions taken and the reasons behind each decision. Detailed and transparent recordkeeping during ESI preservation will become vital if the opposing party files a motion for sanctions due to the deletion of ESI, including spoliation of evidence.

Spoliation is the deletion, destruction, and/or significant alteration of evidence.[18] To establish spoliation, the party seeking relief must demonstrate: (1) a duty existed to preserve the information at issue; (2) a breach of that duty; and (3) prejudice as a result of that breach.[19] Texas courts require a level of scienter to sustain a finding of spoliation, and mere negligence is often insufficient.[20] Similarly, the Fifth Circuit requires a showing of bad faith or culpable conduct on the part of the alleged spoliator.[21] It

18. *Rimkus Consulting Group, Inc. v. Cammarata*, 688 F. Supp. 2d 598, 612 (S.D. Tex. 2010).

19. *Trevino v. Ortega*, 969 S.W.2d 950, 954-55 (Tex. 1998).

20. *See Aguirre v. S. Tex. Blood & Tissue Ctr.*, 2 S.W.3d 454, 457-58 (Tex. App.—San Antonio 1999, pet. denied).

21. *See Condrey v. SunTrust Bank of Georgia*, 431 F.3d 191, 203 (5th Cir. 2005).

is increasingly rare for courts to find bad faith, especially where counsel has diligently documented his extensive preservation efforts.

Legal holds should also include contingency plans for custodians who might not fully understand their obligations or employees who alter or delete records due to self-interest. An astute practitioner will proactively consider this possibility before and after instituting a legal hold and identify alternative measures to preserve the ESI.

Lawyers and employers alike are best served if ESI issues are initially investigated in employee exit interviews. Employers should determine whether the departing employee is already subject to a legal hold. If so, the company can immediately take steps to preserve the departing employee's ESI. If not, the employer should confirm that all computers and storage devices used by the employee during his or her employment have been returned and access to cloud-based services has been removed. The employer should also secure a written verification from the departing employee stating that he has returned all the employer's confidential and proprietary information.

Failing to take proper steps to gather and preserve ESI can derail your case into a fight over ancillary issues.

7-2:5 BASIC TYPES OF INFORMATION

Because any lawyer can easily become lost in the myriad technical terms and aspects of ESI, adding a comprehensive guide to data storage on your bookshelf is a wise idea. Craig Ball's "A Lawyer's Guide to the Language of Data Storage and Networking"[22] is a good reference on ESI. All practitioners should commit to expanding their knowledge of ESI because of its undisputed importance in litigation today. To start, below are some basic descriptions of

22. *See generally* Craig Ball, *Geek Speak: A Lawyer's Guide to the Language of Data Storage and Networking*, at 1 (2009), http://www.craigball.com/GeekSpeak.pdf.

the types of information that can be used as evidence in a departing employee case.

7-2:5.1 ACTIVE DATA

Active data is computer data that can be accessed without any restoration. Active data includes "works in progress that are created and subject to change until the desired work product is reached."[23] This is the most common type of data produced in litigation. The most recent version of a Microsoft Outlook Calendar, the latest version of a document or database, and a company-wide memorandum are all examples of possible active data. This kind of data can be examined and analyzed without the native application using basic applications. However, it is more likely that each file will need to be viewed within the computer application where it originated.

7-2:5.2 METADATA

Metadata is often defined as "data about data" or "information describing the history, tracking, or management of an electronic file [that] is usually not apparent to the reader viewing a hard copy or screen image."[24] This type of data generally consists of descriptive, structural, and administrative information. Similarly, embedded data is "draft language, editorial comments, and other deleted matter . . . not apparent to the reader."[25] Both metadata and embedded data are discoverable in Texas.[26]

Metadata and embedded data can provide counsel with a treasure trove of information. Metadata, for example, often reveals revisions to key documents or alterations to important email communications. Litigators no longer have to rely on a witness's imperfect

---

23. Donald C. Massey, *Discovery of Electronic Data from Motor Carriers—Is Resistance Futile?*, 35 Gonz. L. Rev. 145, 149 (2000).

24. Fed. R. Civ. P. 26(1) (*see* advisory committee's note to the 2006 amendments).

25. *Id.*

26. *See, e.g., In re Honza*, 242 S.W.3d 578, 584 (Tex. App.—Waco 2008, no pet.).

memory to authenticate a document because metadata can provide a document's full history. This data will also inform the lawyer in discovery about whether the opposing party has properly preserved documents during the litigation process. If a document is missing, metadata can expose exactly when it was deleted.

A more streamlined review of documents is also possible with metadata. In departing employee cases, when a lawyer must review thousands of documents in a short period of time, he or she can utilize software review programs that apply metadata in order to efficiently sort, search, and locate "hot" documents.

7-2:5.3 ARCHIVAL DATA

Archival data is information that the user of the computer system can no longer readily access. This kind of data is typically stored on a hard drive or other storage device (such as a CD or thumb drive) to be used for future reference. It is static, preserving earlier and original versions of documents or databases. Archival data may also include automatic back-ups of files. Some archival systems may not be immediately accessible to the user of a computer system, whereas other systems will require an IT professional to access and mine the data.

7-2:5.4 RESIDUAL DATA

Residual data is a type of data that is not active within a computer system. This data can include: (1) data found on media free space; (2) data found in file slack space; and (3) data within files that has functionally been deleted in that it is not visible using the application to which it was created without special recovery techniques. Residual data may contain copies of deleted files and other memory files, which can usually be recovered by a forensic expert. Certainly, most lawyers realize that "deleted" files can now be recovered because the data resides on the hard drive in slack space or other available storage areas. Furthermore, an email system's cache memory can usually be forensically recovered and subsequently used to provide strong evidence against the departing employee. Typically, the computer forensic expert will take an "image" of the departing employee's hard drive and retrieve data from her devices that is otherwise hidden from plain view.

7-2:5.5 HOW MUCH DATA?

Once the practitioner has performed the "five Ws" and identified the custodians, locations, and types of data relevant to his case, she or he must then decide whether to manage the data in-house or with a litigation vendor. A lawyer can easily start scrambling when trying to translate the world of Megabytes, Gigabytes and Terabytes into pages of documents. Below is a helpful guide to understanding the volume of ESI:

Boxes of Paper	Total Pages	Megabytes; Gigabytes; Terabytes
1	2,500	50 Megabytes
10	25,000	500 Megabytes
20	50,000	1 Gigabyte
100	250,000	5 Gigabytes
200	500,000	10 Gigabytes
300	750,000	15 Gigabytes
400	1,000,000	20 Gigabytes
500	1,250,000	25 Gigabytes
1,000	2,500,000	50 Gigabytes
2,000	5,000,000	100 Gigabytes
5,000	12,500,000	250 Gigabytes
10,000	25,000,000	500 Gigabytes
20,000	50,000,000	1 Terabyte
40,000	100,000,000	2 Terabytes
60,000	150,000,000	3 Terabytes

As the chart demonstrates, 5 Gigabytes is exponentially different (and bigger) than 50 Megabytes.

7-2:6 OBTAINING ESI FROM THE DEPARTING EMPLOYEE

Under both the Texas Rules and Federal Rules, the plaintiffs must normally wait several weeks before conducting discovery. While the Texas Rules were recently amended, effective January 1, 2021, to cut down on the time a defendant has to respond to discovery after suit is filed, in federal court a party must often still wait until after a Rule 26 conference and scheduling order is entered before seeking discovery. However, in the incredibly time-sensitive departing employee case, every day spent waiting may mean the loss of customers or a greater misappropriation of vital company secrets. Thus, expedited discovery is often required.

To obtain ESI immediately, the practitioner should file a Motion for Expedited Discovery along with the Application for a Temporary Restraining Order. The application will likely include an order from the judge requiring the preservation and/or return of all ESI in the employee's possession. While the Motion for Expedited Discovery can be drafted within the application, a better practice is to make the motion a separate document.[27]

Counsel should demonstrate to the judge that obtaining discovery (*e.g.*, depositions, requests for production, and interrogatories) is essential prior to the temporary injunction hearing. However, you should show the judge that the request is for a reasonable amount of discovery by limiting the amount of depositions and discovery requests. For example, a proposed order that permits three depositions, ten interrogatories, and ten requests for production sufficiently demonstrates an understanding of what is reasonable. Counsel should also be ready to identify the proposed deponents

---

27. *See* Form 1-011 for a Motion for Expedited Discovery form.

to the judge. In the event the judge seeks to review the requests, the focused discovery requests (which should specifically identify the categories, forms, and location of ESI) need to be prepared in advance. Do not forget about text messages and social media platforms such as Facebook and Twitter. Critical evidence can often be found in a string of text messages or buried in Facebook comments.

When obtaining ESI from a departing employee, be mindful of admissibility of certain information and its authenticity. Often, metadata or other information will self-authenticate the document or communication. Nevertheless, consider how you will introduce the information to the court and what steps you will need to take to use the ESI when it counts.

7-2:7 CONFER AND COOPERATE

As soon as possible, reach out to opposing counsel to set expectations. This is often achieved with a letter or email roughly a week before any formal conference. Identify key issues for your opponent and be specific about what you seek in a concise, clear list. Craig Ball advocates covering the following list of questions:[28]

1. What is the case about?
2. Who are the key players?
3. What events and intervals are relevant?
4. When do preservation duties begin and end?
5. What data are at greatest risk of alteration and destruction?
6. What steps have been or will be taken to preserve ESI?

28. Craig Ball, *Piecing Together the E-Discovery Plan: a Plaintiff's Guide to Meet and Confer*, at 4-12 (2008), http://www.craigball.com/Ball_Piecing%20Together%20the%20EDD%20Plan.pdf .

7. What nonparties hold information that must be preserved?
8. What data require forensically sound preservation?
9. What metadata are relevant, and how will it be preserved, extracted, and produced?
10. What are the defendant's data retention policies and practices?
11. Are there legacy systems to be addressed?
12. What are the current and prior email applications?
13. Are personal email accounts and computer systems involved?
14. What electronic formats are common and in what anticipated volumes?
15. How will the parties handle voicemail, instant messaging and other challenging ESI?
16. What relevant databases exist and how will their contents be discovered?
17. Will paper documents be scanned, and with what resolution, either OCR or metadata (or both)?
18. Are there privilege issues unique to ESI?
19. What search techniques will be used to identify responsive or privileged ESI?
20. If keyword searching is contemplated, can the parties agree on keywords?
21. How will de-duplication be handled, and will data be re-populated for production?

22. What forms of production are offered or sought?
23. How will the parties handle redaction of privileged, irrelevant or confidential content?
24. Will load files accompany document images, and how will they be populated?
25. How will the parties approach file naming and Bates numbering?
26. What ESI will be claimed as not reasonably accessible, and on what bases?
27. Can costs be minimized by shared providers, neutral experts, or special masters?

The practitioner is wise to act reasonably and communicate with the opposing counsel in a respectful manner. Should an ESI dispute turn ugly, the correspondence between the parties will likely be attached as an exhibit to a discovery motion. A paper trail showing cooperation and transparency will allow you to wear the white hat on the day of the hearing.

7-2:8 PROCESSING THE COLLECTED (OR RECEIVED) INFORMATION

Once you have collected discovery, there are several steps you can take to efficiently—and accurately—process the collected information. First, the practitioner must determine whether or not he should hire an e-discovery expert. An expert in this area is helpful for many reasons—most importantly, to help the practitioner avoid common ESI pitfalls. The following elements should be considered when you and your e-discovery expert are planning the next steps[29]:

1. De-duplication (the removal of identical

29. Shannon Armstrong, *et al*, *Texas Perspectives on E-Discovery*, 168-69 (State Bar of Texas 2013).

information) can save the practitioner time that would otherwise be wasted on reviewing the same document multiple times.

2. A great deal hinges on counsel's ability to search the ESI efficiently and accurately. If, for example, counsel can run a global search for terms, he will not have to enter and search each individual document for the same terms. However, a common pitfall will ensnare those who rely too heavily on an impressive database search because, regardless of advances in technology, the ability to make a document searchable is only as strong as the actual quality of the document itself. Therefore, use caution that you do not overlook common misspellings or abbreviations when searching the ESI database. Develop an expansive list of search terms and adapt the list as the documents are reviewed.

3. Whether you choose to use the Bates-numbering system (a standard practice in many firms) or a different system, developing a user-friendly manner of document identification is essential. Then, the collected documents can be easily tracked and managed as they are used throughout the case.

4. Processing data can alter metadata. Take steps to preserve your metadata.

5. Codifying allows you to organize the document's objective and subjective data. Objective data includes elements like the document's date and author. Subjective

data includes elements like the document's relevance, privilege, and notes from the attorney. After codification, searching through the documents is faster and the results are more specific.

6. ESI, in some instances however, can slow efficiency. For example, if you need to open a document's native file (*i.e.*, a spreadsheet in Excel), minutes can be wasted waiting for the new program to open and load. This lag does not exist when flipping through hard copies of excel spreadsheets.

When preparing for production, comply with the applicable rules and produce the ESI in either the ordinary course of business or categorically. Whichever method you choose, make sure it is defensible and the opposing party cannot make accusations of an intentionally disorganized production or data dump. If possible, index your production or effectively use document management software to track the production. Identify "hot" documents and issue code documents in a manner that will make your hearing preparation and brief writing more manageable.

Navigating the world of ESI in any case is challenging. The departing employee case is no different and sometimes even more difficult because of expedited discovery. Be proactive. Engage your client, opposing counsel, and experts early in the process to make the collection and discovery of ESI as streamlined as possible.

7-3 INFORMAL DISCOVERY[30]

Regardless of changes in technology, one fact remains constant: attorneys and their clients seek efficient litigation practices. Such practice includes informal litigation. Because cases are

30. The author thanks Greg P. McAllister, an associate at Littler Mendelson, P.C., for contributing this section of the chapter.

distinguishable from one another, it is best to tailor informal discovery to each case's facts and circumstances.

7-3:1 INITIAL CONSIDERATIONS

The most attractive characteristics of informal discovery are the potential to (1) uncover relevant facts and (2) lower costs of formal discovery in litigation. This potential is often realized for multiple reasons.

7-3:1.1 FOCUS AND NARROW ISSUES

Uncovering available information before, or shortly after, a lawsuit is filed allows a party to focus its goals. Understanding what is known—and what is unknown—helps clarify issues and define the nature of a lawsuit or potential lawsuit. In employment litigation, employers may rush to get a restraining order or injunction based on their fear that a former employee is improperly disclosing confidential information, soliciting customers or employees, or competing with the former employer. But mere fear of breaching a noncompetition agreement is insufficient for such injunctive relief.[31] Instead, employers and their counsel are better served by first analyzing available data.

7-3:1.2 ASSESS CLAIMS, ISSUES, AND DAMAGES

Analyzing and understanding the available information allows for a better assessment of a lawsuit and its damages. Such understanding supports early trial planning and applications for injunctive relief. As practitioners often experience, a judge's determination regarding injunctive relief after an employee

31. *See Shoreline Gas, Inc. v. McGaughey*, No. 13-07-364-CV, 2008 Tex. App. LEXIS 2760, at *34 (Tex. App.—Corpus Christi Apr. 17, 2008, no pet.) (mem. op.) ("Fear or apprehension of the possibility of injury" is "insufficient to establish a probability of irreparable injury as would support a temporary injunction." The employer "produced no evidence that [defendant] had actually breached or violated any covenant or undertaking contained in the Agreement, or even that [defendant] had threatened to breach or violate any such undertakings.").

departs often turns on the lawsuit's most pertinent facts, specific details regarding actions taken and to be enjoined, and specific damages sustained—or imminent—at the time injunctive relief is requested. Of course, understanding relevant facts also supports a more realistic litigation budget.

7-3:1.3 PRESERVE AND UTILIZE OWN INFORMATION

To find available information, employers should start by preserving and utilizing their own information. A departing employee's electronic communications should be immediately preserved and analyzed. Indeed, attorneys usually send preservation letters to clients to support discovery and to develop a case's facts. If a former employer has a specific idea regarding a potential wrongdoing, then keyword searches of email are often productive. Also, analysis of the departing employee's deleted email and sent email may contain relevant information. Employee calendars may provide insight regarding an employee's preparations to leave and join a competitor. Web browsing history and other related electronic information may be relevant and provide useful information. However, a practitioner should be careful not to alter the original data when reviewing a departing employee's activity as it could later be used as evidence. Be aware that not all potentially relevant information is electronic. A former employee may leave hard copies or other relevant notes behind on her desk. Depending on circumstances, interviewing a departed employee's former supervisors, staff, peers, and other co-workers may provide insight and reveal information. Many employees will describe how and when they were solicited for other employment by a departed employee. Interviewing clients is usually much more sensitive, depending on the client, employer, and circumstances. Some clients are more than willing to support litigation on behalf of a party, especially when the client's interests are relevant. But many clients are busy or justifiably concerned about becoming involved in someone else's litigation.

7-3:1.4 PREVENT SURPRISES; IDENTIFY DEFENSES AND COUNTERCLAIMS

Obtaining information possessed by the client is crucial to preventing unwanted surprises located in a client's documents, files, and communications. Also, a departing employee is often able to identify defenses and counterclaims through informal discovery. For example, former employees may review their final payments to discover that they were underpaid.

7-3:2 KNOW THE CLIENT'S BUSINESS

"The more you engage with customers the clearer things become and the easier it is to determine what you should be doing."
—John Russell, President, Harley Davidson.

Before informal discovery and forensic investigation begin, attorneys should understand their client's industry and business. Researching the client's industry provides the attorney with a context for informal discovery. Understanding such context is crucial in employment litigation involving a departing employee because the attorney must understand whether a departed employee is truly competing with her former employer. An attorney might assume that a departing employee is competing simply by working for another company in the same industry. A closer look, however, may show that, while the new employer may be involved in the former employer's industry, the departed employee's job duties are materially different than his or her prior duties and the new employer's services may be dramatically different than the former employer.

For example, some clients (*e.g.*, law firms and hospitals) have unique ethical constraints. So, attorneys for such types of clients must understand that these clients may have unique ethical constraints. A law firm attempting to enforce a noncompetition agreement must be advised regarding attorney ethics.[32] Also,

32. *See e.g.*, Tex. R. Disc. P. 5.06 (Restrictions on Right to Practice: "A lawyer shall

physicians have special ethical guidelines. The Health Insurance Portability and Accountability Act (HIPAA) privacy rules are the most obvious. Hospitals and physicians are also aware of other guidelines regarding physicians' social media use that may be relevant in litigation.[33] These issues may affect both informal and formal discovery.

Understanding clients' businesses includes knowing their policies and procedures. Conversations should often begin with discussion about a relevant noncompetition agreement, but the conversation should eventually turn toward discussion of other agreements (*e.g.*, nondisclosure agreements, jury waivers, arbitration agreements, and employee handbooks). Also, attorneys and clients should communicate regarding publicity. Paula Deen faced an employee's discrimination claims and was likely advised regarding the advantages and risks of a public lawsuit.[34] Her deposition comments became a lightning rod for criticism that threatened her entire career, regardless of the lawsuit's outcome. It is increasingly common, and ethically concerning, for deposition videos to be uploaded to YouTube and web-based video sites. It is certainly a matter of time before looping deposition clips or trial testimony are posted on Facebook or Instagram accounts. Indeed, due to the pandemic era, Texas courts now regularly stream remote

---

not participate in offering or making: (a) a partnership or employment agreement that restricts the rights of a lawyer to practice after termination of the relationship, except an agreement concerning benefits upon retirement; or (b) an agreement in which a restriction on the lawyer's right to practice is part of the settlement of a suit or controversy, except that as part of the settlement of a disciplinary proceeding against a lawyer an agreement may be made placing restrictions on the right of that lawyer to practice.").

33. *See e.g.*, Federation of State Medical Boards, *Model Policy Guidelines for the Appropriate Use of Social Media and Social Networking in Medical Practice* (Apr. 2012), https://meridian.allenpress.com/jmr/article/98/2/27/212515/Model-Policy-Guidelines-for-the-Appropriate-Use-of. ("Social media has enormous potential for both physicians and their patients. It can be used to disseminate information and forge meaningful professional relationships. However, these benefits must occur within the proper framework of professional ethics, and physicians need information on the importance of maintaining the same professional and ethical standards in their online activity or communications using other forms of electronic media.").

34. *See* Corinne Lestch, *Paula Deen's sexual harassment, discrimination lawsuit dismissed*, New York Daily News (Aug. 24, 2013), http://www.nydailynews.com/entertainment/gossip/paula-deen-discrimination-lawsuit-dismissed-article-1.1435396.

hearings to YouTube, increasing the public exposure of litigation. Your clients may be wary of lawsuits that cast them in a negative light and threaten their relationships with customers; such lawsuits are often a source for informal discovery in future litigation.

It is increasingly common for Twitter users and bloggers to provide links to newly filed lawsuits, especially regarding unique concerns or cutting-edge issues. Such attention may assist—or hinder—informal discovery.

Attorneys should also know a client's history and experience. There are several questions that you can ask your clients. Does the client routinely litigate issues regarding departing employees? What are the client's expectations and how do they differ from the client's goals? Does the client understand the importance of consistently enforcing restrictive covenants against departing employees that breach those covenants? What is the client's ability, sophistication, and understanding of informal and formal discovery? What is the client's budget constraints and concerns regarding discovery?

7-3:3 WHERE TO LOOK

7-3:3.1 EMPLOYERS' WEBSITES

When looking for information related to either a new or former employer, reviewing the employer's website is a solid starting point. Biographical profiles often provide insight regarding potential witnesses, corporate representatives, identification of fiduciaries and supervisors, titles, roles, obligations, and other relevant information. Also, some employers will assert that some information is "confidential" but will have posted that "confidential" information on their website. A company's mission statement could indicate its current status as (or plans to become) a competitor of another company. In restrictive covenant cases, employers' websites could show clients in limited or wide-ranging places, and thus a departing employee could claim that geographic restrictions related to her former employer's business are overbroad and/or unreasonable. Analysis of an employer's website should not be limited to the current webpage, but also archived files, potentially accessible through information retrieval websites (*e.g.*, Wayback Machine), which may provide useful information.[35]

A departing employee's biographical information on an employer's website may provide insight. A new employer may show that an employee's duties are similar to that employee's duties for a former employer—thus showing duties that are related to competition or solicitation of a former employer's customers. Also, an employee's biographical page could include information related to his or her department and representative clients. A departing employee's profile that remains on the *former* employer's website could communicate many different messages to a judge in an injunction hearing. Departing employees may complain that they did not give permission to a former employer to continue posting the employee's picture. The former employer may claim that it was so surprised by an employee's sudden departure that the departed employee's profile was not taken down before a temporary restraining order was sought by the former employer.

35. *See Sam's Riverside, Inc. v. Intercon Solutions, Inc.*, 790 F. Supp. 2d 965, 980 (S.D. Iowa 2011) ("The Internet Archive has created a service known as the 'Wayback Machine' which 'makes it possible [for users] to surf more than 120 billion pages stored in the Internet Archive's web archive.'" . . . "Christopher Butler is an employee of the Internet Archive who has personal knowledge about how the Wayback Machine works. . . . Other courts have concluded that an affidavit from an Internet Archive employee is sufficient to authenticate screen shots taken from Archive.org. . . . [T]he Butler Affidavit is sufficient to authenticate the specific screen shots that are mentioned in—and attached to—the Butler Affidavit. However, none of the Contested Screen Shots are attached to the Butler Affidavit; therefore, the Butler Affidavit does not authenticate any of the Contested Screen Shots. . . . Therefore, Plaintiff may not rely upon the Contested Screen shots in order to avoid summary judgment.").

7-3:3.2 EMPLOYERS' PUBLICLY AVAILABLE CORPORATE INFORMATION

Publicly available company data can provide significant insight. Companies register information regarding formation, location, agents for service, and other valuable information.

In Texas, whether a company is filing or responding to a lawsuit, the plaintiff-company needs to be registered with the Secretary of State.[36] This requirement is Texas's "closed door" statute. Thus, whether advising a plaintiff-company or a defendant-company, attorneys should check the Texas Secretary of State website to determine whether the plaintiff filing a lawsuit is registered in Texas.[37]

Another valuable publicly available source is data, such as SEC filings, regarding publicly held companies. For example, the Electronic Data-Gathering, Analysis, and Retrieval (EDGAR) system is often a valuable tool to determine a company's past, future, and present employment agreements, actions, and plans.[38]

36. Tex. Bus. Orgs. Code § 9.051(b) ("A foreign filing entity or the entity's legal representative may not maintain an action, suit, or proceeding in a court of this state, brought either directly by the entity or in the form of a derivative action in the entity's name, on a cause of action that arises out of the transaction of business in this state unless the foreign filing entity is registered in accordance with this chapter. This subsection does not affect the rights of an assignee of the foreign filing entity as: (1) the holder in due course of a negotiable instrument; or (2) the bona fide purchaser for value of a warehouse receipt, security, or other instrument made negotiable by law.").

37. Texas Secretary of State, *SOS Direct* (last visited June 20, 2013), http://www.sos.state.tx.us/corp/sosda/.

38. EDGAR, http://www.sec.gov/investor/pubs/edgarguide.htm. ("The SEC's EDGAR database provides free public access to corporate information, allowing you to quickly research a company's financial information and operations by reviewing registration statements, prospectuses and periodic reports filed on Forms 10-K and 10-Q. You also can find information about recent corporate events reported on Form 8-K but that a company does not have to disclose to investors. EDGAR also provides access to comment and response letters relating to disclosure filings made after August 1, 2004, and reviewed by either the Division of Corporation Finance or the Division of Investment Management. On May 22, 2006, the staffs of the Divisions of Corporation Finance and Investment Management began to use the EDGAR system to issue notifications of effectiveness for Securities Act registration statements and post-effective amendments, other than those that become effective automatically by law.").

7-3:3.3 EMPLOYERS' PUBLICLY ACCESSIBLE "CONFIDENTIAL" INFORMATION ON THE INTERNET

Consideration for restrictive covenants may include the provision of "confidential information." Also, claims against departing employees may include misappropriation of trade secrets. At the same time, a former employer's social media account may zealously reach out to clients and the public and potentially undermine the confidentiality of any related "confidential information" and "trade secrets." It may be argued that it is inconsistent to assert that a client list is confidential if that same client list is publicly available.

In *Sasqua Group Inc. v. Courtney*, a recruiting firm asserted the confidentiality of clients as a trade secret, but the defendant persuasively argued that "virtually all personnel in the capital markets industry that [Plaintiff] serves have their contact information on Bloomberg, LinkedIn, Facebook or other publicly available databases."[39] Based on that argument and others, the court noted, "[a]t the very least, Plaintiffs have failed to prove that the general contact information for [Plaintiff] clients is not readily ascertainable through outside sources, such as the Internet or telephone books, or directories of firms in the financial services industry, like the ones demonstrated by the Defendants at the hearing."[40] Although that case is distinguishable, it highlights that the disclosure of alleged confidential information, especially on publicly accessible websites, may render the information not as confidential as a party asserts.

Regas Christou, R.M.C. Holdings, LLC v. Beatport, LLC demonstrates that courts may be persuaded to at least deny summary judgment because a company's list of social media "friends" is

39. *Sasqua Grp. Inc. v. Courtney*, No. 10-528 (ADS) (AKT), 2010 U.S. Dist. LEXIS, at *10 (E.D.N.Y. Aug. 2, 2010).

40. *Sasqua Grp. Inc. v. Courtney*, No. 10-528 (ADS) (AKT), 2010 U.S. Dist. LEXIS, at *42 (E.D.N.Y. Aug. 2, 2010).

"actually akin to a database of contact information."[41] The court explained that

> [T]rade secret is not merely the list of names but their email and contact information as well as the ability to notify them and promote directly to them via MySpace accounts. Plaintiffs argue that 'the critical information consisting of these friends' personal contact information and their permission to be contacted cannot be compiled from publicly available sources.' The names themselves, readily available to the public, are not the important factor. The ancillary information connected to those names cannot be obtained from public directories and is not readily ascertainable from outside sources, and thus this militates in favor of trade secret classification.

Accordingly, departing employees—and their new employers and potential co-defendants—accused of misappropriating confidential information should analyze a former employer's publicly accessible social media accounts. Potential sources include Facebook friends, Twitter and Instagram followers, LinkedIn connections, and more. Also, departing employees should look to their own accounts. Were they encouraged or discouraged by a former employer to engage with clients via friending or the like? If so, was there an expectation that the employee's account was owned by the employer? Further, departing employees should look to other sources such as employers' blogs, EDGAR profiles, and other publicly accessible sources.

41. *Christou v. Beatport, LLC*, 849 F.Supp. 2d 1055, 1074 (D. Colo. 2012) (list of "friends" on MySpace was alleged trade secret; claim survived motion for summary judgment).

7-3:3.4 DEPARTING EMPLOYEES' PUBLICLY ACCESSIBLE INFORMATION ON THE INTERNET

Departing employees' publicly accessible information may also be valuable. Indeed, former employers might first be alerted to departing employees' actions by social media activity. A departing employee might violate nonsolicitation clauses by soliciting former co-employees in messages via social media. Also, a former employer might see that a departing employee's new Facebook friend or LinkedIn connection is a client of the former employer. Although simply connecting with a former employer's client might not show solicitation, the connection can signal to the employer to look for other potential signs of solicitation or competition.

Departing employees' messages to former clients are significant, but the message's language may be closely scrutinized. For example, a Massachusetts court noted that there is a difference between a hairstylist with a noncompetition agreement contacting former clients and a Facebook announcement:

[T]he evidence that [a departing employee] solicited [former employer]'s clients, or misused its confidential information, is thin. [Former employer] first cites the case of its client Wendy Goodwin Kaiser. Four days after [the departing employee] resigned from [former employer], David Paul Salons, her new employer, posted a 'public announcement' on [the departing employee]'s Facebook page, noting [the departing employee's] new affiliation with David Paul. In the comment section below that post, Ms. Kaiser posted a comment which said, See you tomorrow [the departing employee]!' Ms. Kaiser then canceled her appointment at [the former employer] for the next day. But it does not constitute "solicitation" of [the former employer]'s customers to post a notice on [the departing employee]'s Facebook page that [the departing employee] is joining David Paul Salons. It would be a very different matter if [the departing employee] had contacted

Ms. Kaiser to tell her that she was moving to David Paul Salons, but there is no evidence of any such contact.[42]

Former employers may also benefit from analyzing a departing employee's social media account to assert other claims and defenses. If the Fair Labor Standards Act (FLSA) is raised by a departing employee, the former employer may look at times and dates of employees' past social media posts to determine whether such posts were made during working hours. Also, former employers facing counterclaims may benefit from social media research. In one case, a former employer was granted summary judgment against a former employee who was fired after posting Facebook pictures while on leave under the Family and Medical Leave Act (FMLA).[43] In another case, a plaintiff's case alleging sexual harassment was undermined by her Facebook posts that were sexual in nature.[44]

Other potential sources include Freedom of Information Act requests, personnel files, court filings, Public Access to Court Electronic Records (PACER), property records, and LexisNexis for relevant data.

Former employers may want to consider user terms of a social media account. First, the retention policy may be significant. Also, if a former employee misrepresents his past experience or his current profile, the former employer may want to report that information as inaccurate.[45]

---

42. *Invidia, LLC v. DiFonzo*, 30 Mass. L. Rep. 390 (Mass. Super. Ct. 2012) (emphasis added).

43. *Jaszczyszyn v. Advantage Health Physician Network*, 504 Fed. Appx. 440, 444 (6th Cir. 2012) (unpublished).

44. *Targonski v. City of Oak Ridge*, 921 F. Supp. 2d 820, 834 (E.D. Tenn. 2013).

45. *See e.g.*, LinkedIn, *Reporting Inaccurate Information on Another Member's Profile*, https://www.linkedin.com/help/linkedin/answer/30200?lang=en (last visited February 8, 2021) (complete a "Notice of Inaccurate Profile Information" claim). Employers must be wary of issues regarding accusations of perjury, retaliation, defamation, libel, tortious interference, and related claims.

7-3:3.5 FORENSICS — FORMER EMPLOYEES' RETURNED DATA

Forensic analysis is discussed more thoroughly in a preceding chapter, but a few notes should be made here regarding informal discovery. Former employers conduct forensic analysis of electronic devices and data accessed by a departing employee. The former employee's work computer should be imaged and preserved. Former employees' work email accounts, as well as related calendars and contact lists, and inner-company messaging activity (i.e., Slack or Microsoft Teams) are often excellent sources of discovering information.

Forensic review may show that a former employee utilized a "cleaner" or "eraser" program to delete information from a computer's hard drive. Courts are taking note that running such programs (*e.g.*, the "Evidence Eliminator") may indicate a departing employee's improper actions. A Virginia court explained:

> For [Plaintiff] to download and run a program whose express purpose is deletion of evidence in direct response to the Magistrate Judge's order that his computer be produced for inspection was to blatantly disregard his duties in the judicial system under which he sought relief. The Court finds [Plaintiff]'s conduct to be egregious and highly contemptuous of the inspection order. [Plaintiff] has forfeited his right to pursue his claims with this Court any further. [Plaintiff]'s attempt to create a distinction between "running" Evidence Eliminator and "using it to destroy documents" is not convincing in the least. Nor is [Plaintiff]'s argument that he was not reasonably aware that his work computer might contain information related to his employment discrimination claims.[46]

46. *Taylor v. Mitre Corp.*, No. 1:11-cv-1247, 2012 U.S. Dist. LEXIS 161318, at *6 (E.D.

Further, a transaction log may show a departing employee's web history while on a former employer's computer. It would be interesting to discover if the employee visited a post on Lifehacker titled, "How Can I Save All My Emails for a Personal Backup?"[47] On that post, the posed question was: "Dear Lifehacker, I'm leaving my job and want to take my work emails with me. I've been burned at jobs before, and it became very useful to have an email paper trail behind me. **How can I save all the emails so I can access them in the future, just in case I need them?** Signed, Paranoid Worker Bee." The author responded by explaining how to save work emails to and from various email servers, like Gmail and Outlook.[48]

7-3:3.6 INTERVIEW THE CLIENT

Interviewing a client is a crucial aspect to understanding a lawsuit or potential lawsuit. An employer's representatives are often the attorney's main contact. However, it is just as common that others—a principal, executive, human resources administrator, manager, supervisor, or co-worker—are more directly involved and also understand the relevant facts. These initial interviews provide attorneys with the ability to understand a matter, develop proof, and assess issues. Interviews with the client and its employees should touch on the elements of the case.

A former employer may seek greater insight from co-workers to determine whether a departing employee was encouraging others to join her at a new employer. Also, supervisors should

Va. Nov. 8, 2012).

47. M. Pinola, *How Can I Save All My Emails for a Personal Backup?*, Lifehacker (Mar. 14, 2013), http://lifehacker.com/5990556/how-can-i-save-all-my-work-emails-for-a-personal-backup.

48. After the author's initial post—in response to commentators—she updated the article by writing, "As a number of commenters have pointed out, your company owns your work email. To avoid any legal ramifications, check with your IT department or supervisor about doing this. (Also, if you batch download all of your emails at once, it could raise some eyebrows, as About's Human Resources site points out). It's also worth noting that, of course, these methods all work for personal email as well, so these tricks are useful no matter what you're trying to back up."

be able to provide insight regarding any clients contacted before an employee departed. The former employer's investigations may seem very abrupt if there are time constraints related to seeking an injunction for a recently departed employee.

Interviewing departing employees requires an understanding of their likely current situation. Changing jobs is often stressful, and being sued for changing jobs is even more stressful. Also, departing employees may have some guilt or concern for their new employers because the employees may feel as though they have created a problem—instead of a good impression. The employees also might be subject to an injunction that prevents or impedes their ability to earn commissions and certain bonuses. It is often vital to impress upon departing employees that any "bad" facts must be disclosed to their attorneys immediately—an attorney would almost certainly prefer to hear perceived "bad" facts from the client than from an adverse party.

New employers should be made aware that interviews may often be significant for multiple reasons. First, there may be a recently filed lawsuit that seeks rapidly approaching injunction hearings. There may also be expedited discovery to produce documents and seek a corporate representative's deposition. Thus, the interviews should have an eye toward designated topics, so the attorney can identify the proper deponents for upcoming depositions on the new employer's behalf.

Regardless of the client (former employer, new employer, or departing employee), the focus of the first interview is often:

1. Establish your working relationship and understand your client's concerns.
2. Listen to the client's version of the facts. An early chronological explanation of facts often provides context for an entire case—although it is not unusual for the

chronology to shift during a lawsuit as facts are recalled.

3. Ask questions that you anticipate the adverse party will ask. This structure allows the client to understand facts, outlines a broader view of the lawsuit, and begins to develop a strategy.

7-3:4 HOW TO LOOK (AND HOW NOT TO LOOK) FOR WEB-BASED DATA

The best starting point to find relevant web-based information is often Google and other search engines.

Clients may want to assist with such searches to help reduce costs, but there are always concerns from both litigation and business perspectives when clients get involved in anything beyond notifying their attorney of sources of evidence. Also, a client's nonexempt employees should not assist off-the-clock unless the employer is willing to pay overtime. Attorneys should be wary regarding being logged in to a social media account because some accounts (*e.g.*, LinkedIn) may show the names of persons that viewed an account.

Ethically, publicly accessible information may be searched. Attorneys should not create fake accounts to contact adverse parties and/or witnesses. Similarly, neither paralegals nor other third parties should make such a friend request of adverse parties.[49] The key consideration is what advice is given. Also, attorneys should not advise clients to scrub accounts.[50] And

49. *See, e.g.*, Phila. Bar Ass'n Prof'l Guidance Comm., advised in Opinion 2009-02 (Mar. 2009).

50. *See, e.g.*, Margaret DiBianca, *Complex Ethical Issues of Social Media*, American Inns of Court: The BENCHER (Nov./Dec. 2010) ("Suppose you discover that your client's Facebook page does, in fact, contain several unsavory images or comments that the opposing party would be delighted to use in litigation. Your initial reaction upon viewing this potentially negative evidence may be to instruct the client to delete the content or even her Facebook account. [ABA] Model Rule 3.4(a) may prohibit the lawyer from making this recommendation. Model Rule 3.4(a) prohibit lawyers from unlawfully altering or

attorneys should be wary of overzealous investigation; for example, they should not log in to former employees' personal social media accounts.[51]

7-4 RULE 202

In the departing employee case, pre-suit depositions are often useful tools for the former employer who believes (but cannot prove) there has been nefarious activity. Rule 202 governs pre-suit depositions.[52] A Rule 202 proceeding, however, is not a separate lawsuit. Instead, it functions either in anticipation of a separate lawsuit[53] or as a means to investigate a claim.[54] Rule 202 depositions can be powerful tools not only to obtain information but also to act as a "shot across the bow" where you suspect someone of misbehaving.

7-4:1 TWO REASONS TO TAKE RULE 202 DEPOSITIONS

Courts have held that "a deposition under Rule 202 can be taken for two distinct and separate reasons: (1) to perpetuate or obtain testimony for use in an anticipated suit; or (2) to investigate a potential claim."[55]

The order granting a Rule 202 petition must contain one of the

---

destroying evidence and from assisting others from doing so. Lawyers have an ethical duty to preserve electronic evidence, including social networking profiles. And the failure to preserve can lead to significant sanctions. Instructing a client to delete evidence, including the client's Facebook page, may constitute spoliation of evidence, which could result in an adverse-inference instruction to a jury or sanctions against the attorney. The better alternative is to have the client set her profile page as 'private.' The opposing party will not have direct access to the contents of her page but could request the evidence through formal discovery channels. That is, of course, if the opposing counsel is diligent.").

51. *See* Tex. Civ. Prac. & Rem. Code § 143.001; Tex. Pen. Code § 33.01 *et seq*. (Harmful Access by Computer Act).

52. Tex. R. Civ. P. 202.

53. Tex. R. Civ. P. 202.2(d)(1).

54. Tex. R. Civ. P. 202.2(d)(2).

55. *In re Denton*, No. 10-08-00255-CV, 2009 Tex. App. LEXIS 1322, at *1 (Tex. App.—Waco Feb. 25, 2009, no pet.) (mem. op.)

following findings: (1) that allowing the deposition may prevent a failure or delay of justice in an anticipated suit; or (2) that the likely benefits of allowing the deposition to investigate a potential claim outweigh the burden or expense of the procedure.[56] The findings cannot be implied but rather must be explicitly stated by the court.[57]

A Rule 202 pre-suit deposition is not "an end within itself."[58] Rather, its role is ancillary. The purpose of a Rule 202 deposition is to aid the anticipated suit or claim. In fact, discovery and depositions under Rule 202 are restricted to the same discovery and depositions that would occur "if the anticipated suit or potential claim had been filed."[59]

The Texas Supreme Court has cautioned that Rule 202 depositions are not for routine use, even though they are an increasingly popular discovery tool in Texas.[60] Resolving a split in authority among the courts of appeals, the Court held that Rule 202 depositions are not permitted before an expert report is filed.[61]

As previously stated, a Rule 202 petition may be filed in anticipation of suit or to investigate a potential claim.[62] The petition's requirements vary slightly, depending on the intended function.

---

56. Tex. R. Civ. P. 202.4(a); *see, e.g., In re Hewlett Packard*, 212 S.W.3d 356, 363 (Tex. App.—Austin 2006, orig. proceeding) (petitioner did not show that benefit of potentially avoiding lawsuit outweighed burden of disclosure of trade secrets).

57. *In re Does*, 337 S.W.3d 862, 865 (Tex. 2011).

58. *In re Wolf*, 341 S.W.3d 932, 933 (Tex. 2011).

59. *Id.*

60. *See In re Jorden*, 249 S.W.3d 416, 423 (Tex. 2007) (orig. proceeding).

61. *Id.*

62. However, other Circuits are in disagreement as to whether the Rule authorizes two distinct, mutually exclusive depositions. *See In re Denton*, No. 10-08-00255-CV, 2009 Tex. App. LEXIS 1322, at *1 (Tex. App.—Waco Feb. 25, 2009, no pet.) (mem. op.), *contra In re Emergency Consultants, Inc.*, 292 S.W.3d 78, 79 (Tex. App.—Houston [14th Dist.] 2007, orig. proceeding) (per curiam).

7-4:1.1 IN ANTICIPATION OF A SUIT

If filed in anticipation of a suit, the Rule 202 petition must state: "The petitioner anticipates the institution of a suit in which the petitioner may be a party."[63] In addition to the aforementioned wording, the petition must also identify the subject matter of the anticipated action and explain the petitioner's interest in it.[64]

The names, addresses, and telephone numbers of any persons potentially opposing the petitioner in the anticipated suit must also be included. If the potential opposition's personal information is not included on the petition, the petition must, at the very least, contain a description of those persons and a statement affirming the information will be ascertained through diligent inquiry.[65]

On the other hand, a Rule 202 petition filed in anticipation of a suit is not required to allege a specific cause of action.[66]

7-4:1.2 TO INVESTIGATE A POTENTIAL CLAIM

If filed to investigate a potential claim, the Rule 202 petition must state: "The Petitioner seeks to investigate a potential claim by or against the petitioner."[67]

Unlike a Rule 202 petition in anticipation of a separate suit, a Rule 202 petition to investigate a potential claim is not required to identify persons with an adverse interest.[68]

Moreover, because the rules do not require this type of petitioner to actually expect a separate lawsuit in order to investigate a

63. Tex. R. Civ. P. 202.2(d)(1).

64. Tex. R. Civ. P. 202.2(e).

65. Tex. R. Civ. P. 202.2(f).

66. *City of Houston v. U.S. Filter Wastewater Grp.*, 190 S.W.3d 242, 245 n.2 (Tex. App.—Houston [1st Dist.] 2006, no pet.).

67. Tex. R. Civ. P. 202.2(d)(2).

68. *See* Tex. R. Civ. P. 202.2(f).

potential claim, a prudent practitioner is able to make good-faith inquiry before determining whether or not a suit should be filed.[69]

7-4:2 NOTICE AND SERVICE REQUIREMENTS

Other requirements of Rule 202 procedure include notice and service. Notice of the hearing must be served on the intended deponent, as well as any potential adverse parties named in the petition, at least fifteen (15) days prior to the hearing.[70] Successively, any deponent or potential adverse party may object to the deposition—first by appearing at the hearing and later by filing a motion to vacate the order. A Rule 202 proceeding cannot be removed to federal court.[71]

After the hearing, the court must make one of two required findings:

> (1) Allowing the deposition may prevent a failure or delay of justice in an anticipated suit; or (2) the likely benefits of allowing the deposition to investigate a potential claim outweigh the burden or expense of the procedure.[72]

7-4:3 DETAILS OF DEPOSITION

The court order must state the type of deposition (*i.e.*, oral or written) to be conducted and may also state the time and place the deposition will occur.[73] Listing the time and place information in the notice is also sufficient. Some courts have interpreted Rule 202 as prohibiting any form of pre-suit discovery other than the

---

69. *See* Tex. R. Civ. P. 13.

70. Tex. R. Civ. P. 202.3(a).

71. *Texas v. Real Parties in Interest*, 259 F.3d 387, 394 (5th Cir. 2001); *Mayfield-George v. Texas Rehab. Comm'n*, 197 F.R.D. 280, 283 (N.D. Tex. 2000) (same).

72. Tex. R. Civ. P. 202.4; *In re Emergency Consultants, Inc.*, 292 S.W.3d 78, 79 (Tex. App.—Houston [14th Dist.] 2007, orig. proceeding).

73. Tex. R. Civ. P. 202.4.

deposition, including the production of documents.[74] However, several courts have held that "there is nothing in the language of Rule 202" which inhibits the petitioner from including a request for document production in addition to the deposition.[75]

7-4:3.1 DOCUMENTS UNDER RULE 202

The Texas court in Anand seems to suggest that there is nothing stopping a petitioner from including a request for document production in addition to the deposition, but this is not a definitive conclusion to the issue. However, a few Texas courts have ruled that allowing document discovery in the context of a Rule 202 petition is improper.[76] In *Pickrell*, the court found that the trial court abused its discretion in ordering the production of documents.[77] More recently, courts have held that *Anand*'s holding is "more sound reasoning" than *Pickrell* and concluded that document discovery is permissible in the context of Rule 202.[78] Thus, the current weight of authority is slightly in favor of allowing document discovery.

While Rule 202 is silent on its face about document production, many Texas practitioners include document requests with requests for permission to take Rule 202 depositions, and with notices regarding such depositions. *Pickrell* provides appellate authority opposing that practice, finding that Rule 202 does not provide for such document discovery nor imply that it might be

74. *In re Akzo Nobel Chem., Inc.*, 24 S.W.3d 919, 921 (Tex. App.—Beaumont 2000, orig. proceeding).

75. *See, e.g.*, *In re Anand*, No. 01-12-01106-CV, 2013 Tex. App. LEXIS 4157, at *8 (Tex. App. Houston 1st Dist. Apr. 2, 2013, no pet.) (mem. op.) (per curiam).

76. *In re Pickrell*, No. 10-17-00091-CV, 2017 Tex. App. LEXIS, at *1 (Tex. App.—Waco Apr. 19, 2017, no pet. h.); *In re Akzo Nobel Chem., Inc.*, 24 S.W.3d 919, 921 (Tex. App.— Beaumont 2000, no pet.).

77. *In re Pickrell*, No. 10-17-00091-CV, 2017 Tex. App. LEXIS, at *1 (Tex. App.—Waco Apr. 19, 2017, no pet. h.).

78. *In re City of Tatum*, 567 S.W.3d 800, 808 (Tex. App.— Tyler 2018); *City of Dallas v. City of Corsicana*, No. 10-14-00090-CV, 2015 WL 4985935, at *6 (Tex. App. Aug. 20, 2015).

available.[79] There are cases on both sides of this issue, and the Texas Supreme Court has not yet settled the dispute.

7-4:4 CONTESTING A RULE 202 PETITION

In re Hewlett Packard adequately demonstrates how a Rule 202 petition can be fiercely contested.[80] The case began when Dell filed a verified petition against its chief competitor, Hewlett-Packard, to conduct pre-suit depositions on three former Dell employees suspected of misappropriating company trade secrets. The trial court granted Dell's petition. The appellate court was tasked with deciding whether or not the lower court abused its discretion, when it granted a petition that, in effect, made Dell privy to any Hewlett-Packard trade secrets revealed in the depositions.

Hewlett-Packard argued the same concern after Dell filed its Rule 202 petition to "investigate potential claims it may have against various parties,"[81] asserting that information pertaining to the work the deponents were doing for Hewlett-Packard (the information that Dell sought to discover in the depositions) included trade secrets. Nonetheless, the trial court's balancing test found the "likely benefit of allowing Dell, Inc. to take the requested depositions to investigate potential claims [outweighed] the burden or expense of this procedure."[82] The trial court also resolved the issue of potential confidential disclosures by finding that a protective order would adequately safeguard the confidential information.[83]

The case then progressed to the appellate court on mandamus. In front of this court, Hewlett-Packard argued the balancing test

79. *In re Pickrell*, No. 10-17-00091-CV, 2017 Tex. App. LEXIS, at *1 (Tex. App.—Waco Apr. 19, 2017, no pet. h.).

80. *See generally In re Hewlett Packard*, 212 S.W.3d 356 (Tex. App.—Austin 2006, no pet.).

81. *In re Hewlett Packard*, 212 S.W.3d 356, 360 (Tex. App.—Austin 2006, no pet.).

82. *Id.* at 360.

83. *Id.*

required a different result, specifically that the burden the depositions placed on the company and the deponents outweighed the potential benefit to Dell. Moreover, Hewlett-Packard argued that the trial court erred in permitting the disclosure of trade secrets because Dell had not adequately established a need for discovering them.[84]

First, the appellate court concluded that mandamus was the appropriate remedy to review the trial court's order because it found that an order (pursuant to Rule 202) is not a final appealable order.[85] The court then noted that the "trial court shall authorize a pre-suit deposition if, and only if, the court finds that 'the likely benefit of allowing petitioner to take the requested deposition to investigate a potential claim outweighs the burden or expense of this procedure.'"[86] In arguing the benefits of the requested deposition, Dell maintained there were positive outcomes for discovering the existence of misappropriation of its trade secrets, as well as for finding no misappropriation had occurred at all. If the former were revealed, Dell's following lawsuit would be well founded. Alternatively, if the latter were discovered, both parties would benefit from "saved expense of prosecuting and defending a lawsuit."[87]

In arguing the burdens of the requested deposition, Hewlett-Packard maintained the disclosure of trade secrets would not only cause "grave and irreparable harm" to the company, but would also give Dell a competitive advantage and provide Hewlett-Packard creditors with confidential information about its business.[88]

In its decision, the appellate court noted that Dell did not refute the allegations made by Hewlett-Packard regarding confidential

84. *Id.*

85. *Id.*

86. *Id.* at 361.

87. *Id.*

88. *Id.* at 361-362.

information. Each of the deponents had signed confidentiality or nondisclosure agreements for Hewlett-Packard. It was undisputed that the deponents might be required to disclose trade-secret information in their depositions and, therefore, violate those agreements.[89]

The appellate court then rejected Dell's burden-benefit analysis as insufficient, maintaining Dell needed to better demonstrate that the "substantial burden to Hewlett-Packard and the proposed deponents, as well as the danger the potential litigants could use Rule 202 for anti-competitive purposes,"[90] was outweighed by the value Dell would receive from the requested depositions. In addition, the court employed a traditional trade-secret analysis, saying that a party seeking trade-secret information "must demonstrate with specificity exactly how the lack of information will impair the presentation of the case on the merits to the point that an unjust result is a real, rather than a merely possible, threat."[91]

In its discussion, the court stated that a Rule 202 proceeding to investigate potential claims "does not involve the adjudication of any claim or defense."[92] It also noted that Dell's claims against its former employees or Hewlett-Packard did not exist yet and were "potential claims only."[93] Therefore, because a lawsuit was not yet pending, the court held that "Dell [had] not established the necessity of discovering Hewlett-Packard's trade-secret information as required by Texas law."[94]

In re Hewlett Packard illustrates the often competing considerations in a Rule 202 action. In such an action, courts have held they must be mindful of due process consideration, "strictly

89. *Id.* at 362.

90. *Id.*

91. *Id.* at 363 (citing *In re Bridgestone/Firestone, Inc.*, 106 S.W.3d 730, 733 (Tex. 2003)).

92. *Id.*

93. *Id.*

94. *Id.*

limit and carefully supervise pre-suit discovery to prevent abuse of the rule,"[95] and strictly meet the requirements of Rule 202. Consequently, a practitioner must include the required statements in a Rule 202 petition, which must be verified by a person with knowledge of the facts and supported by a witness with knowledge of the facts at the hearing. [96]

All in all, a Rule 202 proceeding is a useful, albeit technical, tool in the hands of a prudent practitioner.

95. *In re Wolfe*, 341 S.W.3d 932, 933 (Tex. 2011).

96. Tex. R. Civ. P. 202.2(c).

Chapter 8
Texas Anti-SLAPP Protection

Edited by Bennett Hamilton, Josh Sandler, and Holly Stubbs

8-1 TEXAS CITIZENS PARTICIPATION ACT

If an individual is sued based on the content of a communication, the Texas Citizens Participation Act (TCPA) may allow the individual to seek a quick dismissal of that claim and, if successful, the award of reasonable attorney's fees and court costs.

8-1:1 WHY THE TCPA MATTERS TO EMPLOYERS

A business's most valuable asset is its good name, its brand, and reputation.[1] Consequently, employers must make efforts to protect their company's brand reputational value; particularly in the age of social media when anyone can post negative communications about a business. And as one can imagine, an ideal time for an employee to engage in a negative communication about their employer—whether that communication is via social media, distributed by way of email, or even made orally—is at the end of the employment relationship.

1. Brigham, Alexander F. and Stefan Linssen, *Your Brand Reputational Value Is Irreplaceable. Protect It!,* Forbes, Feb. 1, 2010, http://www.forbes.com/2010/02/01/brand-reputation-value-leadership-managing-ethisphere.html.

In such an instance and without the help of a nondisparagement agreement, an employer harmed by a departing employee's negative communication may look to causes of actions like defamation or business disparagement as a means to protect the company's good name. Indeed, prior to 2011, companies could file such lawsuits against departing employees with little recourse for the employee to dismiss the claims early and avoid protracted litigation.

In 2011, the Texas Legislature passed the TCPA, which "provid[ed] a special procedure for the expedited dismissal" of retaliatory suits that seek to intimidate or silence citizens on matters of public concern.[2] The TCPA was "considered by most practitioners to be the broadest anti-SLAPP (strategic lawsuits against public participation) law in the country."[3]

After nearly a decade of the TCPA's existence, questions regarding the efficacy and functionality of the TCPA brought "powerful lobby groups" together to amend the statute "so that it could no longer be used improperly as a litigation tactic to thwart its purpose."[4] In June 2019, Governor Greg Abbott signed H.B. 2730 into law, overhauling the existing structure and substance of the TCPA.[5] The purpose of the amendments was to narrow the focus of the TCPA to the protection of freedom of speech and association, while preserving the integrity and underlying policy goals of the law. Stating their intent in proposing H.B. 2730—the 2019 amendments to the TCPA ultimately passed into law—the authors and sponsors of the bill explained that:

---

2. *In re Lipsky, 460 S.W.3d 579, 586 (Tex. 2015).*

3. Matthew Simmons, Amendments Would Add Clarity to Texas Anti-SLAPP Law, LITTLER MENDELSON P.C. (May 22, 2019), https://www.littler.com/publication-press/publication/amendments-would-add-clarity-texas-anti-slapp-law (explaining the possible effects of the new law).

4. Laura Lee Prather & Robert T. Sherwin, *The Changing Landscape of the Texas Citizens Participation Act,* 52 Tex. Tech L. Rev. 163, 164 (2020).

5. Act of May 17, 2019, 86th Leg., R.S., ch. 378, §§ 1–12 (codified at Tex. Civ. Prac. & Rem. Code Ann. § 27.001–.012).

> Certain statutory provisions relating to expedited dismissal procedures for lawsuits involving the exercise of free speech, the right of association, and the right to petition lend themselves to unexpected applications because they are overly broad or unclear. H.B. 2730 seeks to remedy this issue by clarifying the scope and applicability of those provisions.[6]

While the 2019 amendment narrowed the focus of the TCPA, it still protects a wide range of conduct and communications. Businesses can still sue former or departing employees who engage in negative communications about them. But under the TCPA, such a suit can still be dismissed. Therefore, employers should familiarize themselves with the TCPA so they can be prepared to defend and defeat a motion to dismiss filed by a former or departing employee under the statute.

8-1:2 OVERVIEW OF CHANGES TO TCPA

Although courts have yet to fully grapple with the 2019 amendments,[7] the changes involved critical areas: (1) what the TCPA covers and (2) how it can be used. The TCPA still protects a departing employee from meritless claims brought against a party for exercising its right of free speech. However, the breadth of protection has been narrowed in some instances. Additionally, the legislature amended various procedural components of the TCPA to reflect the timelines and evidentiary standards of a summary judgment proceeding.

6. S. Comm. on State Affairs, Engrossed Bill Analysis, Tex. H.B. 2730, 86th Leg., R.S. (2019).

7. The Texas Legislature stated that the amendments applied only to an action filed on or after the effective date of the Act, September 1, 2019, and that any action filed before that date is governed by the law in effect before that date. Act of May 17, 2019, 86th Leg., R.S., ch. 378, § 11, 2019 Tex. Gen. Laws 684, 687.

8-1:3 PURPOSE OF THE TCPA

The 2019 amendments have not changed the purpose of the TCPA. The TCPA is an anti-SLAPP statute, which means it protects individuals (e.g., departing employees) who exercise their First Amendment rights when engaging in protected communications. The purpose of the TCPA is to "encourage and safeguard the constitutional rights of persons to petition, speak freely, associate freely, and otherwise participate in government to the maximum extent permitted by law and, at the same time, protect the rights of a person to file meritorious lawsuits for demonstrable injury."[8] The Supreme Court of Texas has noted that "the TCPA's purpose is to identify and summarily dispose of lawsuits designed only to chill First Amendment rights, not to dismiss meritorious lawsuits."[9]

8-2 WHAT THE TCPA COVERS: FIRST AMENDMENT RIGHTS COVERED UNDER THE TCPA

The TCPA, codified in Chapter 27 of the Texas Civil Practice & Remedies Code, states that a person may file a motion to dismiss a legal action if that action is:

> based on or is in response to a party's exercise of the right of free speech, right to petition, or right of association or arises from any act of that party in furtherance of the party's communication or conduct described by Section 27.010(b). A party under this section does not include a government entity, agency, or an official or employee acting in an official capacity.[10]

A "legal action," as defined by the TCPA, is a:

8. Tex. Civ. Prac. & Rem. Code Ann *§ 27.002.*

9. *Lipsky, 460 S.W.3d at 589.*

10. Tex. Civ. Prac. & Rem. Code Ann. § 27.003(a).

lawsuit, cause of action, petition, complaint, cross-claim, or counterclaim or any other judicial pleading or filing that requests legal, declaratory or equitable relief. The term does not include:

(A) a procedural action taken or motion made in an action that does not amend or add a claim for legal, equitable, or declaratory relief;

(B) alternative dispute resolution proceedings; or

(C) post-judgment enforcement actions.[11]

The 2019 amendments to the TCPA made several changes to the types of actions that fall under the TCPA. First and foremost, the language "relates to" was stricken from Section 27.003(a). This change was among the most consequential of all the 2019 amendments, as the term permitted parties to file TCPA motions to dismiss in almost any situation.[12] The TCPA also now includes language clarifying that the definition of "party" "does not include a government entity, agency, or an official or employee acting in an official capacity."[13]

Additionally, the legislature modified which actions fall under the TCPA by amending the definition of "legal action." First, particular actions and proceedings once subject to the TCPA, such as motions for sanctions,[14] mediation proceedings, and

---

11. Tex. Civ. Prac. & Rem. Code Ann. § 27.001(6).

12. *See, e.g., Erdner v. Highland Park Emergency Ctr., LLC, 580 S.W.3d 269, 278 (Tex. App.—Dallas 2019, pet. filed) (Whitehill, J., concurring in part and dissenting in part) (entitling a section from his opinion "'Related to' = Tangentially Related to = Very Broad"); Robert B. James, DDS, Inc., v. Elkins, 553 S.W.3d 596, 606 (Tex. App.—San Antonio 2018, pet. denied) (stating the legislature's intent for "relates to" to be broad).*

13. Tex. Civ. Prac. & Rem. Code Ann. § 27.003(a). *Before this addition, at least one court had held that "the TCPA's plain language does not preclude its application to government officials sued in their official capacity." Roach v. Ingram, 557 S.W.3d 203, 220 (Tex. App.—Houston [14th Dist.] 2018, pet. denied). The new language in Section 27.003(a) effectively overturns Roach.*

14. *See, e.g., Hawxhurst v. Austin's Boat Tours, 550 S.W.3d 220, 231–32 (Tex. App.—*

writs of execution no longer fall under the TCPA.[15] Second, legal and equitable relief are no longer the only forms of relief that fall under the purview of the TCPA—declaratory relief is now included, codifying what most Texas appellate courts had already held.[16]

Accordingly, although narrowed somewhat by the 2019 amendments, the TCPA still protects the following First Amendment rights, all of which have distinct meanings under the TCPA:

1. the exercise of the right of free speech;
2. the exercise of the right to petition; and
3. the exercise of the right of association.[17]

8-2:1 EXERCISE OF THE RIGHT OF FREE SPEECH

Much of the TCPA's protections for the right of free speech remain. The TCPA broadly defines the "exercise of the right of free speech" as a "communication made in connection with a matter of public concern."[18] "Communication," as utilized in the TCPA, "includes the making or submitting of a statement or document in any form or medium, including oral, visual, written, audiovisual, or electronic."[19] The TCPA applies even if the defendant denies making the communication underlying the plaintiff's claims.[20]

Austin 2018, no pet.) (concluding that a pleading labeled a counterclaim or motion for sanctions was a legal action under the previous version of the TCPA).

15. Tex. Civ. Prac. & Rem. Code Ann. § 27.001(6).

16. Prather & Sherwin, *supra note 4, at 170 n. 59.*

17. Tex. Civ. Prac. & Rem. Code Ann. § 27.003(a).

18. Tex. Civ. Prac. & Rem. Code Ann. § 27.001(3); *Avery v. Baddour*, No. 04-16-00184-CV, 2016 WL 4208115, at *2 (Tex. App.—San Antonio Aug. 10, 2016, pet. denied).

19. Tex. Civ. Prac. & Rem. Code Ann. § 27.001(1).

20. *Tatum v. Hersh*, No. 16-0096, 2017 WL 2824394 (Tex. Jun. 30, 2017) (overruling *Pickens v. Cordia*, 433 S.W.3d 179, 188 (Tex. App.—Dallas 2014, no pet.) ("since Michael denied sending the email, there can be no evidence the lawsuit was related to Michael's exercise of free speech and no chapter 27 basis for dismissing the claim"); *Rauhauser v. McGibney*, 508 S.W.3d 377, 385 (Tex. App.—Fort Worth 2014, no pet.) ("[t]he TCPA cannot apply to protect free speech when the defendant denies making the

However, the definition of a "matter of public concern" was amended. A "matter of public concern" under the TCPA is now defined as:

> a statement or activity regarding:
>
> (A) a public official, public figure, or other person who has drawn substantial public attention due to the person's official acts, fame, notoriety, or celebrity;
>
> (B) a matter of political, social, or other interest to the community; or
>
> (C) a subject of concern to the public.[21]

The new definition is taken in part from the 2011 United States Supreme Court case *Snyder v. Phelps*.[22] Indeed, State Senator Bryan Hughes, a co-sponsor of the 2019 TCPA amendments, stated that the "tests for what counts as a matter of public concern are taken from *Snyder v. Phelps*."[23] In *Snyder*, the father of a soldier killed in the line of duty filed state tort law claims against the Westboro Baptist Church (WBC) for picketing the funeral of his son.[24] The signs held up near the funeral by the protesters were inflammatory and controversial to say the least.[25] In an 8–1 decision, the Court held on narrow grounds that the First Amendment did protect WBC's speech.[26] And one of the key

statement at issue"); *Am. Heritage Capital, LP v. Gonzalez,* 436 S.W.3d 865, 881 n.5 (Tex. App.—Dallas 2014, no pet.) ("[w]e recently held that a defendant could not rely on Chapter 27 as to a particular claim because his defense was that he did not publish the speech allegedly giving rise to the claim"); and *Culbertson v. Lykos*, 790 F.3d 608, 632 (5th Cir. 2015)).

21. Tex. Civ. Prac. & Rem. Code Ann. § 27.001(7).

22. 562 U.S. 443, 448–50 (2011).

23. S.J. of Tex., 86th Leg., R.S. 2024 (2019).

24. *Snyder, 562 U.S. at 448–50.*

25. *Id.* at 448 ("[The signs] stated, for instance: 'God Hates the USA/Thank God for 9/11,' 'America is Doomed,' 'Don't Pray for the USA,' 'Thank God for IEDs,' 'Thank God for Dead Soldiers,' 'Pope in Hell,' 'Priests Rape Boys,' 'God Hates Fags,' 'You're Going to Hell,' and 'God Hates You.'").

26. *Id. at 460–61.*

justifications for the Court's holding was that WBC's picketing, albeit "hurtful and its contribution to public discourse may [have] be[en] negligible," "*addressed matters of public import*"[27]—i.e., matters of public concern.

Thus, the amendments serve to make the TCPA more closely mirror federal First Amendment protections. In accordance with that goal, the amendments expressly expand the definition of "matter of public concern" to encompass "activit[ies]" in addition to "statement[s]."[28]

The legislature also replaced five nonexhaustive categories of "matter[s] of public concern" and added statements or activities regarding "a public official, public figure, or other person who has drawn substantial public attention due to the person's official acts, fame, notoriety, or celebrity"; "a matter of political, social, or other interest to the community"; and "a subject of concern to the public."[29] This change represents a major legislative shift. While there may be significant overlap of what constitutes a "matter of public concern" under the current and pre-2019 amendment versions of the TCPA, the new statutory language provides sturdier guideposts for Texas courts in identifying such matters under the TCPA.

Both the U.S. Supreme Court and the Texas Supreme Court have issued rulings on what constitutes matters of public concern under *Snyder*. These cases shed light on what may be considered matters of public concern under the amended TCPA. Below is a list of examples of matters of public concern under *Snyder*:

---

27. *Id. at 460 (emphasis added in second quotation).*

28. While the U.S. Supreme Court has "rejected 'the view that an apparently limitless variety of conduct can be labeled "speech" whenever the person engaging in the conduct intends thereby to express an idea,'" the Court has "acknowledged that conduct may be 'sufficiently imbued with elements of communication to fall within the scope of the First . . . Amendment[].'" *Texas v. Johnson, 491 U.S. 397, 404 (1989) (citation omitted) (first quoting United States v. O'Brien, 391 U.S. 367, 375 (1968); and then quoting Spence v. Washington, 418 U.S. 405, 409 (1974) (per curiam)).*

29. Tex. Civ. Prac. & Rem. Code Ann. § 27.001(7)(A)–(C).

- "[C]ommission of crime, prosecutions resulting from it, and judicial proceedings arising from the prosecutions"[30];
- Press coverage containing misrepresentations[31];
- Speech regarding "information related to or learned through public employment"[32];
- Speech which advocates for, *inter alia*, "wage and tax increases, cutting spending 'to Wall Street financial institutions,' and reforms to . . . pension and tax systems"[33];
- Reporting that "a corporation and its principal stockholder 'had links to organized crime and used some of those links to influence the State's governmental process'"[34];
- Disclosing "misbehavior by public officials is a matter of public interest . . . , especially when it concerns the operation of a police department"[35]; and
- Actions of a police chief toward other officers "in response to the officers . . . tick-et[ing] his son."[36]

Although *Snyder* and its progeny provide guidance on how Texas courts may apply the amended language, several unknowns

30. *Cox Broadcasting Corp. v. Cohn, 420 U.S. 469, 492 (1975).*

31. *Time, Inc. v. Hill, 385 U.S. 374, 387–88 (1967).*

32. *Lane v. Franks, 573 U.S. 228, 236 (2014).*

33. *Janus v. Am. Fed'n of State, Cty., & Mun. Emps., Council 31*, 138 S. Ct. 2448, 2475 (2018).

34. *Brady v. Klentzman, 515 S.W.3d 878, 884 (Tex. 2017) (quoting Phila. Newspapers, Inc. v. Hepps, 475 U.S. 767, 769 (1986)).*

35. *Id. (internal quotations marks omitted) (quoting Brawner v. City of Richardson, 855 F.2d 187, 191–92 (5th Cir. 1988)).*

36. *Id.*

remain. For example, the new amendments' impact on whether the communication at issue must be public is unclear. Under the prior version of the TCPA, the communication could be either public or private so long as it is made in connection with a public concern.[37] Although courts may decline to apply the TCPA to private communications, attempts to incorporate a bright line rule were rejected in the legislative process.[38] Nonetheless, courts may be called on to clarify whether communications that are not made to the public at large still fall under Section 27.001(7).

8-2:2 EXERCISE OF THE RIGHT TO PETITION

The right to petition, as protected by the TCPA, was not changed by the 2019 amendments. According to the TCPA, the exercise of the right to petition includes five different types of communications. The first type of communication is a communication in or pertaining to:

1. a judicial proceeding;[39]
2. an official proceeding, other than a judicial proceeding, to administer the law;[40]

---

37. *Lippincott v. Whisenhunt*, 462 S.W.3d 507, 510 (Tex. 2015) (we must presume that the Legislature broadly included both public and private communication); *see also* Tex. Civ. Prac. & Rem. Code Ann. § 27.011 ([the TCPA] shall be construed liberally to effectuate its purpose and intent fully").

38. Compare Tex. H.B. 2730, 86th Leg. R.S. (2019) (which passed), with Tex. S.B. 1981, 86th R.S. (2019) (which did not pass and would have required a legal action to be based on the exercise of constitutional rights "in a place or context that is open to the public.").

39. *See, e.g., Serafine v. Blunt*, 466 S.W.3d 352, 360 (Tex. App.—Austin 2015, no pet.); *James v. Calkins*, 446 S.W.3d 135, 147 (Tex. App.—Houston [1st Dist.] 2014, pet. filed); *Watson v. Hardman*, 497 S.W.3d 601, 606 (Tex. App.—Dallas 2016, no pet.) ("a Rule 202 proceeding is a 'judicial proceeding' for Chapter 27 purposes . . . [and thus,] an exercise of the right to petition under Chapter 27"); *Long Canyon Phase II & III Homeowners Ass'n, Inc. v. Cashion*, 517 S.W.3d 212, 220 (Tex. App.—Austin 2017, no pet.) (pre-suit notice pursuant to the Texas Property Code is not a communication pertaining to a judicial proceeding); *Levatino v. Apple Tree Cafe Touring, Inc.*, 486 S.W.3d 724, 729 (Tex. App.—Dallas 2016, pet. denied) (attorney's demand letter is not a communication pertaining to a judicial proceeding); *Youngkin v. Hines*, No. 10-15-00194-CV, 2016 WL 3896494, at *5 (Tex. App.—Waco July 13, 2016, pet. granted) (the exercise of the right to petition under the TCPA includes an attorney's in-court communications).

40. *Tervita, LLC v. Sutterfield*, 482 S.W.3d 280, 283–84 (Tex. App.—Dallas 2015, pet. denied) (former employee's employment discrimination and conspiracy claims should be

3. an executive or other proceeding before a department of the state or federal government or a subdivision of the state or federal government;[41]
4. a legislative proceeding, including a proceeding of a legislative committee;
5. a proceeding before an entity that requires by rule that public notice be given before proceedings of that entity;
6. a proceeding in or before a managing board of an educational or eleemosynary institution supported directly or indirectly from public revenue;
7. a proceeding of the governing body of any political subdivision of this state;
8. a report of or debate and statements made in a proceeding described by Subparagraph [1], [2], [3], [4], or [5]; or
9. a public meeting dealing with a public purpose, including statements and discussions at the meeting or other matters of public concern occurring at the meeting.[42]

The term "official proceeding" means "any type of administrative, executive, legislative, or judicial proceeding that may be conducted before a public servant."[43] As used in the preceding sentence, the term "public servant" refers to a:

---

dismissed under TCPA because they are "based on, relate [ ] to, or [are] in response to" former employer's exercise of its right to petition, which consisted of testimony and participation in Texas Department of Insurance, Division of Worker's Compensation hearing).

41. *See, e.g.*, *KBMT Operating Co., LLC v. Toledo*, 434 S.W.3d 276, 282 (Tex. App.—Beaumont 2014, pet. granted); *Tervita*, 482 S.W.3d at 283–84.

42. Tex. Civ. Prac. & Rem. Code Ann. § 27.001(4)(A).

43. Tex. Civ. Prac. & Rem. Code Ann. § 27.001(8).

> person elected, selected, appointed, employed, or otherwise designated as one of the following, even if the person has not yet qualified for office or assumed the person's duties: an officer, employee, or agent of government; a juror; an arbitrator, referee, or other person who is authorized by law or private written agreement to hear or determine a cause or controversy; an attorney or notary public when participating in the performance of a governmental function; or a person who is performing a governmental function under a claim of right but is not legally qualified to do so.[44]

Second, a communication "in connection with an issue under consideration or review by a legislative, executive, judicial, or other governmental body or in another governmental or official proceeding" is also included within the TCPA's definition of the exercise of the right to petition.[45] The term "governmental proceeding" means a "proceeding, other than a judicial proceeding, by an officer, official, or body of this state or a political subdivision of this state, including a board or commission, or by an officer, official, or body of the federal government."[46]

The third type of communication involved in the exercise of the right to petition involves one that is "reasonably likely to encourage consideration or review of an issue by a legislative, executive, judicial, or other governmental body or in another governmental or official proceeding."[47]

Fourth, the TCPA states that a communication "reasonably likely to enlist public participation in an effort to effect consideration of an issue by a legislative, executive, judicial, or other governmental

---

44. Tex. Civ. Prac. & Rem. Code Ann. § 27.001(9).

45. Tex. Civ. Prac. & Rem. Code Ann. § 27.001(4)(B); *Tervita*, 482 S.W.3d at 283–84.

46. Tex. Civ. Prac. & Rem. Code Ann. § 27.001(5).

47. Tex. Civ. Prac. & Rem. Code Ann. § 27.001(4)(C); *see also Lipsky*, 411 S.W.3d at 542.

body or in another governmental or official proceeding" is also included within the definition of the right to petition.[48]

Finally, "any other communication that falls within the protection of the right to petition government under the Constitution of the United States or the constitution of this state" is embodied within the definition of the exercise of the right to petition as defined by the TCPA.[49]

8-2:3 EXERCISE OF THE RIGHT OF ASSOCIATION

The third type of First Amendment right protected by the TCPA is the exercise of the right of association, which "means to join together to collectively express, promote, pursue, or defend common interests relating to a governmental proceeding or a matter of public concern."[50]

The 2019 amendments made two key changes to the TCPA's definition of this right. The "exercise of the right of association" is no longer "a communication between individuals who join together"—it simply occurs when individuals "join together." This aligns the TCPA's "right of association" more uniformly with the federal constitutional right.[51] Although the contours of the federal constitutional freedom of association are not entirely clear, it is generally considered to be "the right to choose whether to associate with another person"[52] and "reflects the notion that

48. Tex. Civ. Prac. & Rem. Code Ann. § 27.001(4)(D).

49. Tex. Civ. Prac. & Rem. Code Ann. § 27.001(4)(E); *Cashion*, 517 S.W.3d 212, 220 (Tex. App.—Austin 2017, no pet.) (pre-suit notice pursuant to the Texas Property Code is an "exercise of the right to petition under the TCPA because it falls under subsection (E) of the TCPA's definition of the 'exercise of the right to petition,' which is 'any other communication that falls within the protection of the right to petition government under the Constitution of the United States or the constitution of this state.'") (quoting Tex. Civ. Prac. & Rem. Code Ann. § 27.001(4)(E)).

50. Tex. Civ. Prac. & Rem. Code Ann. § 27.001(2).

51. Prather & Sherwin, *supra note 4, at 168.*

52. Neil Gotanda, *A Critique of "Our Constitution Is Color-Blind,* 44 Stan. L. Rev. 1, 9 (1991).

individual rights of expression can be made more effectual by collective action."[53]

While the wording change of the TCPA's "exercise of the right of association" away from "a communication between individuals who join together" may appear stylistic, given the Texas Supreme Court's clear directive for courts to "interpret the [TCPA] according to its plain meaning"[54] and the Texas Legislature's command to construe the TCPA "liberally to effectuate its purpose and intent fully,"[55] the volume of TCPA litigation relating to the "exercise of the right of association" may increase dramatically as a result of the 2019 amendments.[56]

The second change to Section 27.001(2) is that the "common interests" being "collectively express[ed], promote[d], pursue[d], or defend[ed]" must "relat[e] to a governmental proceeding or a matter of public concern."[57] This modification narrows the scope of the "exercise of the right of association," but the degree to which it does so is unclear. The TCPA defines "governmental proceeding[s]" and "matter[s] of public concern," but, as is discussed above, what constitutes a matter of public concern is still unsettled (but is likely far-reaching).[58] Until courts begin applying

53. Noah R. Feldman & Kathleen M. Sullivan, Constitutional Law 1418 (20th ed. 2019).

54. *Lippincott v. Whisenhunt, 462 S.W.3d 507, 509 (Tex. 2015) (per curiam) (citing Leland v. Brandal, 257 S.W.3d 204, 206 (Tex. 2008)).*

55. Tex. Civ. Prac. & Rem. Code Ann. § 27.011(b).

56. For a brief summary of the federal constitutional right of association, *see generally Vincent Blasi, The Pathological Perspective and the First Amendment, 85* Colum. L. Rev. 449, 495–96 (1985). The Supreme Court has reviewed the right of association in various contexts, which (nonexhaustively) include: government "outlaw[ing] an organization or membership in it," government requiring an organization or a member in it to "disclose information about group membership," government "restrict[ing] activities centrally linked to the purpose of an association," government "deny[ing] governmental benefits or privileges to members of certain associations," and the individual right "not to associate." Feldman & Sullivan, *supra note 53, at 1418–19.*

57. Tex. Civ. Prac. & Rem. Code Ann. § 27.001(2)

58. For example, the Fort Worth court of appeals compiled a list of cases applying the right of association in the TCPA context. See *Kawcak v. Antero Res. Corp.*, 582 S.W.3d 566, 568 n.9 (Tex. App.—Fort Worth 2019, pet. denied). Whether these cases square with the post-2019 amendments version of Section 27.001(2) remains to be seen, but "there is no question" that the amended definition of the "exercise of the right of association"

the amended version of Section 27.001(2), the provision's reach remains uncertain.

8-3 HOW TO USE THE TCPA: MOTION TO DISMISS PROCEDURE UNDER THE TCPA

If an individual, such as a former or departing employee, engages in a negative communication about his or her former employer, the negative communication is protected by the TCPA, and that same individual is sued by the former employer based on the content of the negative communication, the former or departing employee may utilize the motion to dismiss function codified in the TCPA.[59] Under the 2019 amendments, the majority of the procedural steps to file a motion to dismiss under the TCPA remain the same, but the amendments changed certain procedures and appear to align them more closely with the standards for a motion for summary judgment.

8-3:1 WHERE TO FILE THE MOTION TO DISMISS

The former or departing employee must file a motion to dismiss with the court in which the legal action is pending.[60]

8-3:2 WHEN TO FILE THE MOTION TO DISMISS

The motion to dismiss must be filed not later than the 60th day after the date of service of the legal action.[61] The court retains discretion to extend the time to file a motion to dismiss under the TCPA upon a showing of good cause.[62] The 2019 amendments also added that the parties, upon mutual agreement, may extend

"will exclude many cases that came under the old version of the [TCPA]." Prather & Sherwin, *supra* note 4, at 198.

59. Tex. Civ. Prac. & Rem. Code Ann. § 27.003(a).

60. Tex. Civ. Prac. & Rem. Code Ann. § 27.003(b).

61. *Id.*

62. *Id.*

the time to file a motion under this section.[63] Once a motion to dismiss under the TCPA is filed, all discovery in the legal action is suspended until the court can rule on the motion to dismiss.[64]

8-3:3 MOTION TO DISMISS HEARING

A hearing on the TCPA motion to dismiss must be set not later than 60 days after the date the moving party (e.g., the former or departing employee) serves the nonmoving party with the motion to dismiss.[65]

However, the moving party may obtain a later hearing date, but only (1) if the court's docket conditions require a later hearing (for which the court may take judicial notice); (2) upon a showing of good cause; or (3) if the parties agree to obtain a later hearing date.[66] If the moving party obtains a later hearing date, the hearing on the motion to dismiss must not occur more than 90 days after the moving party serves the nonmoving party with the motion.[67]

The 2019 amendments further clarified the deadlines for noticing the hearing and filing a response. Under the 2019 amendments, the moving party must provide written notice of the date and time of the hearing not later than 21 days before the date of the hearing unless otherwise provided by agreement of the parties or an order of the court.[68] The responding party must then file a response, if any, not later than seven days before the date of the hearing on the motion to dismiss.[69]

---

63. *Id.*

64. Tex. Civ. Prac. & Rem. Code Ann. § 27.003(c).

65. Tex. Civ. Prac. & Rem. Code Ann. §§ 27.004(a), (b).

66. Tex. Civ. Prac. & Rem. Code Ann. § 27.004(a).

67. *Id.*

68. Tex. Civ. Prac. & Rem. Code Ann. § 27.003(d).

69. Tex. Civ. Prac. & Rem. Code Ann. § 27.003(e).

8-3:4 SPECIFIED AND LIMITED DISCOVERY

The court may allow specified and limited discovery relevant to the motion to dismiss.[70] The specified and limited discovery may only be obtained by (1) a motion by a party or on the court's own motion and (2) a showing of good cause.[71]

If the court permits limited discovery, it may extend the hearing date on the motion to dismiss.[72] However, in that situation, the hearing on the motion to dismiss must occur within 120 days after the moving party served the nonmoving party with the motion to dismiss.[73]

8-3:5 EVIDENCE

From an evidentiary standpoint, the new amendments clarify that courts may consider only the types of evidence that would be admissible in a summary judgment proceeding. At the hearing, the court must consider (1) the pleadings; (2) evidence a court could consider under Rule 166a of the Texas Rules of Civil Procedure; (3) supporting affidavits stating the facts on which the liability is denied; and (4) opposing affidavits stating the facts on which the liability is based.[74] The TCPA does not require a movant to present testimony or other evidence to satisfy the movant's evidentiary burden.[75]

---

70. Tex. Civ. Prac. & Rem. Code Ann. § 27.006(b).

71. *Id.*

72. Tex. Civ. Prac. & Rem. Code Ann. §§ 27.004(c); 27.006(b).

73. *Id.*

74. Tex. Civ. Prac. & Rem. Code Ann. § 27.006(a); *D Magazine Partners, L.P. v. Rosenthal*, No. 05-14-00951-CV, 2015 WL 5156908, at *5, n.5 (Tex. App.—Dallas Aug. 28, 2015, pet. filed); *Lipsky, 460 S.W.3d 579, 592–93* (Tex. 2015) (TCPA affidavit is conclusory when it fails to provide underlying facts).

75. *Hicks v. Group & Pension Administrators, Inc.*, No. 13-14-00607-CV, 2015 WL 5234366, at *4 (Tex. App.—Corpus Christi Sept. 3, 2015, no. pet. h.). There is nothing in the TCPA, however, that precludes live testimony. *See generally Moldovan v. Polito, No. 05-15-01052-CV, 2016 WL 4131890, at *16 (Tex. App.—Dallas Aug. 2, 2016, no pet.).*

Under the previous iteration of the statute, courts could consider only "the pleadings and supporting and opposing affidavits stating the facts on which the liability or defense is based."[76] The ability for courts to examine valid summary-judgment evidence in ruling on a TCPA motion to dismiss will allow courts to consider the claims more fully and parties to make their cases more readily.

8-4 BURDEN SHIFTING UNDER THE MOTION TO DISMISS

8-4:1 FIRST BURDEN SHIFT

The 2019 amendments to the TCPA lowered the evidentiary burden required to prevail on a motion to dismiss. Under these amendments, a former or departing employee who brings a motion to dismiss under the TCPA must demonstrate that the legal action is:

1. based the right of free speech;
2. in response to the party's exercise of free speech;
3. based on the right to petition;
4. in response to the party's right to petition;
5. based on the right of association; or
6. in response to the party's right of association.[77]

Convincing a court to grant a TCPA motion to dismiss under the prior evidentiary burden—a preponderance of the evidence standard—proved to be difficult, so the removal of that standard

76. Citizens Participation Act, 82d Leg., R.S., ch. 341, § 2, 2011 Tex. Gen. Laws 961, 961 (amended 2019) (current version at Tex. Civ. Prac. & Rem. Code Ann. § 27.006(a)).

77. Tex. Civ. Prac. & Rem. Code Ann. § 27.005(b)(1). A court shall also dismiss a legal action against the moving party if the moving party demonstrates that the legal action is based on or is in response to the acts described in section 27.010(b). Tex. Civ. Prac. & Rem. Code Ann. § 27.005(b)(2).

likely enhances a former or departing employee's ability to meet his or her initial burden.

8-4:2 SECOND BURDEN SHIFT

If the former or departing employee meets this burden, the burden then shifts to the nonmoving party (e.g., the former employer), who must establish by clear and specific evidence a prima facie case for each essential element of the claim in question.[78] Clear and specific evidence includes direct evidence as well as relevant circumstantial evidence.[79] If the former employer meets this burden (and the former or departing employee is unable to meet his shifting burden, as specified more fully below), the court may not dismiss the legal action in question by granting the motion to dismiss on the challenged claim(s).[80]

8-4:3 THIRD BURDEN SHIFT

If the former employer establishes this burden, the burden then shifts once more back to the moving party (e.g., the former or departing employee) who must establish an affirmative defense or other grounds on which the moving party is entitled to judgment as a matter of law.[81] Under the 2019 amendments, the process for

78. Tex. Civ. Prac. & Rem. Code Ann. § 27.005(c); *see also KTRK Television, Inc. v. Robinson*, 409 S.W.3d 682, 688 (Tex. App.—Houston [1st Dist.] 2013, pet. denied) ("[t]he Legislature's use of 'prima facie case' in the second step of the inquiry implies a minimal factual burden: '[a] prima facie case represents the minimum quantity of evidence necessary to support a rational inference that the allegation of fact is true'") (quoting *Rodriguez v. Printone Color Corp.*, 982 S.W.2d 69, 72 (Tex. App.—Houston [1st Dist.] 1998, pet. denied).

79. *Lipsky*, 460 S.W.3d at 584 (clear and specific evidence means that the plaintiff "must provide enough detail to show the factual basis for its claim"); *see also Andrews Cty. v. Sierra Club*, 463 S.W.3d 867, 867 (Tex. 2015) (the clear and specific standard "neither imposes a heightened evidentiary burden nor categorically rejects the use of circumstantial evidence when determining the plaintiff's prima-facie-case burden under the Act"). At least one court has held that a plaintiff may not rely solely on the allegations in its petition to meet its prima facie burden. *See Buzbee v. Clear Channel Outdoor, LLC*, No. 14-19-00512-CV, 2020 WL 6738021, at *10 (Tex. App.—Houston [14th Dist.] Nov. 17, 2020, no pet. h.).

80. Tex. Civ. Prac. & Rem. Code Ann. § 27.005(c).

81. Tex. Civ. Prac. & Rem. Code Ann. § 27.005(d); *Patterson v. T.V. Channel 25*

a moving party to establish an affirmative defense also appears to more closely resemble summary-judgment practice. If the former or departing employee meets this burden, the court must dismiss the legal action in question by granting the motion to dismiss.[82]

8-4:5 STATUTORY EXEMPTIONS UNDER THE TCPA

The 2019 TCPA amendments made sweeping changes to the types of actions to which the TCPA does not apply.

The first four exemptions remain from the prior statute. Namely, (1) the TCPA does not apply to an enforcement action brought in the name of the State of Texas or a political subdivision of the state by the attorney general, a district attorney, a criminal district attorney, or a county attorney.[83] (2) The TCPA does not apply to a legal action brought against a person primarily engaged in the business of selling or leasing goods or services, if the statement or conduct arises out of the sale or lease of:

1. goods;
2. services;
3. an insurance product;
4. insurance services; or
5. a commercial transaction in which the intended audience is an actual or potential buyer or customer.[84]

(3) The TCPA does not apply to a legal action seeking recovery for bodily injury, wrongful death, or survival or to statements

Broad. Station, 489 S.W.3d 589, 591-92 (Tex. App.—Texarkana 2016, no pet.) (even if the nonmoving party established a prima facie case of defamation by clear and specific evidence, the movant TV station is entitled to dismissal under the TCPA's motion to dismiss because it established by a preponderance of the evidence that the nonmovant's claim was barred by its affirmative defense of statute of limitations).

82. Tex. Civ. Prac. & Rem. Code Ann. § 27.005(d).

83. Tex. Civ. Prac. & Rem. Code Ann. § 27.010(a)(1).

84. Tex. Civ. Prac. & Rem. Code Ann. § 27.010(a)(2).

made regarding that legal action.[85] (4) The TCPA does not apply to a legal action brought under the Insurance Code or arising out of an insurance contract.[86]

In addition to the above exemptions, the 2019 amendments exempted eight additional legal actions:

(5) Legal actions arising from an officer, director, employee-employer, or independent contractor relationship that:

(A) seeks recovery for misappropriation of trade secrets or corporate opportunities; or

(B) seeks to enforce a nondisparagement agreement or a covenant not to compete;[87]

(6) Legal actions filed under Title 1, 2, 4, or 5, Family Code, or an application for a protective order under Chapter 7A, Code of Criminal Procedure;[88]

(7) Legal actions brought under Chapter 17, Business & Commerce Code, other than an action governed by Section 17.49(a) of that chapter;[89]

(8) A legal action which a moving party raises a defense pursuant to Section 160.010, Occupations Code, Section 161.033, Health and Safety Code, or the Health Care Quality

85. Tex. Civ. Prac. & Rem. Code Ann. § 27.010(a)(3).

86. Tex. Civ. Prac. & Rem. Code Ann. § 27.010(a)(4).

87. Tex. Civ. Prac. & Rem. Code Ann. § 27.010(a)(5).

88. Tex. Civ. Prac. & Rem. Code Ann. § 27.010(a)(6).

89. Tex. Civ. Prac. & Rem. Code Ann. § 27.010(a)(7).

Improvement Act of 1986 (42 U.S.C. 11101 et seq.);[90]

(9) An eviction suit brought under Chapter 24, Property Code;[91]

(10) A disciplinary action or disciplinary proceeding brought under Chapter 81, Government Code, or the Texas Rules of Disciplinary Procedure;[92]

(11) A legal action brought under Chapter 554, Government Code;[93] or

(12) A legal action based on a common law fraud claim.[94]

The eight new exemptions will likely change TCPA litigation significantly, removing many types of disputes from the TCPA's purview that formerly complicated application of the TCPA.

However, the 2019 amendments contain exemptions to the exemptions, which reflect the legislature's intent to apply the TCPA to situations that might otherwise have been excluded from TCPA coverage.

First, the TCPA applies to a legal action against a person arising from any act of that person related to "gathering, receiving, posting or processing" information for communication to the public, whether or not that information is actually communicated to the public;[95] and to a legal action against a person related to communication of consumer opinions or commentary, evaluations of consumer complaints or reviews or ratings

90. Tex. Civ. Prac. & Rem. Code Ann. § 27.010(a)(8).

91. Tex. Civ. Prac. & Rem. Code Ann. § 27.010(a)(9).

92. Tex. Civ. Prac. & Rem. Code Ann. § 27.010(a)(10).

93. Tex. Civ. Prac. & Rem. Code Ann. § 27.010(a)(11).

94. Tex. Civ. Prac. & Rem. Code Ann. § 27.010(a)(12).

95. Tex. Civ. Prac. & Rem. Code Ann. § 27.010(b)(1).

of businesses.[96] Under this new provision, members of old and new media and companies involved in online business reviews and ratings may now utilize the TCPA. None of the claims arising out of these communications must relate to matters of public concern.[97]

Second, the TCPA amendments ensure that TCPA motions to dismiss are available to address claims regarding family and dating violence.[98] This provision "allows victims of family violence, dating violence, and revenge porn to invoke the TCPA in response to suits brought against them."[99]

8-5 COMMERCIAL SPEECH EXEMPTION

The 2019 amendments did not alter the commercial speech exemption to the TCPA.[100] Some courts have stated that the commercial speech exemption to the TCPA applies only where a statement is made to a limited audience and not the public at large.[101]

The First Court of Appeals in Houston uses the following test to determine whether the commercial speech exemption applies:

---

96. Tex. Civ. Prac. & Rem. Code Ann. § 27.010(b)(2).

97. Prather & Sherwin, *supra note 4, at 173.*

98. *See* Tex. Civ. Prac. & Rem. Code Ann § 27.010(c).

99. Mark C. Walker, *The Essential Guide to the Texas Anti-SLAPP Law, the Texas Defamation Mitigation Act, and Rule 91a, in State Bar of Tex. 36th Annual Litigation Update Inst., ch. 4.1, at 26 (2020).*

100. Tex. Civ. Prac. & Rem. Code Ann. § 27.010(a)(2); *see also Backes v. Misko*, No. 05-14-00566-CV, 2015 WL 1138258, at *10 (Tex. App.—Dallas Mar. 13, 2015, pet. filed) (individuals at issue were not primarily engaged in business of selling or leasing goods or services in the quarter horse business and thus, commercial speech exemption under the TCPA did not apply); *NCDR, L.L.C. v. Mauze & Bagby, P.L.L.C.*, 745 F.3d 742, 752–55 (5th Cir. 2014) (law firm's advertising campaign to solicit owner of dental clinics' former patients as potential clients fell within commercial speech exception of the TCPA); *Schimmel v. McGregor*, 438 S.W.3d 847, 857–8 (Tex. App.—Houston [1st Dist.] 2014, pet. denied) (commercial-speech exemption not applicable where, although defendant provided legal services to plaintiff at the time he made statements at issue, his intended audience was City of Galveston, not a potential buyer or customer of attorney's services).

101. *Better Bus. Bureau of Metro. Houston, Inc. v. John Moore Services, Inc.*, 441 S.W.3d 345, 354 (Tex. App.—Houston [1st Dist.] 2013, pet. denied).

1. the cause of action is against a person primarily engaged in the business of selling or leasing goods or services;
2. the cause of action arises from a statement or conduct by that person consisting of representations of fact about that person's or a business competitor's business operations, goods, or services;
3. the statement or conduct was made either for the purpose of obtaining approval for, promoting, or securing sales or leases of, or commercial transactions in, the person's goods or services or in the course of delivering the person's goods or services; and
4. the intended audience for the statement or conduct [is an actual or potential buyer or customer].[102]

8-6 RULING ON THE MOTION TO DISMISS

The TCPA requires the court to rule on the motion to dismiss within 30 days of the conclusion of the hearing on the motion.[103] This is a mandatory deadline and gives the trial court no discretion to grant an extension of time.[104] The ruling on the motion to dismiss may be made orally, so long as its announcement rendering judgment is "made as a present act and not as an intention

---

102. *Newspaper Holdings, Inc. v. Crazy Hotel Assisted Living, Ltd.*, 416 S.W.3d 71, 88-89 (Tex. App.—Houston [1st Dist.] 2013, pet. denied) (citing *Simpson Strong-Tie Company, Inc. v. Gore* (2010) 49 Cal.4th 12, 30 [109 Cal.Rptr.3d 329, 343, 230 P.3d 1117, 1129]); *see also Lamons Gasket Co. v. Flexitallic L.P.*, 9 F. Supp. 3d 709, 711 (S.D. Tex. 2014) (citing *NCDR*, 745 F.3d at 753–54)).

103. Tex. Civ. Prac. & Rem. Code Ann. § 27.005(a). However, the TCPA's 30-day deadline to rule on a motion to dismiss does not deprive a trial court of authority, after timely granting a TCPA dismissal motion, from exercising its plenary authority to reconsider and vacate its prior order after the deadline has passed. *In re Panchakarla, 602 S.W.3d 536, 541 (Tex. 2020).*

104. *Inwood Forest Cmty. Improvement Ass'n v. Arce*, 485 S.W.3d 65, 70 (Tex. App.—Houston [14th Dist.] 2015, pet. denied).

to render judgment in the future."[105] However, the court's ruling on the motion is not admissible as evidence at any later stage of the case, and no burden of proof shall be affected by the ruling.[106]

8-7 AWARDING DAMAGES AND COSTS UNDER THE MOTION TO DISMISS

If the moving party (e.g., the former or departing employee) prevails on the motion to dismiss under the TCPA and the court orders dismissal of a legal action, the court must award to the moving party:

1. court costs; and
2. reasonable attorney's fees.[107]

The new TCPA language makes all sanctions awards discretionary. The court may award sanctions against the party who brought the legal action as the court deems fit to deter the party who brought the legal action from bringing similar actions described in this chapter.[108] The court may also award sanctions of reasonable attorney's fees upon the dismissal of a compulsory counterclaim if the court finds that the counterclaim is frivolous or solely intended for delay.[109]

On the other hand, if the court finds that a motion to dismiss brought under the TCPA is either frivolous or solely intended to delay, the court may award to the nonmoving party (e.g., the former employer)[110]:

---

105. *Id.* (quoting *State v. Naylor*, 466 S.W.3d 783, 788 (Tex. 2015)).

106. Tex. Civ. Prac. & Rem. Code Ann. § 27.0075.

107. Tex. Civ. Prac. & Rem. Code Ann. § 27.009(a)(1).

108. Tex. Civ. Prac. & Rem. Code Ann. § 27.009(a)(2).

109. Tex. Civ. Prac. & Rem. Code Ann. § 27.009(c).

110. "A motion to dismiss under the TCPA is frivolous if it has no basis in law or fact and lacks a legal basis or legal merit." *Baxter Constr. Co., LLC v. Senior Care Living VII, LLC, No. 02-19-00308-CV, 2020 WL 6165412, at *3 (Tex. App.—Fort Worth Oct. 22, 2020, no pet. h.).*

1. court costs and
2. reasonable attorney's fees.[111]

If the court awards sanctions, the court must issue findings.[112] If a party has requested the court to issue findings, the court must "issue findings regarding whether the legal action was brought to deter or prevent the moving party from exercising constitutional rights and is brought for an improper purpose, including to harass or to cause unnecessary delay or to increase the cost of litigation."[113] These findings must be issued within 30 days of the date of the request to issue such findings.[114]

Because of these amendments, trial courts will no longer be forced to award nominal sanctions against parties the trial court does not believe need to be deterred from filing future similar cases, and appellate courts will avoid wrestling with the question of whether failing to award any sanctions is reversible error.[115]

8-8 APPEALING THE RULING ON THE MOTION TO DISMISS

If the court does not rule on a motion to dismiss under the TCPA within 30 days after the hearing on the motion, the motion is considered to have been denied by operation of law and the moving party may appeal.[116] While appellate courts exercise interlocutory appellate jurisdiction over an appeal of a denial of a motion to dismiss under the TCPA[117], appellate courts do

---

111. Tex. Civ. Prac. & Rem. Code Ann. § 27.009(b).

112. Tex. Civ. Prac. & Rem. Code Ann. § 27.007(a).

113. *Id.*

114. Tex. Civ. Prac. & Rem. Code Ann. § 27.007(b).

115. *See, e.g., Prather & Sherwin, supra* note 4, at 178–79.

116. Tex. Civ. Prac. & Rem. Code Ann. § 27.008(a).

117. Tex. Civ. Prac. & Rem. Code Ann. § 27.008(b); *Better Bus. Bureau of Metro. Dallas, Inc. v. BH DFW, INC.*, 402 S.W.3d 299, 306 (Tex. App.—Dallas 2013, pet. denied); *Better Bus. Bureau of Metro. Houston, Inc. v. John Moore Svcs., Inc.*, 441 S.W.3d 345, 352 (Tex. App.—Houston [1st Dist.] 2013, pet. denied); *KTRK Television, Inc. v. Robinson,* 409 S.W.3d 682, 688 (Tex. App.—Houston [1st Dist.] 2013, no pet. h.).

not have jurisdiction over an interlocutory appeal from an order granting a motion to dismiss under the TCPA.[118]

Furthermore, appellate courts must expedite an appeal or other writ—whether interlocutory or not—from a trial court order on a motion to dismiss or from a trial court's failure to timely rule on the motion to dismiss.[119] Appellate courts conduct a de novo review.[120] Like the trial court, the appellate court considers the "pleadings and supporting and opposing affidavits stating the facts on which the liability or defense is based."[121] However, the appellate court reviews those pleadings and evidence in a light favorable to the nonmovant.[122]

8-9 CONCLUSION

Although the 2019 amendments to the TCPA narrowed aspects of the statute's application, the TCPA still applies to a wide range of business-related conduct. As such, businesses should familiarize themselves with the TCPA when considering legal action against a departed employee. It is not uncommon for an employer to ask his or her employees to sign an agreement stating that the parties agree not to disparage each other in the event one or both parties end the employment relationship. Some employers do this at the beginning of the employment relationship. Others do it at the end of the employment relationship in the form of a separation package. Irrespective of when a nondisparagement agreement is

---

See also D Magazine Partners, 2017 WL 1041234, at *9 (if the trial court partially grants a motion to dismiss—dismissing some, but not all claims—the trial court should award the moving party with attorney's fees as to the dismissed claims).

118. *Fleming & Associates, L.L.P. v. Kirklin,* 479 S.W.3d 458, 460 (Tex. App.—Houston [14th Dist.] 2015, pet. denied).

119. Tex. Civ. Prac. & Rem. Code Ann. § 27.008(b).

120. *Patterson, 489 S.W.3d at 591.*

121. *Id.* (quoting Tex. Civ. Prac. & Rem. Code Ann. § 27.006(a)).

122. *Epperson*, 2016 WL 4253978, at *9 (citing *Newspaper Holdings, Inc. v. Crazy Hotel Assisted Living, Ltd.*, 416 S.W.3d 71, 80 (Tex. App.—Houston [1st Dist.] 2013, pet. denied)); *but see Tatum v. Hersh*, 493 S.W.3d 675, 681 (Tex. App.—Dallas 2015) *rev'd on other grounds*, No. 16-0096, 2017 WL 2824394 (Tex. Jun. 30, 2017).

executed within the employment relationship, it is important for an employer to at least consider obtaining one from its employees, particularly in the current era of social media in which we live.

Regardless of whether a former or departing employee makes a negative communication in the form of a social media posting, print publication, or even by word of mouth, without an employee's agreement not to disparage his or her former employer, the employer is undoubtedly more vulnerable to damaging negative communications by its former or departing employee.

PART II

LITIGATION STRATEGY

Chapter 9
Preliminary Considerations

Edited by Robert Wood

9-1 THE BASICS

Your client comes to you with a controversy involving a departing employee. Likely, this client is one of the following people: the former employer, the new employer, or the affected employee. Your client is seeking your advice on what to do and, ultimately, your assessment of the most practical and expedient steps that can be taken to protect his or her interest. The adage "time is of the essence" is particularly true in situations where trade secrets and other confidential information are vulnerable. This chapter will provide guidance as to the initial steps that should be taken to determine whether and when a suit should be filed, or alternatively, whether another strategy would better serve the client's interests.

9-2 DEFINING THE ENGAGEMENT

It sounds simple, but one of the most important things the lawyer must first establish is who his actual client is. In a situation with the former employer, the issue should be fairly straightforward: the client is the former employer. Nonetheless, the prudent lawyer always asks probing questions about the corporate structure in order to confirm that the situation is as straightforward as it seems. During this questioning process, the issue of corporate affiliates often arises. An employee may have worked for multiple affiliates and, more importantly, may have entered into contracts with or obtained confidential information from multiple affiliates. As a result, any agreements between the departed employee and the corporate affiliates (whether parents or subsidiaries) will need to be taken into account. Even if counsel does not ultimately represent all such affiliates, their respective interests must still be accounted for in these conflicts.

The situation can become even more complicated when either the departing employee or the new employer (or both) is the source of the representation. The new employer may engage counsel to represent its affected employee. Although the employee may technically be the client, the employer will also be deeply involved in the representation. The prudent lawyer should take care that any communications with the new employer do not violate or waive the lawyer's attorney-client privilege with the affected employee. Typically, this can be accomplished with a joint defense agreement.[1] The employer may ask counsel to represent both the new employer and one or more departing employees, particularly in a situation where both the employer and the employee(s) have been sued. Provided there is no conflict of interest, it is completely permissible for counsel to represent both the employer and the employee(s).[2] However, if representing both the employer and the employee(s), counsel should take great care in determining whether a conflict of interest exist and the probability of a conflict of interest arising in the future. Then, presuming counsel is satisfied that no conflict exists, counsel can represent multiple parties in the controversy. At the onset, counsel should require

1. *See* Appendix B-1 for a joint defense agreement form.

2. *See* Tex. Disciplinary R. Prof 'l Conduct I .06(d).

each of the clients to sign a well-drafted engagement letter clearly outlining the parameters of the representation.[3]

Irrespective of time constraints and the ever-present pressures of litigation; it is absolutely essential that counsel fully explain each detail of the engagement letter to the clients. The explanation should cover the following aspects of the engagement letter:.

9-2:1 WHAT IS CONFIDENTIAL?

The parties (particularly the employees) should understand that, although the confidences between themselves and counsel in the context of the representation are confidential from the outside world, they are *not* confidential *among the parties*. As a result, the parties need to understand that any confidences shared with the attorney will be shared among co-defendants.

9-2:2 WHAT HAPPENS IF A CONFLICT ARISES?

Usually, the engagement letter will provide that in the event one party develops a conflict with the other represented parties, that party will seek alternative representation. However, the conflict will not disqualify counsel from representing the remaining defendants. This provision greatly benefits the remaining parties who have already invested time, money, and energy into the current counsel. Alternatively, the other parties might not be able to retain counsel after the conflict in some situations, a reality that should also be explained when discussing the engagement letter.

9-2:3 WHO IS RESPONSIBLE FOR FEES?

Are the various clients jointly and severally responsible for the attorney's fees, or are they only responsible for their respective portions? In the case where the employer has agreed to pay the fees, what occurs when the employer and the new employee

---

3. *See* Appendix B-2 for a sample multi-party engagement letter.

develop some sort of conflict? Almost always, the new employer no longer wishes to pay the employee's attorney's fees.

9-3 PRELIMINARY FACT GATHERING

When a dispute arises concerning a departing employee, there are four steps that are almost always necessary. The steps are as follows:

1. Counsel should gather all relevant agreements. Typically, the employee will have signed various confidentiality agreements, non-disclosure agreements, employment agreements, inventions agreements, or other agreements which may not be named intuitively (but which may be relevant to the subject matter).
2. Counsel should review the documents to determine which of the various company policies may apply. These policies can often be found within handbooks and may include sections about non-disclosure, loyalty, ethics, or other applicable matters.
3. Counsel should isolate all potentially relevant electronic information. This information may be found on the former employee's hard drive, in email folders, on the company's network, or elsewhere. It is essential that care is taken to isolate and preserve any such information. It cannot be deleted.
4. Counsel should issue a "litigation hold", which communicates what is required of each affected person in the company in terms of preserving information (electronic

> or otherwise) once a controversy occurs or it is deemed likely one will occur.[4]

9-4 CONDUCTING A "FACT BLITZ"

Because departing employee controversies are typically time sensitive, quickly grasping the core facts of a particular case becomes extremely important. Usually, the first indication that a controversy exists is a call or other communication from a client regarding an emergency involving a former employee's conduct. This initial communication gives counsel a general flavor for the important issues in the case. Additionally, this preliminary rendition of the client's story will assist counsel in forming a plan of attack, which often includes a critical review of the relevant documents (described below):

> Depending on the nature of the controversy, the various agreements signed by the employee can often be of paramount importance. Such agreements may contain one or more non-disclosure agreements, an employee agreement containing restrictive covenants (such as a covenant not to compete, a covenant not to solicit customers, and/or covenant not to solicit employees). Frequently, there are multiple versions of such documents, particularly in cases where an employee has significant tenure, and to make matters more complicated-the restrictive covenants might not appear in the most obvious places. Therefore, counsel should take care to investigate purchase or sale documents, stock option agreements, restrictive stock agreements, and other documents which may contain restrictive covenants.[5]

4. *See* Appendix B-3 for a sample litigation hold memo.

5. *See Newell Rubbermaid, Inc.* 1'. *Storm,* No. CV 9398-VCN, 2014 Del. Ch. LEXIS 45 (Del. Ch. Mar. 27, 2014) (mem. op.) (not released for publication) (employer could enjoin a former employee with a TRO based on her violation of restrictive covenants in

9-5 ANALYZE COMPANY POLICIES

Company policies can often supplement the agreements signed by employees. Moreover, various sections of the company policies or handbook, such as those dealing with prohibited conduct or arbitration clauses, may become highly relevant.

9-6 INTERVIEW PERSONS WITH KNOWLEDGE OF FACTS

This seems fairly obvious, but counsel in a time-sensitive departing employee controversy may rely upon her initial contact to obtain most of the preliminary information about the case. However, such an approach can easily result in missteps. Almost invariably, information reported upward through a chain becomes less accurate, even though each link may believe it is correctly reporting the information. Ultimately, the employer must prove or disprove the allegations in a case through witnesses who have actual, firsthand knowledge of the transactions or occurrences in question. Direct communication early on with primary witnesses (and not just to their manager) will improve the quality of counsel's overall representation and help counsel avoid misunderstanding and missteps.

9-7 CONDUCT A FORENSIC REVIEW

The integrity and preservation of confidential, proprietary, and business information is almost always at the forefront of actual or potential departing employee litigation. Accordingly, counsel should strongly encourage her client to immediately engage in a forensic review of any relevant information-particularly confidential and proprietary information-that might be at risk. An IT professional can determine the following:

1. Has the departed employee sent information to his personal email address? Have all

contained in stock agreements, which she agreed to on a third-party website).

forms (whether electronic or hard copy) of confidential and proprietary information been returned?

2. Were any devices ever attached to the former employee's computer(s) that would indicate unauthorized copying or transferring of confidential, proprietary, or business information?
3. Have all PDAs (smartphones, tablets, and other devices) been examined to determine whether they have or might have contained company information?
4. What additional information do the former employee's email accounts, folders, and other electronic information indicate might be useful in the event of a lawsuit?

9-8 OTHER USEFUL INFORMATION

The nature and extent of this inquiry is usually determined by the surrounding controversy. If the controversy is merely an alleged breach of restrictive covenant (with no suspicion that confidential information has been compromised), a more low-level review may be sufficient. On the other hand, if there are legitimate and pressing concerns regarding preservation of confidential information, a significantly more detailed review may be necessary. The IT professional conducting the review should be carefully selected. He or she must be thorough, competent, knowledgeable, and even a good potential witness. In addition, consider carefully whether an "in-house" IT professional is adequate, or whether an outside professional may provide a more credible testimony.

9-9 WARNING/DEMAND LETTERS

As noted in Chapter 1,[6] it will occasionally be appropriate or useful to send a warning letter prior to initiating a lawsuit. For example, a letter may be appropriate when a competitor is unaware that a new hire either is subject to restrictive covenants (or potentially violating some). A warning letter will likely result in the former employee, the new employer, or both parties, acting more carefully in their subsequent dealings. The letter may additionally provide evidence that the former employer is taking prudent steps to protect its confidential information, contractual rights, or common-law rights. Finally, the letter can double as a "demand letter," which is a prerequisite to recovery under the Texas Attorney's Fee Statute.[7] However, as discussed earlier, an employer should take care to ensure a warning/demand letter is not an unintended first step toward waiver.[8]

9-9:1 TEXAS ATTORNEY'S FEE STATUTE

In certain instances, one or more of the agreements between the parties may provide for recovery of attorney's fees. In fact, courts will generally enforce contracts where the parties have contracted for recovery of attorney's fees.[9] However, many contracts are silent as to potential recovery of attorney's fees. Practitioners should be aware that some courts have held that Section 15.51 of the Texas Business and Commerce Code preempts Chapter 38 of the Texas Civil Practice & Remedies Code, and precludes recovery of attorneys fees under a declaratory judgment theory or prevailing party provision in the employment agreement.

---

6. *See* discussion in Chapter I , § 1-3:3 *(Ally Fin., Inc. v. Gutierrez,* No. 02-13-00108-CV, 2014 Tex. App. LEXIS 792, at *7-8 (Tex. App.-Fort Worth Jan. 23, 2014, no pet.) (mem. op.).

7. Tex. Civ. Prac. & Rem. Code Ann. § 38.001 .

8. *See* discussion in Chapter I , § 1-3:3 *(Allv Fin., Inc. v. Gutierrez,* No. 02-13-00108-CV, 2014 Tex. App. LEXIS 792, at *7-8 (Tex. App. -Fort Worth Jan. 23, 2014, no pet.) (mem. op.).

9. *See Intercontinental Grp. P'ship v. KB Home Loan Star L P* , 295 S.W3d 650, 653 (Tex. 2009).

However, the employer may recover under Chapter 38 or prevailing party provision if the employer prevails under a different breach of contract claim outside of the Texas Noncompete Act (e.g. breach of confidentiality) or under an independent cause of action that provides for recovery of attorneys fees (e.g. Texas Uniform Trade Secrets Act).[10]

9-10 POSSIBLE EARLY RESOLUTION

Often, parties to an impending departing-employee lawsuit will want to determine if a satisfactory business solution can be reached before commencing a costly litigious process. Consequently, counsel should be prepared to explore all available strategies which could achieve that efficient result. Some of the available strategies are outlined in the following sections.

9-10:1 INFORMAL SETTLEMENT CONFERENCE

If there is not an immediate, irreparable harm that would require a temporary restraining order, the parties may choose to sit down and have an informal settlement discussion regarding mutually satisfactory approaches to the issue at hand. If counsel are already involved, they may confer to determine if early resolution is possible. Because the Rules provide that these settlement discussions are inadmissible in the event of subsequent litigation, counsel should document such discussions as protected.[11] Even if settlement discussions do not result in an agreement between the parties, they almost invariably allow each party to better understand the other party's position.

9-10:2 MEDIATION

As a more formal procedure, mediation may allow the parties to reach a compromise and ultimately avoid litigation. The value of

10. *See, e.g. Traina v. Hargrove and Associates Inc.* Court of Appeals of Texas, Houston (14th Dist.). July 27, 2021 —S.W.3d —2021 WL 3161482

11. *See* Tex. Evid. R. 408; *See also* Appendix B-4 for a sample Rule 408 letter.

a mediator, as an objective third-party to help the parties reach a resolution, should not be underestimated. Departing employee litigation can often be highly emotional, and a mediator can help the parties focus on the business issues and the benefits of reaching a settlement. Additionally, even if a full settlement is not reached, the mediator may be able to help the parties reach a partial settlement, which may delay or likewise preclude the need for litigation. As with informal settlement discussions, mediation communications are considered confidential by statute and may not be used in subsequent litigation.[12]

9-10:3 ARBITRATION

As previously stated, many employers already have predispute arbitration agreements with their employees or arbitration clauses in their handbooks or company policies. It is important to understand that these agreements to arbitrate are routinely enforced by the courts in departing employee situations.[13]

In addition, the parties are free to enter into a post-dispute arbitration agreement. In that instance, the parties may design any arbitration procedure they so choose. Properly designed, an arbitration procedure can have the salutatory effect of providing the parties with a quicker, more streamlined, and ultimately less-expensive path to dispute resolution. In such an arbitration agreement, the parties can draft an agreement which meets their needs and may include the following items:

1. selection of the arbitrator;
2. selection of the arbitration service provider;
3. limitations on discovery;
4. the scope of the dispute;

12. Tex. Civ. Prac. & Rem. Code Ann. § 154.053.

13. *See* discussion in Chapter 4. § 4-1.

5. extended or accelerated time limits for taking action;
6. the scope of the arbitrator's authority;
7. the type of award to be issued by the arbitrator; and
8. any other matters important to the parties.

A carefully drafted post-dispute arbitration agreement offers the opportunity for the parties to address their primary concerns, which almost always include mitigating the burdens and costs of litigation.

Chapter 10

Whether to Seek an Injunction

Edited by Shelby Taylor

10-1 INTRODUCTION

More often than not, litigation involving departing employees includes making an early determination of whether the plaintiff(s)—typically, the departing employee's former employer—will seek an injunction. Departing employee lawsuits can be highly emotional, and impassioned clients will often come into your office with the desire to "slap them with a TRO" without understanding the rather involved process of obtaining one.

10-2 WHETHER TO SEEK A TEMPORARY RESTRAINING ORDER

A Temporary Restraining Order (TRO) gives an employer emergency relief, allowing it to preserve the status quo until a temporary injunction hearing is held.[1] This preservation of the status quo until the court-specified date of the temporary injunction hearing is the purpose of a TRO. Not surprisingly, preparing the appropriate papers to obtain a TRO is both time consuming

1. *Texas Aeronautics Comm'n v. Betts*, 469 S.W.2d 394, 398 (Tex. 1971).

and expensive. Therefore, before beginning the process of obtaining a TRO, care should be taken to determine whether one is even necessary. While TROs can be granted without notice, the local rules of many jurisdictions require that notice is given either to opposing parties or to their counsel or, alternatively, certification is given as to why such notice cannot be given.[2] The court determines whether to grant a TRO based on the written evidence provided by the movant. Upon a review of the pertinent facts and documents, counsel should (as a threshold matter) determine that:

1. Injunction, particularly a TRO, is the appropriate remedy; and
2. Grounds for the restraining order exist. These are typically found in either a statute or under principals of equity.

10-3 DO PRINCIPLES OF EQUITY APPLY?

Typically, principals of equity are applicable where there is:

1. An actual or anticipated violation of an existing right;
2. Substantial or irreparable injury unless the restraining order is issued; and
3. The injunctive relief is the only adequate remedy.

10-4 POTENTIAL SETBACK

Even if a TRO appears to be appropriate, prudent counsel should still determine the wisdom of seeking a restraining order. These considerations would include the likelihood of obtaining such an order. Courts can be highly reluctant to grant TROs in close cases, and an unsuccessful attempt at obtaining a TRO—especially after

2. *See generally* Chapter 2.

a large expenditure of time, money, and effort—could be viewed as a setback by your client (and by opposing parties).

10-5 THE COST AND DISRUPTION OF SEEKING A TRO

Gathering the information and preparing an application for a TRO is often a time-consuming, costly process, which can be disruptive to the client's business. For example, your client will need to understand and be willing to post either a cash bond or a surety bond as required by the court's local rules.[3] Thus, at the outset, lawyer and client should determine whether the time and cost associated with seeking a TRO are justified, given the harm that would otherwise occur if the TRO were not granted. Accordingly, the client's knee-jerk reaction to "slap them with a TRO" should be tempered by a rational cost-benefit analysis.

The potential cost and disruption of a TRO is real and should be discussed frankly with your client.

10-6 PREPARING A TRO APPLICATION

All petitions for injunctive relief must be based on verified petitions.[4] Because a restraining order is granted on the pleadings (and attachments to the pleadings) alone, this is an absolute requirement. This verification requirement can either be met by actual verification of the pleading or by a supporting affidavit or declaration under penalty of perjury.[5] To have an effective application for a restraining order, you and your client must gather and verify all the necessary facts for the granting of a TRO. All

3. *See* discussion *supra* Chapter 2 § 2-8; *see also* discussion *infra* Chapter 13 § 13-8:4.

4. *See* Tex. R. Civ. P. 682.

5. *See* Tex. Civ. Prac. & Rem. Code § 132.00.

the technical requirements for receipt of a TRO must be also met for the Order to be granted.[6]

Before you file your first Application for a TRO, review this checklist to be sure your filing meets the minimum requirements of the Texas Rules of Civil Procedure.[7] If you are defending against a TRO, be sure your opposing counsel has met each of the minimum requirements. Additionally, below are some best practices that should aid you in litigating your injunctive relief case.

Checklist for TRO:

1. What are the causes of action? Do those causes of action support injunctive relief?
2. Are you applying for a TRO? Make sure you also apply for a Temporary Injunction.
3. Have you properly identified the parties you seek to enjoin? Be sure to effect service on every individual and corporation you expect to comply with the TRO.
4. Where does the opposing party reside? Make sure you file in the enjoined party's county of residence or be prepared to argue Civil Prac. & Rem. Code § 65.023 does not apply.
5. Do you have a Verified Petition or Application? Either a Verification or an Affidavit will suffice.
6. Does the person who verified the Petition/ Application have personal knowledge of

6. *See* checklist below.

7. This checklist is from Michael E. Coles's address at the State Bar of Texas "Soaking Up Some CLE, A South Texas Litigation Seminar" (May 16-17, 2013), entitled *TROs and Injunctions—Avoiding Pitfalls*, and is reprinted here with permission.

the facts in the Petition/Application? That person will likely be deposed on the facts contained in the Petition/Application.

7. Does your TRO include facts that support the Court's decision to enter the TRO? Those facts should mirror the facts in your Petition/Application.
8. Does your TRO have a bond? An expiration date? A date for the hearing on the Application for Temporary Injunction?
9. Do you have a Motion for Expedited Discovery? Is your limited discovery drafted and attached for the Court to review?
10. Have you drafted a Motion to Extend the TRO to provide ample time for discovery?

Because the Rules specifically provide that a temporary injunction must be heard within a short period of time after the TRO is entered, the parties consume a significant amount of financial and other resources when preparing for the hearing. The parties have a limited time to gather all the necessary evidence before the hearing[8], and so they usually seek expedited discovery, interrogatories, requests for productions, and depositions to address the injunctive relief. Moreover, all this information must be assimilated in order to prepare for the temporary injunction hearing, which is often dispositive of the issues in the case.

10-7 TEMPORARY INJUNCTION

Whether or not a TRO is issued, a temporary injunction can still be granted. As previously stated, the purpose of a temporary injunction is to preserve the status quo, which is defined as the last "peaceable, non-contested status which preceded the

8. See Tex. R. Civ. P. 680.

pending controversy."[9] Temporary injunctions and TROs serve similar functions and are based on the same elements of proof. However, since temporary injunctions are more like a trial on the merits, counsel's approach to temporary injunctions is often quite different than their approach to TROs. During temporary injunction hearings, courts must accept evidence as they would when it is presented in trial.[10] One Texas appellate court case has held that affidavits can be offered and, if the court is accepting of the evidence, may single-handedly support a temporary injunction.[11] However, that case appears to be a slight aberration, and litigants should only introduce evidence that is admissible pursuant to the Texas Rules of Evidence.

---

9. *In re Newton*, 146 S.W.3d 648, 651 (Tex. 2004).

10. *Millwrights Local Union No. 2484 v. Rust Eng'g* Co., 433 S.W.2d 683, 686-88 (Tex. 1968).

11. *Pierce v. State*, 184 S.W.3d 303, 306-07 (Tex. App.—Dallas 2005, no pet.).

Chapter 11
Procedural Considerations

Edited by Shelby Taylor

11-1 INTRODUCTION

Just as in any other case, counsel seeking to file suit in a departing employee case must make some initial determinations. Two such important determinations are where to file suit (jurisdiction and venue) and what causes of action should be included. This chapter will discuss both issues, as well as additional procedural considerations.

11-2 JURISDICTION

The Texas district courts are constitutional courts of general jurisdiction.[1] A district court has original jurisdiction over civil matters when the amount in controversy is more than $500 (exclusive of interest).[2] The district court is the ultimate Texas trial court, with "exclusive, appellate and original jurisdiction of all actions, proceedings and remedies, except in cases where exclusive, appellate or reasonable jurisdiction may be conferred

1. Tex. Const. Art. 5, §§ 1, 8.

2. Tex. Gov. Code § 24.007.

by the Constitution or other law on some other court, tribunal, or administrative body."[3] Therefore, unless the case is removed to or filed in federal court, most departing employee suits are tried in district court.[4]

11-3 PERSONAL JURISDICTION

Texas residences can bring departing employee suits in Texas courts so long as they can obtain personal jurisdiction over the defendant(s). A Texas court's exercise of personal jurisdiction over nonresident defendants is controlled by the Texas long-arm statutes.[5] In order to determine whether a nonresident defendant can be subjected to personal jurisdiction in a Texas court, the Texas Supreme Court has formulated a three-part test for due process in "specific jurisdiction" cases. Specific jurisdiction occurs when a nonresident defendant only has a single or a few contacts with a forum. In these cases, due process requires that *all* the following conditions are met before a court can properly exercise personal jurisdiction over a nonresident defendant:

1. The nonresident must purposefully do some act or consummate some transaction in Texas;
2. The cause of action must arise from or be connected with the act or transaction, particularly if the nonresident's contacts with the state are few; and
3. The assumption of jurisdiction by the state must not offend traditional notions of fair play and substantial justice.[6]

---

3. Tex. Const. Art. 5, § 8; *see also Subaru of America v. David Nissan*, 84 S.W.3d 212, 220 (Tex. 2002).

4. Departing employees may also be brought in county courts provided they otherwise meet the jurisdictional prerequisites.

5. Tex. Civ. Prac. & Rem. Code §§ 17.041-045.

6. *O'Brien v. Lanpar Co.*, 399 S.W.2d 340, 342 (Tex. 1966).

11-4 VENUE

The term "venue" generally refers to whether a suit can be brought in a particular county.[7] Venue can be waived.[8]

11-4:1 APPLICABLE TEXAS VENUE PROVISIONS

11-4:1.1 TEXAS STATE COURT VENUE

Assuming a court has both subject matter and personal jurisdiction, then counsel must determine which venue is proper. Some Texas venue statutes are characterized as "mandatory," meaning that venue *must* be brought in a certain county. Conversely, some statutes are more permissive and state that venue *may* be brought in a certain county. Moreover, there may be one or more of these permissive venue statutes that allow the plaintiff to file suit in multiple counties. The general venue statute requires that all lawsuits are brought in one of the following counties:

1. The county in which all or a substantial part of events or omissions giving rise to the claim occurred;
2. The county of the defendant's residence at the time the cause of action accrued, if the defendant is natural person;
3. The county of the defendant's "principal office" in Texas, if the defendant is not a natural person; or
4. The county in which the plaintiff resided at the time of accrual of the cause of action, if the rules in paragraphs (1), (2), and (3), above, do not apply.[9]

---

7. *Kshatrya v. Texas Workforce Com'n*, 97 S.W.3d 825, 830 (Tex. App.—Dallas 2003, no pet.).

8. *Id.*

9. Tex. Civ. Prac. & Rem Code § 15.002(a).

Additionally, in some circumstances venue is permitted in a county designated by a written contract expressly providing that the contractual obligation should be performed there.[10]

11-4:1.2 GENERAL VENUE

The Texas General Venue Statute is most commonly used to determine venue in departing employee cases.[11] Consequently, venue is usually appropriate in counties where all or a substantial part of the advance or admissions giving rise to the claim occurred.[12] Theoretically, the concept of "substantiality" requires the claimant to demonstrate that the venue has an actual relationship to the dispute.[13] The substantiality requirement does not limit venue to a single county;[14] therefore, it is possible (under the Texas General Venue Statute) for venue to exist in multiple counties.

11-4:1.3 CONTRACT ACTIONS

To meet the substantiality requirements in an action for breach of contract, courts tend to look at where the contract was formed, where the contract was intended to be performed, or where the breach occurred.[15] Venue may be proper in the county where the negotiations that resulted in an agreement were reached, which may involve multiple counties. On the other hand, venue is likely not proper where only the damages occurred in a contract claim.[16]

---

10. Tex. Civ. Prac. & Rem. Code § 15.035.

11. *But see* discussion *infra* 12-4:1.7 (concerning mandatory injunction in some venue cases).

12. Tex. Civ. Prac. & Rem. Code § 15.002(a)(1).

13. *Chiriboga v. State Farm Mut. Auto. Ins. Co.*, 96 S.W.3d 673, 681 (Tex. App.—Austin 2003, no pet.).

14. *S. County Mut. Ins. Co. v. Ochoa*, 19 S.W.3d 452, 457-58 (Tex. App.—Corpus Christi 2000), *on reh'g (May 11, 2000)*.

15. *Cf.* Tex. Civ. Prac. & Rem. Code § 15.035(a).

16. *Haden Co., Inc. v. Johns-Manville Sales Corp.*, 553 S.W.2d 759, 759-60 (Tex. 1977).

11-4:1.4 DEFENDANT'S RESIDENCE

As previously stated, venue is proper in the county where the defendant resides at the time the cause of action accrued, as long as the defendant is a natural person.[17] Of course, a person may have more than one residence. For example, a college student often has a permanent home residence, as well as a dormitory or off-campus housing in the county where the school is located.[18] For the purpose of the general statute, a residence is generally considered to be:

(1) A fixed place of abode within the possession of the defendant,

(2) occupied or intended to be occupied consistently over a substantial period of time, and

(3) permanent rather than temporary.[19]

11-4:1.5 CORPORATIONS, ASSOCIATIONS, AND PARTNERSHIPS: DEFENDANT'S "PRINCIPAL OFFICE"

If the defendant is not a natural person, the defendant may be sued in a "principal office in this state."[20] The term "principal office" means "a principal office of the corporation, unincorporated association, or partnership in this state in which the decision makers for the organization within this state conduct the daily affairs of the organizations. The mere presence of an agency or representative does not establish a principal office."[21] Naturally, an organization may have more than one principal office. "Principal office" usually applies to the office where the organization conducts its "daily affairs." However, an office that

---

17. Tex. Civ. Prac. & Rem. Code § 15.002(a)(2).

18. *Mijares v. Paez*, 534 S.W.2d 435, 436-37 (Tex. Civ. App.—Amarillo 1976, no writ).

19. *Snyder v. Pitts, 241 S.W.2d 136, 140 (Tex. 1951).*

20. Tex. Civ. Prac. & Rem. Code § 15.002(a)(3).

21. Tex. Civ. Prac. & Rem. Code § 15.001(a).

is clearly subordinate to another Texas office cannot itself be a principal office.[22]

11-4:1.6 PLAINTIFF'S RESIDENCE

Normally, the plaintiff's residence cannot be the source of venue. However, if (1) there is no county in Texas in which all or a substantial part of the events or omissions giving rise to the claim occurred, (2) no natural-person defendant has resided in Texas from the time the cause of action accrued, and (3) no defendant that is not an actual person has a principal office in Texas, *then* the plaintiff's residence may be considered as a source of venue.[23]

11-4:1.7 MANDATORY VENUE STATUTE

Because the general venue statute pertains only "as otherwise provided by" mandatory or permissive venue sections,[24] the mandatory venue exception controls if applicable. Therefore, whenever a defendant correctly files a motion to transfer based upon a mandatory venue exception, and the plaintiff is only relying on a permissive venue exception, the trial court is required to grant the defendant's motion to transfer.

11-4:1.7A ACTIONS INVOLVING INJUNCTIONS

The Texas Civil Practice & Remedies Code provides that a writ injunction against a resident of Texas must be tried in the county of the defendant's domicile.[25] When the injunction request is ancillary to a cause of action and the party's primary interest, the mandatory venue statute does not apply.[26] As previously

---

22. *In re Missouri Pacific R. Co.*, 998 S.W.2d 212, 220 (Tex. 1999).

23. Tex. Civ. Prac. & Rem. Code § 15.002(a)(4).

24. Tex. Civ. Prac. & Rem. Code § 15.002(a).

25. Tex. Civ. Prac. & Rem. Code § 65.023(a).

26. *In re Adan Volpe Props.*, 306 S.W.3d 369, 377 (Tex. App.—Corpus Christi 2010, no pet.).

mentioned, in cases where injunctions are ancillary, the lawsuit will determine the venue and the request for injunction.[27]

11-4:1.8 UNDER TEXAS LAW, "DOMICILE" AND "RESIDENCE" MEAN THE SAME THING[28]

Section 65.023 only applies where the primary relief being sought is purely or primarily injunctive.[29] Therefore, where an injunction is merely ancillary to the underlying cause of action's main purpose, this mandatory provision of the Texas Civil Practice & Remedies Code does not apply.[30] When this mandatory injunctive venue provision does not apply, venue is determined by the otherwise applicable venue provision.

11-4:1.9 MAJOR TRANSACTIONS — VENUE BY AGREEMENT

The question of major transactions imbeds a slight wrinkle into the venue selection clause.[31] A "major transaction" is one where there is a written agreement in which someone pays or receives (or is obligated to pay or receive) aggregate consideration of a value equal to or greater than $1,000,000. However, there are exceptions to the applicability of the statute.[32] For example, the

---

27. *In re City of Corpus Christi*, No. 13-12-00510-CV, 2012 WL 3755604, at *5 (Tex. App. Aug. 29, 2012) (mem. op.) (" . . . the possibility that the trial court will resort to injunctive relief to enforce a judgment rendered in this case does not by itself transform the suit into one for a 'writ of injunction' within the meaning of [Tex. Civ. Prac. & Rem. Code §] 65.023(a). In short, based on the pleadings and relief sought, we cannot conclude that the relief sought by [petitioner] in this matter is 'purely or primarily injunctive.' Accordingly, [Tex. Civ. Prac. & Rem. Code §] 65.023 does not apply to compel mandatory venue in Nueces County.") (citations omitted); See discussion supra 2-7.

28. *Snyder v. Pitts*, 241 S.W.2d 136, 140 (Tex. 1951).

29. *O'Quinn v. Hall*, 77 S.W.3d 452, 455-56 (Tex. App.—Corpus Christi 2002, no pet.).

30. *See Hogg v. Prof'l Pathology Associates, P.A.*, 598 S.W.2d 328, 330 (Tex. Civ. App.—Houston [14th Dist.] 1980, writ dism'd w.o.j.).

31. Tex. Civ. Prac. & Rem. Code § 15.020(d).

32. Tex. Civ. Prac. & Rem. Code § 15.020(a).

statute does not apply to forum selection clauses that are not considered major transactions.[33]

Under the statute, an action arising from a major transaction *must* be brought in a particular county if the defendant has already agreed in writing that an action arising from that transaction must be brought in that county.[34] This situation has been characterized as a mandatory venue provision.[35] Conversely, an action may not be brought in a particular county when the plaintiff has agreed in writing that any action arising from the transaction may not be brought in that county. In the same way, no action can be brought in a particular county if the plaintiff has agreed in writing that the action must be brought in another county.[36]

11-4:2 FORUM SELECTION CLAUSES

Counsel should always determine whether there is any agreement that might constitute a forum selection clause. Many employee agreements with restrictive covenants contain certain choice of law and or forum selection provisions for any potential dispute between the parties. Forum selection clauses are only enforceable in Texas if the parties have contractually consented to submit to the exclusive jurisdiction of the state.[37] However, an opposing party can defeat a forum selection clause if it can carry the heavy burden of proof to establish that:

1. Enforcement would be unreasonable or unjust;
2. The clause is invalid due to fraud or overreaching;

33. Tex. Civ. Prac. & Rem. Code § 15.020(e).

34. Tex. Civ. Prac. & Rem. Code § 15.020(b).

35. *In re Tex. Ass'n of Sch. Bds., Inc.*, 169 S.W.3d 653, 654-55 (Tex. 2005).

36. Tex. Civ. Prac. & Rem. Code § 15.020(c).

37. *Faulk & Fish, L.L.P. v. Pinkston's Lawnmower & Equip., Inc.*, 317 S.W.3d 523, 525 (Tex. App.—Dallas 2010, no pet.).

3. Enforcement would contravene a strong public policy of the forum where the suit was brought; or
4. The selected forum would be seriously inconvenient for trial.[38]

Failure to consider a forum selection clause could completely derail your efforts to obtain or maintain injunctive relief in your chosen forum.

Generally, courts will grant a mandatory forum selection clause that is coupled with a covenant not to compete.[39]

11-5 FEDERAL COURT JURISDICTION

A complete discussion of federal procedure is beyond the scope of this book. However, a Texas state court practitioner must be aware of required federal procedure when a federal court has original jurisdiction.[40]

This type of jurisdiction is usually based upon federal question jurisdiction[41] or diversity of citizen jurisdiction.[42] In federal question jurisdiction, federal courts have original jurisdiction when the actions are brought under the United States Constitution or laws or treaties of United States.[43] A case arises under federal law if federal law creates a right or immunity that is an essential ingredient of the plaintiff's claims.[44]

38. *See* footnote 2 in the Texas Insurance Coverage Litigation 2013 book, nos. 1, 2, 3, and 4.

39. *In re Autonation, Inc.*, 228 S.W.3d 663, 669 (Tex. 2007).

40. 28 U.S.C. § 1441a.

41. 28 U.S.C. § 1331.

42. 28 U.S.C. § 1332(a).

43. 28 U.S.C. §§ 1331, 1441(a).

44. *Franchise Tax Bd. of State of Cal. v. Laborers Vacation Tr. For S. California*, 103 S. Ct. 2841, 2847 (1983) (superseded by 28 U.S.C. § 1441(e) on other grounds).

In diversity jurisdiction, federal courts have jurisdiction over claims between citizens of different states, between state citizens and citizens or subjects of foreign states, between citizens of different states (in which foreign states or citizens are additional parties), and between a citizen and a foreign state.[45] This diversity jurisdiction only exists when the amount in controversy exceeds $75,000 (exclusive of interest and costs).[46] In this way, diversity jurisdiction differs from federal jurisdiction, which requires no minimum amount in controversy.[47]

11-6 REMOVAL

As previously stated, practitioners in state court must be cognizant of the removal statute.[48] Removal jurisdiction applies when there is original federal court jurisdiction. Thus, the defendant can remove any civil action brought in state court if the federal district courts have original jurisdiction.[49] There are certain claims that are specifically excepted from the removal statute, but these exceptions are generally not relevant in departing employee cases. In addition, an action may not be removed on grounds of diversity jurisdiction if any defendant resides in the state where the action is brought.[50]

11-6:1 FRAUDULENT JOINDER

Occasionally, a defendant will attempt to join a non-diverse defendant solely for the purposes of defeating removal jurisdiction. However, if the plaintiff can prove that the joinder is improper or fraudulent, the non-diverse party will not be considered, and

---

45. 28 U.S.C. § 1332(a).

46. 28 U.S.C. § 1330(a).

47. 28 U.S.C. § 1331(a).

48. *See* Form 1-009–form of Notice of Removal and Form 1-010–form of notice to state court of removal.

49. 28 U.S.C. § 1441(a).

50. 28 U.S.C. § 1441(b)(2).

federal courts will retain removal jurisdiction.[51] To determine if a joinder is improper, the Fifth Circuit has articulated two tests:

1. Outright fraud in the plaintiff's pleading of the jurisdictional facts; or
2. That there is absolutely no possibility that the plaintiff will be able to establish a cause of action against the non-diverse defendant in state court.[52]

11-6:2 REMOVAL PROCEDURE

To remove an action, a defendant must timely file a notice of removal in the proper federal district court, as well as copies of all process, pleadings, and orders from the State Court proceedings.[53] The notice of removal should contain a short and plain statement of the grounds for removal.[54] Nonetheless, an insufficient notice of removal may be amended any time.[55] When a civil action is correctly removed solely on 28 U.S.C. § 1441(a) grounds, all the defendants who have been properly joined and served must consent to the action's removal.

Removal is effective when a copy of the notice is filed with both the federal court and state court. As soon as the notice is filed in state court, the state court effectively loses jurisdiction.[56] The federal court then takes the case as if events in the state court before removal had occurred in federal court. All orders entered by the state court will remain effective unless they are superseded or expire by their terms.[57]

---

51. 28 U.S.C. § 1441(b)(2).

52. *Travis v. Irby*, 326 F.3d 644, 646-47 (5th Cir. 2003).

53. 28 U.S.C. § 1446(a).

54. 28 U.S.C. § 1446(a). *See* Forms 1-009 and 1-010 for forms of removal.

55. 28 U.S.C. § 1653.

56. 28 U.S.C. § 1446(d); *Dukes v. S.C. Ins. Co.*, 770 F.2d 545, 547 (5th Cir. [Miss.] 1985).

57. 28 U.S.C. § 1450.

11-7 FEDERAL COURT VENUE

In most departing employee cases where federal jurisdiction exits, venue will be based on the general federal venue statute.[58] It states:

> (a) Applicability of Section. Except as otherwise provided by law—
>
> (1) this section shall govern the venue of all civil actions brought in district courts of the United States; and
>
> (2) the proper venue for a civil action shall be determined without regard to whether the action is local or transitory in nature.
>
> (b) Venue in General. A civil action may be brought in—
>
> (1) a judicial district in which any defendant resides, if all defendants are residents of the State in which the district is located;
>
> (2) a judicial district in which a substantial part of the events or omissions giving rise to the claim occurred, or a substantial part of property that is the subject of the action is situated; or
>
> (3) if there is no district in which an action may otherwise be brought as provided in this section, any judicial district in which any defendant is subject to the court's personal jurisdiction with respect to such action.
>
> (c) Residency. For all venue purposes—

58. 28 U.S.C. § 1391.

(1) a natural person, including an alien lawfully admitted for permanent residence in the United States, shall be deemed to reside in the judicial district in which that person is domiciled;

(2) an entity with the capacity to sue and be sued in its common name under applicable law, whether or not incorporated, shall be deemed to reside, if a defendant, in any judicial district in which such defendant is subject to the court's personal jurisdiction with respect to the civil action in question and, if a plaintiff, only in the judicial district in which it maintains its principal place of business; and

(3) a defendant not resident in the United States may be sued in any judicial district, and the joinder of such a defendant shall be disregarded in determining where the action may be brought with respect to other defendants.

(d) Residency of Corporations in States With Multiple Districts. For purposes of venue under this chapter, in a State which has more than one judicial district and in which a defendant that is a corporation is subject to personal jurisdiction at the time an action is commenced, such corporation shall be deemed to reside in any district in that State within which its contacts would be sufficient to subject it to personal jurisdiction if that district were a separate State, and, if there is no such district, the corporation shall be deemed to reside in the district within which it has the most significant contacts.

(e) Actions Where Defendant Is Officer or Employee of the United States—

(1) In general. A civil action in which a defendant is an officer or employee of the United States or any agency thereof acting in his official capacity or under color of legal authority, or an agency of the United States, or the United States, may, except as otherwise provided by law, be brought in any judicial district in which:

(A) a defendant in the action resides;

(B) a substantial part of the events or omissions giving rise to the claim occurred, or a substantial part of property that is the subject of the action is situated; or

(C) the plaintiff resides if no real property is involved in the action. Additional persons may be joined as parties to any such action in accordance with the Federal Rules of Civil Procedure and with such other venue requirements as would be applicable if the United States or one of its officers, employees, or agencies were not a party.

(2) Service. The summons and complaint in such an action shall be

served as provided by the Federal Rules of Civil Procedure except that the delivery of the summons and complaint to the officer or agency as required by the rules may be made by certified mail beyond the territorial limits of the district in which the action is brought.

(f) Civil Actions Against a Foreign State. A civil action against a foreign state as defined in section 1603 (a) of this title may be brought—

(1) in any judicial district in which a substantial part of the events or omissions giving rise to the claim occurred, or a substantial part of property that is the subject of the action is situated;

(2) in any judicial district in which the vessel or cargo of a foreign state is situated, if the claim is asserted under section 1605 (b) of this title;

(3) in any judicial district in which the agency or instrumentality is licensed to do business or is doing business, if the action is brought against an agency or instrumentality of a foreign state as defined in section 1603 (b) of this title; or

(4) in the United States District Court for the District of Columbia if the action is brought against a foreign state or political subdivision thereof.

(g) Multiparty, Multiforum Litigation.

> A civil action in which jurisdiction of the district court is based upon section 1369 of this title may be brought in any district in which any defendant resides or in which a substantial part of the accident giving rise to the action took place.

11-8 CHOICE OF LAW

A covenant not to compete will very often include a choice of law provision. Texas courts are usually skeptical of such provisions.[59] However, the case of *In re Autonation* indicates that the skepticism of a choice of law provision may be overcome with a forum selection clause.[60] In that case,[61] the Court considered a choice of law provision that required the agreement to be construed under Florida law. The Court endorsed the *DeSantis* approach, which does not require the routine application of choice of law provisions. Then, the Court stated that Texas law can only be applied when the following three requirements are met:

> (1) Texas has a more significant relationship to the parties and the transaction than the other state;
>
> (2) Texas has a materially greater interest in enforcing the covenant than the other states does; and
>
> (3) application of the other state's law would be contrary to the fundamental policy of Texas.

As a general rule, any party challenging a forum selection clause should do so early in the litigation or risk waiver.[62]

---

59. *See DeSantis v. Wackenhut Corp.*, 793 S.W.2d 670, 677 (Tex. 1990).

60. *In re Autonation, Inc.*, 228 S.W.3d at 669.

61. *Id. at* 664-65.

62. *See, e.g., Flying Diamond-W. Madisonville L.P. v. GW Petroleum, Inc.*, No. 10-07-

If venue is proper in more than one district,[63] the court "need not decide which district is the 'best' venue or whether one forum has greater contacts than another."[64]

*00281-CV, 2009 WL 2707405, at *11 (Tex. App. Aug. 26, 2009).*

63. *Godwin Gruber, P.C. v. Lambert*, No. 3-03-CV-1095-BD(L), 2004 WL 813229, at *5 (N.D. Tex. Apr. 13, 2004).

64. *Doe v. Kanakuk Ministries*, No. 3:11-CV-0524-G, 2012 WL 715980, at *1 (N.D. Tex. Mar. 5, 2012).

Chapter 12
Initial Pleadings, Petition, and Answer

Edited by Shelby Taylor

12-1 PLEADINGS IN A DEPARTING EMPLOYEE INJUNCTION ACTION

This chapter will attempt to walk the reader through the initial pleadings and motions in a case involving a claim against or by a departing employee or the new employer. Since departing employee cases usually involve injunctive relief, this chapter will include the steps necessary for a party to obtain or challenge injunctive relief.

12-2 PLAINTIFF'S PETITION

In the Forms Appendix, there is a form of a plaintiff's original petition seeking injunctive relief, including a temporary restraining order and a temporary injunction.[1] This chapter will explain each of the elements within such a petition.

1. See forms section for sample motions and pleadings.

12-3 THE CAPTION

Typically, the caption of the petition contains the names and designations of the parties, the file number, the court, the county and state of suit, the number of the judicial district, and often the name of the pleading (such as "Plaintiff's Original Petition").

12-4 THE SALUTATION

Lawyers will generally start a petition with a salutation like "TO THE HONORABLE COURT." This salutation usually follows the caption. However, because it does not place any matters at issue, it is not required for the petition.

12-5 PARTY ALLEGATIONS

Unlike the optional salutation, the petition *must* include the names of the parties and their residences.[2] Effective September 1, 2007, an initial pleading must include the last three numbers of each party's driver license numbers and the last three numbers of each party's social security numbers, if they have them.[3]

12-6 DISCOVERY CONTROL PLAN

Effective January 1, 1999, every civil case must now be conducted under a discovery control plan.[4] To comply, a plaintiff must designate in the first numbered paragraph of every petition whether discovery in the case will be conducted under a Level 1, Level 2, or Level 3 discovery control plan.[5] A Level 3 discovery plan must be requested by court order. Pursuant to Rule 47, the plaintiff must also state that it seeks:

(1) only monetary relief of $250,000 or less,

2. Tex. R. Civ. P. 79.
3. Tex. Civ. Prac. & Rem. Code § 30.014.
4. Tex. R. Civ. P. 190.
5. Tex. R. Civ. P. 190.1.

excluding interest, statutory or punitive damages and penalties, and attorney's fees and costs;

(2) monetary relief of $250,000 or less and non-monetary relief;

(3) monetary relief over $250,000 but not more than $1,000,000; or

(4) monetary relief over $1,000,000; or

(5) only non-monetary relief.[6]

A party that fails to comply with Rule 47(c) may not conduct discovery until the party's pleading is amended to comply.

12-7 JURISDICTION

12-7:1 SUBJECT MATTER JURISDICTION

In order to show the subject matter jurisdiction of the court in which the action is brought, the petition must state the proper facts.[7] However, unless the petition affirmatively demonstrates an absence of jurisdiction, failure to state the jurisdictional matter in the original petition does not deprive the court of jurisdiction.[8] If a suit involves a claim for nonliquidated damages, for example, a petition only needs to state that the "damages sought are within the jurisdictional limits of the court."[9] Items of special damages must be specifically stated.[10]

12-7:2 PERSONAL JURISDICTION

On the other hand, personal jurisdiction is only a matter at issue when the defendant is a nonresident. In that instance, personal

6. Tex. R. Civ. P. 47(c).

7. Tex. R. Civ. P. 90.

8. *See* Tex. R. Civ. P. 47(b).

9. Tex. R. Civ. P. 47(b).

10. Tex. R. Civ. P. 56.

jurisdiction is sufficiently alleged by stating the defendant's residence. Any nonresident defendant, therefore, should carefully allege the sufficient facts required by the appropriate long-arm statute.[11]

12-7:3 VENUE

The plaintiff must plead the applicable venue statute. These statues are often characterized as the general venue rule[12] or as an exception.[13] Unless denied by the adverse party, venue facts are accepted as true.[14]

12-7:4 PLEADING THE ELEMENTS OF THE CAUSE OF ACTION

Rule 45 requires the plaintiff to state a cause of action in plain, concise language. The statement of the cause of action can be short. Its only requirement is to give fair notice of the claim involved. However, because of the existence of the verification requirement when seeking a temporary restraining order or temporary injunction, a well-pleaded claim for injunctive relief goes far beyond simple notice. In fact, the claim must state all the facts necessary to obtain injunctive relief. Furthermore, these facts must be verified.[15]

12-7:5 STATEMENT OF CLAIM

A party may state, separately, a claim he has against a single defendant or multiple defendants.[16] A plaintiff may also plead two or more alternate statements of claims.[17]

---

11. *See* Tex. Civ. Prac. & Rem. Code §§ 17.041-17.045.
12. Tex. Civ. Prac. & Rem. Code § 15.002.
13. Tex. Civ. Prac. & Rem. Code §§ 15.011-15.040.
14. Tex. R. Civ. P. 87(3).
15. Tex. R. Civ. P. 682.
16. Tex. R. Civ. P. 48, 51(a).
17. Tex. R. Civ. P. 48.

12-7:6 PRAYER FOR RELIEF

In general, plaintiffs' petitions must request all relief to which they consider themselves to be entitled.[18] This is often called the "prayer". The prayer can be general or "special." When an injunction and a restraining order are sought in the same petition, a special prayer is required.[19]

12-7:7 EXHIBITS

The Rules allow parties to attach exhibits to a petition.[20] For all intents and purposes, an exhibit is deemed to be a part of the petition.[21]

12-8 APPLICATION FOR INJUNCTIVE RELIEF

When a party seeks a temporary restraining order or a temporary injunction, it must apply for injunctive relief. Usually, the application for injunctive relief is a part of the original petition, but it does not necessarily have to be. Below are the steps to take when applying for injunctive relief.

12-8:1 PRELIMINARY ASSESSMENT

Counsel's first step is to determine whether an injunction is even the appropriate remedy. Therefore, counsel must review the facts and evidence and decide whether grounds for injunctive relief are available by either statute or general principles of equity. Moreover, unless there is no other adequate remedy of law, an injunction is only appropriate where there has been irreparable injury.[22] Furthermore, the client must be capable of providing a surety bond.

---

18. Tex. R. Civ. P. 47.

19. *Fant v. Massie*, 451 S.W.2d 774, 776 (Tex. Civ. App.—Austin 1970, writ ref'd n.r.e.).

20. Tex. R. Civ. P. 59.

21. Tex. R. Civ. P. 59.

22. *Letkeman v. Reyes*, 299 S.W.3d 482, 486 (Tex. App.—Amarillo 2009, no pet.).

Counsel should decide whether a temporary restraining order (with or without notice) is necessary. In that case, counsel needs to determine whether the plaintiff is receiving an ongoing harm which could cause immediate, irreparable damage prior to a hearing on the temporary injunction. However, counsel should also consider what possible damages are available to the adversary under a claim for wrongful injunction, if the restraining order is dissolved.

12-8:2 CONTENTS OF THE RESTRAINING ORDER AND REQUEST FOR INJUNCTION

As mentioned earlier, the application is usually part of the original petition. When an application for injunction is included in the petition, the elements of injunction must be stated. In addition, the application for injunction must include an affidavit verified by a person with knowledge that the facts in the petition (alleged in support of the application) are true and correct.[23] Regarding a temporary restraining order, this requirement is absolute. Because the temporary restraining order is granted on the basis of the verified pleading, this same requirement may not be necessary in an application for a temporary permanent injunction, as long as sworn testimony is given at the hearing.[24]

Prudent counsel should draft the affidavit in support of the application for temporary restraining order or temporary injunction carefully. Often, both counsel and clients are rushed. In addition, clients can unintentionally shade facts in support of their case. Subsequently, this potential failure to be entirely accurate can devastate a case in a deposition or at a temporary injunction hearing.

---

23. Tex. R. Civ. P. 682.

24. *Williams v. City of Tom Bean*, 688 S.W.2d 618, 621 (Tex. App.—Dallas 1985, no writ).

12-8:3 ORDER GRANTING TEMPORARY RESTRAINING ORDER

Before counsel appear at court seeking temporary restraining orders, they need to prepare an order granting the temporary restraining order.[25]

As previously stated, an order granting a temporary restraining order must strictly comply with the requirements of the Rules. To comply, the order must:

1. Be as specific in terms as possible.[26]
2. Explicitly set forth the reasons for issuance of the restraining order.[27]
3. State why the motion is being granted without notice to the adverse party[28] (*i.e,* that a particular, concrete, immediate and irreparable injury, loss, or damage will result to the moving party before notice of the motion for a temporary injunction can be served and a hearing had thereon).[29]
4. Specifically describe the act or acts sought to be prohibited.[30]
5. Fix an amount of security to be given by the moving party for the protection of the party restrained.[31]

---

25. Tex. R. Civ. P. 680, 683, 684; *see* Forms 1-002 for a form of temporary restraining order.

26. Tex. R. Civ. P. 683.

27. Tex. R. Civ. P. 683.

28. Tex. R. Civ. P. 680.

29. Tex. R. Civ. P. 683.

30. Tex. R. Civ. P. 683.

31. Tex. R. Civ. P. 684.

6. Set the "earliest possible date" for hearing the motion for a temporary injunction.[32]

12-8:4 BOND REQUIREMENT

Any order granting a temporary restraining order must also contain the amount of security the applicant will give for the protection of the party restraints.[33] This likewise applies to a temporary injunction. Prior to the application being presented to the court, counsel should take care to confirm that the client is able to post either a cash or surety bond that will support the temporary restraining order. This is imperative because a temporary restraining order is invalid until bond is posted.[34] The local rules of the court you select may have additional requirements for delivery of the bond, so prudent counsel should always confirm that they or their clients will follow any special rules required to ensure proper delivery.

To be sufficient, the bond must meet the following requirements:

1. The bond should be payable to the adverse party.[35] When there are two or more adverse parties, the bond should (more likely than not) be made payable to them jointly and severally.
2. A bond may be issued by a single surety company in compliance with the Texas Insurance Code.[36] There must be at least two good and sufficient sureties.[37] Note, however, that under Chapter 3503 of the

32. Tex. R. Civ. P. 680.

33. Tex. R. Civ. P. 684.

34. *See* Form 1-020 for a form of bond, which may be used to satisfy the bond requirement.

35. Tex. R. Civ. P. 684.

36. Tex. Ins. Code § 3503.002

37. Tex. R. Civ. P. 684.

Insurance Code, a bond issued by a single surety company authorized to do business in Texas in compliance with the statutory requirements of that chapter is sufficient to comply with any legal requirement that a bond or other obligation be executed by one or more sureties.[38] If the bond is issued by such a corporate surety, the form below may be adapted to provide for execution by one party. If the corporate surety does not provide a form, this form may be adapted by altering the signature lines.

3. It should be expressly conditioned that the applicant will abide by the decision and pay all sums of money and costs that may be adjudged against the applicant if the temporary injunction is dissolved (in whole or in part) because of having been wrongfully issued.[39]
4. It should be signed by both the principal and the sureties.

12-9 THE ANSWER

In terms of an answer, a general denial is all that is required. However, to the extent that a party has any defenses under Texas Rules of Civil Procedure 93 or 94, he should plead those as well.[40]

12-10 MOTION TO DISSOLVE A TEMPORARY RESTRAINING ORDER

A motion to dissolve a temporary restraining order needs to state the justification for relief in clear language, concisely

38. *See* Tex. Ins. Code § 3503.002.

39. *See* Tex. R. Civ. P. 684.

40. *See* Tex. R. Civ. P. 93-94.

demonstrating that either the plaintiff is not entitled as a matter of law to have the temporary restraining order or that circumstances have changed and one is no longer necessary.[41] A motion to dissolve only requires two days' notice to the party who obtained the TRO, because the short expiration time period of a TRO requires that the motion to dissolve be filed quite rapidly.[42] While making a motion to dissolve a TRO constitutes a general appearance, courts have held that the filing of that motion will not waive venue rights.[43] A defendant still must timely file the answer, regardless of the court's action on the motion to dissolve. The motion does not provide a substitute.[44] Furthermore, under Texas Rule of Civil Procedure 690, a court will not dissolve an injunction based solely on a denial of the plaintiff's material allegation. The denial must be under oath. An unsworn declaration, under penalty of perjury, will suffice in lieu of verification.[45] If, in fact, the court grants a motion to dissolve an injunction preventing the collection of money, the defendant will be forced to post bond (payable to plaintiff) amounting to twice the sum being restrained. If the injunction is, however, reinstated, the condition dictates that the defendant refunds the applicant costs (including interest) collected prior to the final decision of the court.[46]

12-11 MOTION TO EXTEND A TEMPORARY RESTRAINING ORDER

To extend the order for 14 days, the motion must be granted while the existing TRO is still active. The motion will be granted if the requesting party is able to show either good cause for the extension or is able to secure the consent of the enjoined party.[47]

---

41. *See* 4-50 Dorsaneo, Texas Litigation Guide § 50.103 (2017).

42. *See* 4-50 Dorsaneo, Texas Litigation Guide § 50.103[1][b] (2017).

43. *See* Id.

44. *See* Id.

45. *See* 4-50 Dorsaneo, Texas Litigation Guide § 50.103 [1][c] (2017).

46. *See* 4-50 Dorsaneo, Texas Litigation Guide § 50.103 [1][d] (2017).

47. *See* 4-50 Dorsaneo, Texas Litigation Guide § 50.107 (2017).

Although the Rules do not explicitly require the extension motion be verified, prudent counsel will support the motion by verification or a declaration.[48] An order stating the reason for extension should accompany the motion and should specify the terms of the extension and describe the affected parties.[49]

12-12 MOTION FOR EXPEDITED DISCOVERY

As mentioned previously, counsel will usually draft a motion for expedited discovery (containing his attached discovery request) as well as a proposed order. Typically, the request includes documents, disclosures, interrogatory responses, and depositions on an expedited schedule.[50] Discovery for expedited actions is governed by Texas Rule of Civil Procedure 190.2.[51]

12-13 COUNTERCLAIM FOR WRONGFUL INJUNCTION

When seeking damages due to a wrongful injunction, the defendant should serve a copy of the counterclaim on both the plaintiff's attorney and the surety on the injunction bond.[52] This activates two potential causes of action. The defendant can either file suit on the bond or for malicious prosecution. A claimants choosing action on the bond must establish that:

1. The temporary injunction was issued wrongfully; and
2. The injunction was later dissolved.[53]

Recovery, in this case, is limited to the amount of the bond. Punitive damages and attorney's fees may not be recovered.

---

48. *See Id.*

49. *See* 4-50 Dorsaneo, Texas Litigation Guide § 50.107 (2017).

50. *See* discussion *supra* 2-12:1.

51. *See* Tex. R. Civ. P. 190.2.

52. *See* 4-50 Dorsaneo, Texas Litigation Guide § 50.104 (2017).

53. *See Id.*

On the other hand, claimants choosing an action for malicious prosecution must prove that the injunction:

1. Was prosecuted maliciously;
2. Was prosecuted without probable cause; and
3. Terminated in the claimant's favor.[54]

Recovery, in this case, includes all actual damages. Punitive damages and attorney's fees may not be recovered.

In either cause of action, the pleading should state that the injunction was a proximate cause of the enjoined party's actual loss and state special damages specifically.[55] If the case is that an injunction restrained a party from collecting money, the recovery is ten percent of the enjoined amount—as long as the injunction was later dissolved and it is discovered that it was obtained for delay.[56]

54. *See Id.*

55. *See Id.*

56. *See* Id.

Chapter 13
Judges' Thoughts

Edited by Greg McAllister and Dave Wishnew

13-1 SOUND ADVICE FROM JUDGES

Every judge is unique. However, some sound, fairly universal advice does exist for the counsel seeking a temporary restraining order (TRO) or an injunction—no matter who the judge on the case may be. In his book, *What Judges Want: A Former Judge's Guide to Success in Court*, James M. Stanton highlights various actions a practitioner should take both before and during the process of securing (or defending against) a TRO and/or injunction.[1]

In this chapter, we have included some of Stanton's insights, along with a summary of our interviews with multiple judges that we surveyed on various topics related to TROs and injunctions. Their astute advice follows:

13-2 COMMON PROBLEMS IN PETITIONS FOR TROS

- The lawyer fails to provide notification as required in the local rules.

1. James M. Stanton, *What Judges Want: A Former Judge's Guide to Success in Court* (Texas Lawyer 2013).

- The client does not demonstrate personal knowledge of the facts when providing the affidavits
- The lawyer fails to provide the judge with information sufficient to allow him or her to grant relief to preserve the status quo without being overly broad.
- The lawyer does not help the judge administer justice, so the judge (alone) has to figure out how to fit the facts to the law.
- The lawyer does not follow the specific rules relevant to injunctions. There are very specific steps that a lawyer must take and "magic language" he or she must use.
- The lawyer is unable to articulate why there is an emergency. If there has been some delay, a lawyer must carefully explain the reason for the delay and why the delay should not weigh against a current emergency.
- The lawyer fails to articulate the imminent harm and a lack of an adequate remedy at law (in the form of monetary damages).
- The lawyer fails to state in the petition that the petitioner is willing to post a bond.
- The lawyer is unable to articulate what bond amount would be appropriate and why.

13-3 HOW TO MAKE A TRO MORE USER-FRIENDLY AND MORE LIKELY TO BE GRANTED

- Make certain the judge understands the context of the issue and why you are seeking a TRO.
- Explain how your client was harmed and why a judge should grant the relief.
- Make certain you fully explain the probable right to relief.
- Explain why monetary damages alone will not remedy the problem.
- Make certain that your "woe is me" facts are clear, particularly in an *ex parte* filing.
- Well-reasoned petitions that seek reasonable protections are more likely to be granted.
- Ask for a fair remedy. Seek adequate protection without overreaching.
- Provide case law to support what you are trying to accomplish, as you are probably more knowledgeable about the specific law. Highlighted cases are encouraged.
- A petition should be short and sweet. The longer the explanation, the smaller the likelihood of a favorable verdict.
- In order to be successful at the injunction hearing, it is important that the lawyer be able to identify in detail both the tangible and intangible injuries that will be suffered by his client and third parties in the event that an injunction is not issued.
- The more limited the scope of the remedy

you are seeking, the more likely you are to obtain relief.

- One-sided arguments make a judge weary. Come to court with opposing counsel to assuage suspicion.
- "Cheat sheets" are helpful when they provide an outline of the key facts and legal issues in one or two pages. This is an opportunity to provide the narrative.
- Start with a good elevator speech.
- Explain how you were harmed and why a judge should grant you relief.
- Although your client cannot testify, bringing your client to court is a good idea (as sometimes clients can explain the real business need in a way that lawyers cannot).

13-4 PET PEEVES REGARDING TRO APPLICATIONS

- Lawyers who are not candid.
- Lawyers who misstate the facts or the law.
- Lawyers who try to give the impression that they made every attempt to comply with the local rules regarding notice in order to have the opposing counsel or opposing party in attendance but clearly made no genuine effort.
- Lawyers who fail to explain the damage that will occur to the other side so that a judge can understand and assess any potential harm.

- Lawyers who are not prepared to respond to the question, "What is a reasonable bond?"
- Lawyers who appear to obtain a TRO over the noon hour, or at some other time when the judge to which the case has been assigned may be unavailable, in order to get permission from the court staff to "shop around."

13-5 ADVICE REGARDING MOTIONS FOR EXPEDITED DISCOVERY

- Before you consider filing an application for injunctive relief, it is important to have a streamlined discovery plan drafted. To be fair to the other side (who will tell the judge that you are blindsiding them with your emergent pleadings), the judge will likely provide them at least as much expedited discovery as you get. For this reason, narrowly tailor and, when possible, limit the depositions and written discovery so you can manage it appropriately.
- Motions for expedited discovery are readily granted because they are a good way to narrow the issues before a hearing.
- Make certain your request for expedited discovery is reasonable, practical, and tailored. You are more likely to obtain the relief to conduct one or two depositions than you are the relief to conduct ten.
- Make certain your request for expedited discovery is not one-sided. Your order should allow expedited discovery for both sides.

- *Ex parte* expedited discovery orders are disfavored because both sides should have an opportunity to voice their discovery and scheduling needs.
- Make certain the requested discovery is relevant to the temporary injunction, not the merits of the entire case.

13-6 THE WORST MISTAKES LAWYERS MAKE IN TEMPORARY INJUNCTION HEARINGS

- Lawyers fail to narrow a presentation to the real issues at hand for a temporary injunction hearing.
- Lawyers fail to communicate with each other in order to determine common ground.
- Lawyers underestimate the amount of time necessary for the hearing. Injunctions are difficult for judges because they tend to consume longer amounts of time than the attorneys request. If the hearing will last one day, do not ask for two hours.
- Lawyers do not attempt mediation prior to a temporary injunction hearing.
- Lawyers ask for too much, like putting someone out of work. Judges like to preserve the status quo.
- Most lawyers—whether representing the applicant or respondent—fail to offer any evidence on the potential damage to the respondent and, having received no evidence, the trial court is left with complete discretion on the amount of the bond.

13-7 ASSUMING A WELL-DRAFTED COVENANT NOT TO COMPETE, THE GENERAL PRINCIPLES MORE LIKELY TO BE GRANTED IN AN ORDER

- A fairly universal point among the judges is that they enforce provisions that preserve confidential information, prohibit solicitation of employees, and prohibit solicitation of customers (with whom the former employee had contact while employed with the former employer). Most judges indicated that they would not put someone out of work at the TRO stage.
- Several judges attempt to customize a ruling to be the least restrictive as possible on the respondent, while still preserving the status quo. Other judges grant greater relief in cases of indisputable (and significant) bad-faith conduct.
- Because the law has changed dramatically in the last few years to favor the enforcement of covenants not to compete, some judges are more likely to provide greater enforcement at the TRO stage.
- One aspect that has not changed—and probably never will—is the need for a lawyer to speak to the judge at the TRO and temporary injunction stage more like a juror than in other cases. The judges are trying to rule fairly, and so you need to fully explain why your client deserves relief.

13-8 THE MOST EFFECTIVE EXAMINATION TECHNIQUES TO UTILIZE DURING AN INJUNCTION HEARING

- If the former employer can catch the former employee in a lie, it goes a long way to leveling the playing field.
- Well before the temporary injunction hearing, the attorneys need to know how long each side will have to present evidence and arguments to the court. If the court has a short hearing scheduled, the legal team may need to make some difficult decisions about whether certain witnesses should testify by deposition or, on agreement of the parties, the court may accept affidavits. Knowing the ground rules for the temporary injunction hearing will allow for a well-tailored discovery plan and avoid unnecessary depositions.
- It is amazing what you can find on a cellphone. Lawyers should conduct discovery in this area and examine the witnesses on it. Witnesses will often deny things that can be proved up using cellphone data.
- The most effective examinations are brief, precise, and focused on the need for the temporary injunction. Lawyers should start examining the witnesses on agreed-upon, unrebutted facts.
- Remember that, on some level, this is a trial on the merits. You should treat it as such but keep the facts sufficiently narrowed to those necessary for the temporary injunction.

- On direct examination, make certain that you set the stage to tell your own story.
- On cross examination, try to impeach the witness *only* on important points. It is tiresome, and generally a waste of time, to see a lawyer impeach a witness on trivial issues.
- Demonstrative evidence is very useful. Timelines, enlargements of the important language of a contract, or the highlighting of key text messages or emails all help make the presentation more interesting.
- If information is presented by deposition, a lawyer should eliminate the extraneous information.
- Consider letting the judge read the deposition. Presenting the deposition in question-and-answer format takes longer.
- It is never too early in the litigation process to seize the opportunity to begin developing your case themes—get your ideas and buzzwords in front of the judge and in his or her mind sooner, rather than later.
- Take the time during direct examination to explain the important points: Why is this an emergency? What about this situation gives rise to imminent harm and irreparable injury (excepting restrictive covenants)? What is the harm? Why will a damages award not remedy this issue? What is the remedy you seek to stop the harm and why? The other side should also hone in on these issues during cross examination and try to prove that the relief requested is too

broad or extreme and that there is really no harm (or no harm that cannot be resolved by money damages).

- In order to build credibility at your hearing for a temporary injunction or restraining order, be prepared, be responsive, and be reasonable.
- When you arrive to argue your temporary injunction or restraining order before the court, make sure you have thought about what you want both legally and factually. This helps the judge understand your specific goals at this stage in the litigation.

13-9 FACTS THAT MOTIVATE THE JUDGE TO PROTECT THE EMPLOYER

- Facts that clearly demonstrate the employee is lying and stealing confidential information.
- Facts that clearly demonstrate the employee blatantly violated a well-drafted and reasonable restrictive covenant.
- Facts that show the employee has (or appears to have) breached his or her duty of loyalty prior to leaving, such as emailing customer lists to a personal computer or email account or using confidential information before leaving to prepare to compete.
- Facts that show the employee is "fishing off the former employer's trout line." For example, in one case an employee took all of his former employer's customers and contacted them 30 days in advance,

making a deal with them to "prove" their accounts as soon as he started a new business. However, the noncompete agreement restrained him from calling on the former accounts of the employer. There were several accounts he could have called, other than the exact accounts the restrictive covenant prohibited.

- Facts that show a knowing and willing breach or anticipated breach, such as the employee's contract with the new employer addresses the former employer's restrictive covenant and contains an indemnity in favor of the employee in the event of a breach (plus a "bounty" for each new customer who is successfully solicited in violation of the restrictive covenant).
- Appeal to the judge's desire to do justice—include the likelihood of imminent harm and the inadequacy of adequate legal remedies in your arguments. This is essential to winning your hearing.

Forms

Please Note: Forms are based on Texas rules and case law issued before the book's publication date. The forms are intended as a reference—their application to particular circumstances requires a practitioner's analysis and research.

www.texaslawbookpublishing.com

Index

CPSIA information can be obtained
at www.ICGtesting.com
Printed in the USA
JSHW020934150222
22914JS00001BA/1